A Dictionary of Arabic Idioms and Expressions
Arabic–English Translation

El Mustapha Lahlali and Tajul Islam

Edinburgh University Press is one of the leading university presses in the UK. We publish academic books and journals in our selected subject areas across the humanities and social sciences, combining cutting-edge scholarship with high editorial and production values to produce academic works of lasting importance. For more information visit our website: edinburghuniversitypress.com

© El Mustapha Lahlali and Tajul Islam, 2024

Edinburgh University Press Ltd
13 Infirmary Street
Edinburgh EH1 1LT

Typeset in 14/16 Myriad Arabic by
IDSUK (DataConnection) Ltd, and
printed and bound in Great Britain

A CIP record for this book is available from the British Library

ISBN 978 1 3995 1432 3 (hardback)
ISBN 978 1 3995 1433 0 (paperback)
ISBN 978 1 3995 1434 7 (webready PDF)
ISBN 978 1 3995 1435 4 (epub)

The right of El Mustapha Lahlali and Tajul Islam to be identified as authors of this work has been asserted in accordance with the Copyright, Designs and Patents Act 1988 and the Copyright and Related Rights Regulations 2003 (SI No. 2498).

Acknowledgements

We wish to thank our families, friends and colleagues for their support and encouragement during the compilation of this dictionary. Special thanks go to the anonymous reviewers for their very positive and constructive feedback on the manuscript.

Contents

List of Abbreviations iv
Introduction v
أ 1
ب 54
ت 75
ث 91
ج 93
ح 101
خ 113
د 121
ذ 126
ر 129
ز 138
س 141
ش 149
ص 158
ض 165
ط 171
ظ 179
ع 180
غ 203
ف 207
ق 225
ك 241
ل 258
م 285
ن 321
ه 330
و 336
ي 348

Abbreviations

adj. adjective
adv. adverb
Chr. Christian
e.g. for example
esp. especially
fig. figuratively
foll. following
gram. grammar
Isl. Islamic
jur. juristic
lit. literally
o.s. oneself
prep. preposition
s.b. somebody
s.o. someone
s.th. something

Introduction

This is your one-stop shop for developing your vocabulary, academic writing, translation and comprehension through the acquisition of Arabic idioms and stylistic expressions.

This dictionary provides readers with a comprehensive glossary of Arabic idioms and expressions, translated into English. The wide range of idioms and expressions are very practical for learners, translators and academics who wish to expand their knowledge of Arabic idioms and expressions, and develop their Arabic translation and academic writing skills. This easy-to-access dictionary covers up-to-date idiomatic expressions reflecting different registers.

The main objectives of this dictionary can be summarised as follows:

1. Introduce learners to key idioms and expressions reflecting different registers.
2. Equip learners, translators and academics with a collection of multi-faceted key idiomatic and stylistic expressions to aid them in their translation, writing and comprehension.
3. Enhance awareness of key Arabic idioms and expressions and their translations.
4. Facilitate the task of accessing and using idioms and expressions alphabetically.
5. Develop their Arabic writing style.

Structure and Organisation

In term of the structure and organisation, this dictionary follows conventional dictionary formats and as such there are no breakdown of idioms into sections or themes, but all are listed alphabetically. The entries are organised alphabetically on the *Alif–Yā'* (A–Z) scale. There is no criteria for selecting idiomatic expressions as the dictionary aims to accommodate all genres and types of idioms. In doing so, major modern and classic references and dictionaries such as *Lisān al-'Arab*, *Hans Wehr*, *Oxford Arabic Dictionary*, *al-Mawrid* and other pertinent references have been consulted to ensure a wide range of idioms have been included.

This dictionary is considered a key reference and it is hoped that it will supplement existing textbooks and will be most useful for intermediate and advanced learners of Arabic, native Arabic speakers, translators and interpreters.

Our major drive for developing this idiomatic dictionary is the learners' pressed need for a comprehensive glossary or a dictionary of Arabic idioms and expressions, which will help them in their translation and writing. Our students would often ask us to provide them with translations of idioms to help them with translating and comprehending texts. It was evident on numerous occasions in Arabic classes that current dictionaries are not of much help to students when translating idioms and expressions into English. Some of the dictionaries do not cover all Arabic idioms and often only offer a selection. This dictionary incorporates major modern and classical Arabic idioms and expressions. This will equip learners with a compilation of idioms required for understanding, translating and interpreting Arabic texts, both modern and classical.

The dictionary also makes idiomatic expressions visible to learners and translators, helping them to recognise and identify key idioms and expressions, which are often invisible in existing dictionaries.

With the growing interest in learning Arabic, and with the high demand for translating different texts and registers, this compilation will be very useful for learners of Arabic at the intermediate and advanced levels, translators and interpreters. The dictionary will also be of great benefit to native speakers of Arabic with a special interest in translation and interpreting from Arabic into English. Learners and translators will have at their disposal a comprehensive and easy-to-use dictionary/glossary of idiomatic expressions, organised alphabetically and covering up-to-date idioms. In addition to facilitating the process of mastering formal Arabic, this dictionary aims at developing language skills for learners, translators, interpreters and academics. It is therefore useful for different Arabic language and translation programmes at the undergraduate and postgraduate levels here in the UK and beyond.

This dictionary covers over 8,000 idioms and expressions, both modern and classical, making it one of the most comprehensive in the field of Arabic studies. We therefore believe that it will fill an existing gap in the field. It will certainly contribute to the discipline and supplement available dictionaries and glossaries. What sets this dictionary apart from others is its attempt to provide a comprehensive list of idioms and their translations, covering new idioms in different registers and contexts, including timely themes such as COVID-19. It is hoped that this dictionary will become the foremost reference for Arabic idioms and expressions.

Accessing the Dictionary

Concerning the structure and organisation, this dictionary does not attempt to categorise the entries into sections or themes, but is organised in alphabetical order, from *Alif* to *Yā'*. Organising the entries alphabetically will facilitate the task of searching particular idioms and expressions by looking for the headword of the idiom. To facilitate the task of searching, some entries, especially those that may have more than one vocalisation, are vocalised to ensure that the right meaning and translation are provided.

أ

Handed down from father to son, as s.th. inherited from forefathers	أباً عن جد
Vanities, falsehoods	أباطيل
Before she could say a word, he exclaimed ...	ابتدرها قائلاً ...
To degrade o.s., demean o.s.	ابتذل نفسَه
To rob, fleece s.o., to lift money out of people's pocket, relieve people of their money	ابتزّ أموالَ النَّاس
Forced smile	ابتسامة قهرية
To try to ingratiate s.o.	ابتغى الوسيلةَ (إلى بِ)
To strive for God's grace	ابتغى من فضل الله
Forever and ever	أبد الأبدين
To express one's opinion about	أبدى رأيه في
To express a wish or desire	أبدى رغبةً
To display a hostile, threatening attitude	أبدى عن نواجذه لِـ
To clear o.s. from guilt, exonerate	أبرأ ذمَّتَه
The most outstanding or conspicuous phenomenon	أبرزُ المظاهر
Tardier than Noah's raven, i.e. slower than a ten-year itch	أبطأ من غراب نوح
To escape, run away (abscond)	أبق العبد من سيده
Maintenance of the status quo	إبقاء الحالة على ما كانت عليه
To recover from an illness	أبلَّ من مرض
To report s.th. to the police	أبلغ الشرطةَ بِـ
He did his utmost, but without success	أبلغ نفسَه عُذرَها

Human being, lit. son of Adam	ابن آدم
A man of the world, a sophisticated man, product of his time	ابن الأيام
Native	ابن البلد
Vagabond, tramp, wayfarer, traveller	ابن السبيل
He knows the job from the ground up, inside out, he is the right man for it	ابنُ بُجْدَتِهَا
A famous, well-known man, a celebrity	ابن جلا
Our countryman, our fellow tribesman	ابن جِلْدَتِنا
Illegitimate son	ابن حرام
Legitimate son, decent fellow	ابن حلال
His own son, his offspring	ابن صُلْبِه
Short lived, ephemeral	ابن يومه
Moustached, sporting a moustache	أبو شوارب
Responsible for, answerable for ...	أبو عُذر ...
Hunchback	أبو قُنْبُور
The parents, father and mother	الأبوان
He insisted on doing it	أبى إلا أن يفعله
God willed that ...	أبى الله إلا أن ...
To enjoy an excellent reputation, stand in good repute	ابيض وجهه
To walk slowly, unhurriedly	اتأد في مشيته
In observance of, according to	اتّباعاً لِـ
To pursue a policy	اتّبع سياسة
To follow a school of Islamic law	اتّبع مذهباً فقهيّاً
To keep to the right	اتّبع يمينَه
Unanimity, uniting of views	اتحاد الآراء

اتحاد الكلمة	Concord, agreement, harmony
اتَّخذ التدابير اللازمة	To take the necessary measures
اتَّخذ المعلول علة	To mistake cause and effect
اتَّخذ المُنَاسِبَ	To act in a suitable or appropriate manner
اتَّخذ المواقع الجديدة	To take up new positions (troops)
اتَّخذ خطوةً حاسمة	To take a decisive step
اتَّخذ شكلاً	To take a form or shape
اتَّخذ قراراً	To pass or adopt a resolution
اتَّخذ منه نِبراساً	To take s.o. as an example, model s.o. after s.o.
اتَّخذ منه وسيلةً لـ	To regard s.th. as an expedient for
اتَّخذ موقفاً	To take an attitude, assume a position
اتِّساع في الكلام	Vagueness of expression
اتَّسع الخرق على الراقع	The rent is beyond repair
اتصل به تلفونيا	To get in touch with s.o. by telephone
اتصلت به النار	To catch fire
أتعب سرَّه	To trouble, worry, bother, harass s.o.
اتقد غيرةً (حماساً) على	To burn with zeal (energy) for
اتماماً للنصاب	So as to complete the number, in order to round off the amount
أتى (جاء) شيئاً فرياً	To do s.th. unheard of, do an unprecedented thing
آتى أُكُلَهُ	To bear fruit
أتى ب	To bring, produce, advance
أتى بجديد	To come out with s.th. new
أتى على الأخضر واليابس	To destroy everything, wreak havoc
أتى متلصصاً إلى	To steal, to sneak up to

He met with success, he was successful	أتيحَ له التوفيق
He was given the opportunity, he had the chance	أتيحت له الفرصة
To infuriate s.o., excite s.o.	أثار ثائرَتَهُ
To stir up dust	أثار غباراً
To bring up a question, a problem	أثار مسألةً
To determine s.o.'s identity, identify s.o.	أثبت الشخصَ
To fix the precise wording of a text	أثبت الكلامَ
To prove one's identity	أثبت شخصيتَه
To put s.th. down in writing, get s.th. on paper	أثبته في الورق
To massacre the enemy	أثخن في العدو
To weaken s.o. by inflicting wounds	أثخنه بالجراح
To wallop s.o., give s.o. a sound thrashing	أثخنه ضرباً
To burden s.o. or s.th.	أثقل كاهلَه
To bereave a mother of her son	أثكل الأمَّ ولدَها
To delight, please, gratify s.o.	أثلج صدرَه
It snowed, was snowing	أثلجت السماء
Prices that are beyond competition	أثمان لا تقبل المزاحمة
During, meanwhile, in the course of	أثناء ذلك
To speak in the most laudatory terms of s.o., to extol s.o. to the skies	أثنى عليه عاطرَ الثناء
Favoured, preferred	أثير عند
To comply with s.o.'s request, to respond to s.o.'s demands	أجاب إلى طلبه
In answer to your request	إجابةً لطلبكم
To play (an instrument)	أجاد العزفَ على
To master a language	أجادَ لغةً

أجال الرأيَ في	To weigh s.th. thoroughly, ponder s.th.
أجال النظر	To let one's eyes wander about, look around
اجتاز العقبات	To overcome obstacles
اجتازت شهرتُهُ الآفاقَ	His fame spread throughout the world
اجترّ آلامه	To mull over one's grief
اجترح السيئات	To do evil things
اجتروا أحاديثَهم	They chewed the old cud over, kept saying the same things
اجتمعت كلمتُهم على ...	They united, joined forces, came to an agreement, they were agreed that ...
أجّج النار	To light, kindle, start (a fire)
أجدى نفعاً	To be useful
أجر المثل	Adequate payment or wages
أجر زهيد	A mere pittance
إجراء العمل بِـ	Enforcement, implementation of s.th.
إجراءات رادعة	Deterrence measures
أجراه مجرى	To treat s.th. in the same manner as, put s.th. on equal footing with
أجرة النقل	Transport charges, cartage, carriage, freight
أجرضه بريقه	To alarm s.o., fill s.o. with apprehension
أجرى ألسنتَهُم بِـ	He brought them to the expression of ..., caused them to voice or utter s.th.
أجرى تجربةً	To carry out an experiment
أجرى تحقيقاً	To conduct an investigation
أجرى حديثاً	To conduct an interview
أجرى سراً	To dispense a sacrament

To grant s.o. a subsidy	أجرى له إعانةً
To give generously, open-handedly	أجزل له العطاءَ
Consensus	إجماع في الرأي
There is general convocation that …	الإجماع منعقد على أن …
To sum up I would say …	إجمالا لذلك أقول …
They made a joint decision	أجمعوا أمرَهم
To put one's mind to	أجهد فكرَهُ في
To exert o.s.	أجهَدَ نفسَه
To burst into tears	أجهش بالبكاء
She induced an abortion	أجهضت نفسَها
Tuition fees	أجور الدراسة
Fares	أجور السفر
A few thousand	آحاد الألوف
One-dimensional	أحادي البعد
Premonition, bright expectation	أحاديث النفس
To be wrapped in obscurity, be completely ambiguous	أحاط به الالتباس
To know s.th. thoroughly	أحاط به علماً
Familiarity with, acquaintance with	إحاطة بِ
He let him know about	أحاطه علما بِ
To like about s.o. that he …	أحب له أن …
To be more than found of	أحبّه حُبّاً جَمّاً
To burn with wrath at, over	احتدم غيظاً
Protection from or against	احتراساً من
Caution!	احتَرِسْ!
To be self-respecting	احترم نفسَه
To sacrifice s.th. in anticipation of God's reward in the hereafter	احتسب عند الله الشيء
To give a son, be bereaved of a son	احتسب ولداً
To die	أحتُضِرَ

احتفظ بالوفاء لـ	To remain loyal to s.o.
احتفظ بحقوقه	To maintain, uphold one's rights
احتفظ لنفسه	To keep, appropriate, reserve for o.s.
احتقن وجهُه	His face turned red, his face was flushed
احتكّ في صدره	It impressed him, affected him, touched s.th. inside him
احتلّ أعمالَه	To take over s.o.'s functions
احتلّ المكانَ الأول	To occupy the foremost place
احتلّ مكاناً مكيناً	To have or hold a strong, powerful position
احتمالات	Probabilities, possibilities
أحدّ النظرَ إلى	To look sharply at, stare at
أحدّ بصرَه في	To scrutinise
أحدّ من بصرِه	To glance sharply
أحداث متزامنة	Simultaneous event
أحدث حدثاً	To bring about s.th. evil, do mischief (Isl. Law, to commit a ritual impurity)
أحدق النظر	To fix one's glance on
أحرج موقفَه	To put s.o. under pressure, threaten s.o.'s position
أحرز قصَبَ السبق (والغَلب)	To come through with flying colours, carry the day, score a great success
أحرز نصراً (انتصاراً)	To win a victory
أحرق فحمةَ ليله في …	To spend the night doing s.th., burn the midnight oil over …
أحسّ بالذنب	To feel guilty
إحساس الانحطاط	Sense of inferiority
الأحسن	The best outcome, the happy ending

To make a good choice	أحسن الاختيارَ
To aim accurately	أحسن التسديد
To have a good opinion of	أحسن الظن بِـ
To make a good practical application of s.th.	أحسن تطبيقَه
Better off than they are	أحسن حالاً منهم
To grasp or understand s.th. well	أحسن فهمَه
To give good advice	أحسن مشورتَه
To treat s.o. well	أحسن معاملتَه
Well done! Bravo!	أحسنتَ!
To bring s.th. along	أحضره معه
To help truth come into its own	أحقّ الحقَّ
Is that really so? Really?	أحقاً ذلك؟
God's commands	أحكام الله
To erect solid barriers	أحكم السدودَ
To do s.th. carefully, thoroughly	أحكمَ أمرَه
To plan one's actions precisely, organise well	أحكمَ تدابيرَه
To tie up s.th. tightly	أحكم ربطَه
To lock the door firmly	أحكم قَفْلَ البابِ
To master a language	أحكم لغةً
To pay attention to s.th.	أحل الشيءَ محلَّ العناية
To cause s.o. or s.th. to take the place of s.o. or s.th. else	أحلّه محلَّه
Blood-red, deep-red	أحمر قان
In greater need of s.th.	أحوجُ إلى
To commemorate (a deceased person)	أحيا الذكرى
To burn the midnight oil	أحيا الليلَ
To spend the night in prayer	أحيا الليل صلاةً

أحيا حفلةً	To give a performance
إحياء الموات	Cultivation of virgin land
إحياء لذكرى	In commemoration of, in memoriam
أحياناً	Occasionally, sometimes
أُحِيلَ إلى (على) المعاش	To be pensioned off, be retired, be superannuated
أخبار زائفة	False reports
أخبت إلى الله	To be humble before God
اختار الله إلى جواره	The Lord has taken ... unto Himself
اخترق مسامعَه	To shrill in s.o.'s ears
اخترم الصفوفَ	To break the ranks
اختطف البصرَ	To dazzle the eyes
اختطف الكلامَ	To talk rapidly, half swallowing one's words
اختفى عن الأنظار	To disappear from sight
اختلّ توازنُه	To lose one's balance
اختلّ عقلُه	To be mentally deranged
اختلّت الشروط	The conditions are not fulfilled
اختلج غمّاً	To be filled with sorrow
اختلس الخُطَى إلى	To sneak up on s.o.
اختلس النظر إلى (في)	To glance furtively at s.o.
اختلط الحابل بالنابل	Everything became confused, got into a state of utter confusion
اختلف باختلاف ...	To be different, differ according to the kind of ...
اختياراً	Of one's own accord
أخذ (أعد) عدته لـ	To make one's preparations for, prepare o.s. for
أخذ الباخرة	To go by boat, took a ship
أخذ الثأر	To take revenge
أخذُ الرأي	Voting, vote

The matter was put to a vote	أُخِذَ الرأيُ عليه
To take s.th. seriously	أخذ الشيء مأخذ الجد
To prepare to do s.th.	أخذ العُدَّة لـ
To study under s.o.	أخذ العلم عنه
To make preparations, prepare o.s., get ready	أخذ أُهْبَتَهُ
To take down s.o.'s personal description	أخذ أوصافَه
To adopt modern civilisation	أخذ بأسباب الحضارة الحديثة
To catch everyone's eye	أخذ بالأبصار
To take revenge, avenge o.s.	أخذ بالثأر (أخذ ثأرَه)
To repay like for like	أخذ بالمقابلة
To catch the eye	أخذ بالنظر
To apply o.s. to, attend to, engage in, cultivate, practise s.th.	أخذ بأهداب الشيء
To collar s.o., seize s.o. by the collar	أخذ بتلابيبه
To hold to the letter of the law	أخذ بحرفية القانون
To try to please s.o., to reassure s.o.	أخذ بخاطره
To agree with s.o.	أخذ برأيه
To consider seriously, bear in mind, take into consideration	أخذ بعين الاعتبار
To win or captivate the hearts	أخذ بمجامع القلوب
To help s.o., stand by s.o., look after s.o.	أخذ بناصره
To seize, take by the forelock, tackle properly	أخذ بناصيته
To take revenge	أخذ ثأرَه
To wrest away, take away by force	أخذ جذباً
To be on one's guard, take precautions	أخذ حِذرَه
To receive one's due, get what one deserves	أخذ حقه

أخذ حيطته	To be on one's guard, take precautions
أخذ رأيه	To ask for s.o.'s opinion, consult s.o.
أخذ صورةً	To take a picture
أخذ عدة الشيء	To make preparations for s.th.
أُخِذَ على حينِ غِرَّةٍ	To be taken by surprise, be caught unaware
أخذ على خاطره من	To feel offended by, take offence at
أخذ عليه أنفاسَه	To take s.o.'s breath away
أخذ عليه طريقَه	To obstruct s.o.'s way, hinder s.o. from moving on
أخذ عليه عهداً	To put s.o. under an obligation
أخذ عهداً عليه	To exact a promise from s.o., pledge s.o.
أخذ قياسَه	To take s.o.'s measure (tailor)
أخذ مأخذ فلان	To adopt the same course as s.o., follow s.o.'s example
أخذ مجراه	To take its course
أخذ مجلسَه	To take one's seat, to sit down
أخذ منه كلَّ مأخذ	To completely overcome, overpower, seize s.o. (also, e.g. of fatigue, emotion, sensation)
أخذ منه مأخذاً	To seize s.o., take possession of s.o. (a sensation or the like)
أخذ نَفَسَه	To draw breath
أخذ وأعطى مع	To do business, deal with, maintain relations with
أخذ وجه العَروسة	To consummate marriage
أخذ وجهاً	To win respect, gain prestige
أخذٌ وردٌّ	Discussion, debate
أخذ وعَطاءٌ	Give and take, trade, dealings

I caught sight of a book	أخَذَتْ عَيْنِي كتاباً
She took me in her arms	أخذتني بين أحضانها
We got caught in the rain	أخذَنَا المطرُ
He was overcome with astonishment	أخذه العَجَب
Sleep overwhelmed him	أخذه النوم
To be friendly, be nice to s.o.	أخذه بالحسنى
He took all of it, lock, stock and barrel	أخذه بحذافيره
To punish s.o. for his offence	أخذه بذنبه
To grab s.o. by the throat, to have power over s.o.	أخذه بمَخْنَقِه (بخِناقِه)
To help s.o., stand by s.o.	أخذه بيده
To shoulder s.th., take s.th. upon o.s., assume s.th.	أخذه على عاتقه
The other	الآخَر
Eventually, finally, in the end, after all	آخرَ الأمر
To break wind	أخرج ريحاً
He said what he had intended to say	أخرج ما عنده من بِضاعة
Get out of here!	اخرج من هنا
Grief drove him out of his mind	أخرجه الحزن عن طوقه
To upset, discompose, disconcert s.o.	أخرجه عن طوره
To rob s.o. of his property, dispossess	أخرجه من ثروته
To change, disfigure s.o. or s.th.	أخرجه من صبغته
Beat it! Scram!	اخْسَأ إليك
The most select elite, the crème de la crème	أخصّ الخاصّة

أخطأ اللفظَ	To mispronounce
أخطأ بين الشيئين	He confused the two things, he mistook one thing for the other
أخطأ فأله	His expectations do not come true, are not fulfilled
أخطأ في استنتاجاته	He drew the wrong conclusions
أخطأه التوفيق	He failed, was unsuccessful
أخطأه الشيءُ	He lacked it
أخفّ الضررين	The lesser of two evils
أخفق إخفاقا ذريعاً	To fail miserably
أخفى الصوتَ	To lower one's voice
أخلاط من الناس	Common people, rabble
أخلد إلى الراحة	To rest
أخلص لله دينَه	To worship God faithfully and sincerely
أخلص له الحُبَّ	To love s.o. dearly
أخلص له النية	To be loyally attached to s.o. or s.th.
أخلف الرجاءَ	To disappoint one's hopes
أخلف وعدَه	To fail to keep one's promise, to go back on one's word, to break his word
أخلى السبيلَ لِـ	To open the way for
أخلى بينه وبين ما يقول	To let s.o. say whatever he likes, let s.o. talk freely
أخلى سبيلَه	To release s.o.
أخلى سمعَه لِـ	To be all ears for, listen intently to
أخلى طرفَه	To exonerate s.o.
أخلى مكاناً	To make room
أخو الخير	Benevolent person
أخو ثقة	Trustworthy

His brother on the paternal and maternal side, his brother-german, his full brother	أخوه لأبيه وأمه
The best people, the best of all people	أخيار الناس
Last but not least	أخيراً وليس آخراً
To let one's eyes roam over …	أدار نظره في …
A strong condemnation	إدانة شديدة اللّهجة
The day is over	أدبر النهار
To turn one's back on s.b.	أدبر عن شخص
Inserting amendments	إدخال تعديلات
To save money	ادّخر مالاً
To amend	أدخل تعديلات
To bring about a change in	أدخل تغييراً على
To admit s.o. to hospital	أدخل شخصا إلى المستشفى
Be in vain	أدراج الرّياح
To blacklist s.b.	أدرج شخصا في القائمة السوداء
To include an item in the agenda	أدرج نقطة في جدول الأعمال
He got the point	أدرك الموضوعَ
To be fully aware of s.th.	أدرك شيئاً تمام الادراك
To fall into disuse, pass out of use	أدركه العفاءُ
A false allegation	ادّعاء باطل
False allegations	ادّعاءات كاذبة
To make a statement	أدلى بتصريح
To put forward an argument	أدلى بحجّة
To make one's contribution	أدلى بدلوه في
To greet, salute	أدّى السلام
To testify, give evidence	أدّى الشهادة
To take an examination	أدّى امتحاناً
To render a service	أدّى خدمةً
To fulfil a mission	أدّى رسالةً

أدّى فريضة الصلاة حاضرةً	To perform the prescribed prayer promptly and on time
أدّى مأمورية	To accomplish a task
أدّى واجبَه	To do one's duty
أدّى وظيفةً	To fulfil a function, to fill a post
أدّى يميناً	To take an oath
أديم الأرض	The surface of the earth
أديم الغبراء	Lithosphere, earth's crust
إذا صحّ ما قالته الجرائد من أن ...	If what the newspapers say is true, namely that ...
إذا لم يكن بدٌّ من أن ...	If it is inevitable that ...
أذاع الأخبار	To broadcast news
أذاع برنامجاً	To broadcast a programme
إذاعة تلفزيونيّة	TV broadcast
أذاقه الأمرين	To cause him trouble
أذعن لحكم	To accept a verdict
أذعن لقرار	To respect a decision
أذعن لمطالبه	To give into his demands
أذكى نار الثورة	To fan the flames of revolution
آذن الليل بانتصاف	It was close to midnight
آذن بالسقوط (بالزوال)	To show signs of the imminent downfall (end)
أذّن بالصلاة	To call to prayer
آذنت الشمس بالمغيب	The sun was about to set
الأراضي الواطئة	The Netherlands
أراق ماء وجهه	To sacrifice one's honour, abase o.s., disgrace s.o.
أرباب الكارات	Artisans, craftsmen
أرباح طائلة	Vast profits
ارتباط شخصي	Personal connection
ارتباط وثيق	A strong commitment
ارتدّ على عقبيه	To withdraw, retreat

To abandon his religion	ارتدّ عن دينه
To withdrew, turn back	ارتدوا على أعقابهم
To get dressed	ارتدى ملابس
To be terrified, violent fear or excitement seized him	ارتعدت فرائصه (فريصته)
To shake with fever	ارتعش من الحمى
To tremble with fear	ارتعش من الخوف
A rise in sea level	ارتفاع مستوى سطح البحر
To ascend the throne	ارتقى على العرش
To mount the pulpit	ارتقى منبراً
To make a mistake	ارتكب خطأً
To commit an offence	ارتكب ذنباً
To commit a massacre	ارتكب مذبحة
To lean on one's cane	ارتكز على عصاه
To throw o.s. at s.b.'s feet	ارتمى على شخص
It is most likely, probably	الأرجح أن
Sending letters	إرسال الرسائل
Sending through the mail	إرسال بالبريد
To send out signals	أرسل إشارات
To dispatch a letter	أرسل رسالة
To utter cries	أرسل صيحات
To send letter after letter	أرسل كتاباً تِلو كتاب
Frozen assets	أرصدة مجمّدة
Solid or firm ground	أرض شديدة
Wasteland	أرض قفر
He showered me with kindness	أرضعني أفاويق بِرِّه
To attach a file	أرفق ملفاً
Abler, more capable, more qualified	أرقى كعباً
Stress	إرهاق عصبيّ
To strain one's nerves	أرهق أعصابه
To exhaust s.b.	أرهق شخصاً

أُرهق من شيء	To be worn out by s.th.
أزاغ عني بصره	He looked past me, he snubbed me
أزال شيئاً	To get rid of s.th.
أزال عراقيل	To remove obstacles
إزالة الشكوك	Dispelling doubts
ازدجر عن المنكر	To abstain from vice
ازدحام خانق	Heavy traffic
ازدهار اقتصادي	Economic boom
ازدواج الشخصية	Split personality
ازدواج لغويّ	Diglossia
ازدياد تدريجيّ	Gradual increase
ازدياد مطّرد	Steady increase
أزعج صديقه	To disturb his friend
أزمع على السفر	He decided to travel
الأزمنة الغابرة	Old times, ancient times
أساء استعماله	To abuse, misuse, misemploy s.th.
أساء الظن بـ	To misjudge
أسارير الوجه	Features, facial expression
أساساً	Primarily
أسال أوديةً من الحبر	To pour forth floods of ink
أسأله سؤلَه	To fulfil s.o.'s wish, comply with s.o.'s request
أسباب الراحة	Luxury
أسبغ الوضوء	To perform the ritual ablution properly
أسبوعي (أسبوعياً)	Weekly
استاذ كرسي	Full professor
استأصل شأفتَه	To eradicate s.th., eliminate s.th. radically
استباح حرمتَه	To hurt s.o.'s honour
استباح دمَه	To proscribe, outlaw s.o.

It became clear to him that …	استبان له أن …
To regard s.th. as auspicious	استبشر به خيراً
To be eliminated, drop out (in a competition)	اُسْتُبْعِدَ
Everything went well with him	استتب له الأمر
He went on saying, he continued with the words …	استتلى يقول …
To make s.o. angry	استثار غضبَه
To find s.o. unbearable, dislike s.o.	استثقل ظلَّه
In deference to, in answer to	استجابةً لـ
To recuperate	استجمّ عافيتَه
To gather one's thoughts	استجمع أفكارَه
To gather one's strength	استجمع قُواه
To be good, commendable	اُسْتُحْسِنَ
To know English well	استحسن الإنجليزية
To be ashamed of s.th., to feel embarrassed by	استحيى من
To ask God for proper guidance in	استخار اللهَ في
He got carried away by enthusiasm	استخفت به الحماسةُ
He was beside himself with joy	استخفّه الطَّرَبُ
To learn a lesson	استخلص دروساً
To derive benefit from, profit from	استخلص فائدةً من
To exact a promise from s.o.	استخلص منه وعداً
To secure generous contributions	استدر الأكُفَّ
To get s.b. to admit doing s.th.	استدرج شخصاً للاعتراف بشيء
To lure him into the trap	استدرجه إلى الفخّ
To call a witness	استدعى شاهداً
To summon s.b. to appear in court	استدعى شخصاً للمثول أمام المحكمة
To summon the suspect	استدعى متّهماً
A short break	استراحة قصيرة
To regain consciousness	استرجع وعيَه (عاد إلى وعيه)

استردّ شيئاً من شخص	To reclaim s.th. from s.b.
استردّ قوته	To regain his strength
استرسل في الكلام	To speak at great length
استرق الأنفاس	To gasp, pant
استرق السمع	To eavesdrop, to monitor (radio, telephone, etc.)
استرق النظر إليه	To glance furtively at s.o., give s.o. a surreptitious look
استشاط غضباً	To be or become fuming with rage, flare up, fly off the handle
أُسْتُشْهِدَ	To be martyred, die as a martyr
استشهد على معنى كلمة ببيت	To attest the meaning of a word by a verse
استصدر حكماً	To bring about, obtain s.th., esp. a legal judgement
استصدر مرسوماً	To issue an ordinance
استصغر نفسَه	To feel inferior
استصفى مالَه	To realise all one's assets, to confiscate s.o.'s property
استطاب (استطيب) (ه)	To find or deem s.th. pleasant, good, agreeable
استطرد من ذلك إلى قوله أن ...	Thereupon he proceeded to speak about ..., then he broached the subject of ..., after that he went on to say that ...
استطلاع للرأي	Poll, survey
استطلع خبرَه	To seek information about s.o. or s.th.
استطلعه رأيه	To consult s.o., ask s.o.'s advice or opinion
أُسْتُطِيرَ	To be terrified
أُسْتُطِيرَ عقلُه	To got out of one's mind (with astonishment or fright)

To seek to conciliate, propitiate or win over s.o.	استعطف خاطرَه
He brought severe measures to bear upon him	استعمل معه وسائل القسوة
He brought harsh measures to bear on him	استعمل وسائل القسوة معه
To continue to laugh	استغرق في الضحك
To hide one's head in one's clothes so as not to see or hear	استغشى ثيابَه
I ask God's forgiveness!	استغفر اللهَ
He was unable to speak, he was dumb-struck, he was speechless	استغلق عليه الكلامُ
To cease the opportunity	استغنم الفرصة
To exert o.s., make every effort	استفرغ مجهودَه
To resign, tender one's resignation	استقال من
To keep, stick to s.th.	استقام في
He said the right thing about ..., he talked sense about ...	استقام له الكلامُ في ...
In the future	استقبالاً
It was decided to ..., a resolution was passed on s.th., the decision was reached to ...	استقر الرأي على ...
He finally became ..., he ended up as ...	استقر أمرُه على ...
To be firmly established, be in a secure position	استقر به الحال
To sit down, get seated	استقر به المجلسُ
To settle down permanently, to sit down, not move from one's seat	استقر به المقام (المكان)
His mind dwelled on ...	استقر خاطره على ...
To make up one's mind, decide to ...	استقر رأيُه على ...
To be a positive fact with s.o., be beyond doubt for s.o.	استقر في نفسه
Investigation, examination	استقراء

Things were straightened out, returned to normal	استقرت الأمور في نصابها
His situation had stabilised	استقرت له الأمور
To assume a burden	استقل بحمل
He alone made it, he was the only one who made it	استقل بصنعه
To assume a task (or duty)	استقل بمُهِمَّة (بواجب)
To be entirely self-reliant, be left to one's own devices, to be independent, manage without others, get along by o.s.	استقل بنفسه
To thank s.o.	استكثر بخيره
To unsheathe, draw (a sword)	استل سيفَه
To withdraw gently (s.th. from)	استل كفَّه عن
To arouse or attract s.o.'s attention, catch s.o.'s eye	استلفت نظرَه (أنظارَه)
Death defiance, desperate struggle	استماتة في
To apologise for s.th.	استمح عذراً من
He continued in this tone	استمر على هذه الوتيرة
To keep in touch with s.o.	استمر في اتصاله به
To exhaust, or avail o.s. of, every possibility	استنفد كلَّ وُسعٍ
To take one's way, go one's way	استنهج سبيلَه
He mistook the male camel for a she-camel (proverbially of a mistake)	استنوق الجمل
To let o.s. be guided by the thought	استوحي الفكرةَ
To draw a lesson from	استوحي موعظة من
Farewell! God be with you!	استودعك الله
To fix a moderate price	استوصى بالأجر خيراً
To make s.th. one's concern, to mean well, have the best intentions with	استوصى به خيراً

To embrace s.o. with the arms	استوعبه بين ذراعيه
To arrest the attention	استوقف الانتباه
To catch s.o.'s eye, arouse s.o.'s attention	استوقف نظره
He awoke over the call to prayer, he was awakened by the adhan	استيقظ على الأذان
To extend one's thanks to s.o., thank s.o.	أسدى الشكرَ له
To give s.o. (a word of) advice	أسدى إليه (له) النصح
To make suggestions to s.o., advise s.o.	أسدى إليه الإرشادات
To render s.o. a service	أسدى إليه خدمة
To do s.o. a favour	أسدى إليه يداً
To be beneficial	أسدى فائدة
To whisper in s.o.'s ear	أسر في أذنه
Care for the aged	إسعاف العَجَزة
He had the good fortune to …	أسعده الحظ بِـ
To give s.o. a sharp look	أسفّ النظر إليه
To end, result in	أسفر عن
Revoking of citizenship	إسقاط جنسية
Devaluation of … (currency)	إسقاط قيمة …
To cause loss of hair	أسقط الشعرَ
To forfeit one's right in s.th., waive one's claim to s.th.	أسقط حقَّه في
To quash a complaint, nonsuit a case, to withdraw or drop a complaint	أسقط دعوى
To stand aghast, be at a loss, be bewildered	أسقط في يده
To deprive s.o. of his citizenship	أسقطه من الجنسية
Literary style	أسلوب كتابي
Pen name, nom de plume	اسم الكتابة

أسوة بِـ	Following the model or pattern of, along the lines of, in the same manner as, like
أسود فاحم	Pitch black, jet-black
الأسود والأحمر	All mankind (lit. the black and the red)
اسودّ وجهه	To fall into discredit, be in disgrace
أشاد بذكره	To celebrate, praise, commend s.o. or s.th., speak in glowing terms of s.o. or s.th.
أشباه عمر	People like Omar, men of Omar's quality
أشباهه	The likes of him, his kind
اشبته على	To be doubtful, dubious, obscure to s.o.
اشبته في الأمر	The matter appeared doubtful to him
أشبع الكلامَ فيه	To speak in great detail, at great length about s.th., describe or explain s.th. elaborately
أشبعه تأنيباً	To reprimand, rebuke s.o. severely
أشبعه ضرباً	To give s.o. a sound beating
أشبهُ بِـ	He resembles . . ., more than anything else, he is just like . . .
أشبَهُ شيء بِـ	Very much like . . .
أشبهه تمام الشبَه	To resemble s.th. completely
أشتات المأكول	Varieties of food, different dishes or courses of a meal
أشتاتٌ من	Varieties, various kinds of . . .
اشتبك في	To get entangled, embroiled, implicated in
اشتبك في حديث	To be drawn into a conversation, become engrossed in a discussion
اشتبك في حرب	To become involved in a war

اشتبك مع (بِـ)	To come to blows or to grips with s.o.
اشتبه في	To be in doubt about s.th, to doubt s.th.
اشتد ساعده	To become strong, powerful, vigorous
اشتدت وطأة الشيء	To aggravate
أُشْتُرِطَ لِـ	To be prerequisite, preconditional for
اشترطه على	To impose s.th. as a condition on s.o, to stipulate s.th
اشتعل رأسه شيباً	His hair was, or turned, white
اشتعل غضباً	To be flaming with rage
اشتغل به عن	To be distracted by s.th. from
اشتغل قلبُه	To be uneasy, apprehensive, worried
اشتمله السواد	It was completely black
أشد سواداً	Blacker
أشد غضباً	Angrier, more wrathful
أشد ما يكون	As strong as could be, extremely violent
أشراط الساعة	To portents of the Day of Judgement
أشربه ما لم يشرب	To attribute s.th. wrongly to s.o.
أشرع عينيه إلى	To cast one's eyes on, turn one's glance towards
أشرع قلمَه	To draw one's pen, to prepare to write
أشرك بالله	To set up or attribute associates to God
الأشعة الكونية	Cosmic rays
أشغال شاقة	Hard labour
أشغال عامة	Public works

أشغل البال	To disquiet, disturb, preoccupy
أشفق من	To shun, shirk, be on one's guard against
أشفى به على حافة اليأس	He brought him to the brink of despair
أشهر مزادَ بيعِ شيءٍ	To auction s.th. off, put s.th. up at auction
أشهر من نار على عَلَم	Very famous
أشهق بالبكاء	To burst into tears, break out into loud weeping
أصاب إصابات	To score, make goals
أصاب في عمله	To do right, act properly
إصابة العمل	Industrial accident
أصابه مس من الجنون	He has gone crazy
أصالةً ونيابةً	Directly and indirectly
أصبح أثراً بعد عين	To be destroyed, be wiped out, leave nothing but memory behind
أصبح الحق	Truth has come to light
أصبح الصباحُ	It became morning
أصبح طُعمة النيران	To be destroyed by fire
أصبح على خير	To have a good morning, begin the day happily
أَصْبَحَ فِي	To get into a situation, come to a point where..., to become, grow, turn, to be
أصبح في حكم المقرر	It is all but decided
أصبح في خبر كان	To disappear, become dated, belong to the past, become obsolete
أصبح نافذاً	To become operative, come into force (law)
أصبح نسياً منسياً	To be completely forgotten, fall into utter oblivion
أصبع القدم	Toe

Sectarians, dissenters	أصحاب الاهواء
Those concerned, the important, influential people	أصحاب الشأن
Dubious persons, people of ill repute	أصحاب الشبهات
The Seven Sleepers	أصحاب الكهف
To issue (a command, edict, judgement),	أصدر (أمراً، فتوى، حكماً)
The most reliable, or best, proof for	أصدق برهان على
The most loyal, or best, friend	أصدق صديق
To fix a bridal dower (for a woman)	أصدقها
To fish in troubled waters	اصطاد في الماء العكر
The youngest of his parents' children	أصغر أبويه
To listen, pay attention, lend one's ear to s.th. or s.o.	أصغى إلى
To have s.o. in mind for s.th., choose, select, or single out s.o. for s.th.	أصفاه بالشيء
He grew pale, he turned white	اصفرّ وجهه
The actual reason	الأصل الأصيل
To make s.o. burn in the fire	أصلاه النار
To set s.th. on fire, to fire at s.o. or s.th.	أصلاه ناراً
To make s.o. undergo the most excruciating pangs of jealousy	أصلاه ناراً من الغيرة
To make peace, bring together people	أصلح بين
To mend, improve, ameliorate	أصلح من
To evoke the right intention in one's heart (ethical and religious)	أصلح نية
She made herself up	أصلحت من شأنها
To be hard hit, be grievously afflicted	أصيب إصابة شديدةً

To be stricken, attacked, afflicted, to be killed	أصيب بِـ
To incur multiple wounds	أصيب بجراح
To suffer a loss	أصيب بخسارة
Of sound unerring judgement	أصيل الرأي
To waste time	أضاع الوقتَ
To lose one's mind	أضاع صوابَه
To make s.o. miss an opportunity	أضاع عليه فرصةً
Waste of time	إضاعة الوقت
To annex a noun (the first member of a genitive construction) to another (the second member, gram.)	أضاف اسماً إلى اسمٍ
He added s.th. of his own	أضاف شيئاً من عنده
Similar, like	أضراب
To stop work, to strike	أضرب (عن العمل)
To be prepared for s.th., make up one's mind to take s.th. upon o.s.	أضرب جأشاً لـ
To desist, abstain from	أضرب صفحاً عن
To go on hunger strike	أضرب عن الطعام
To get into a state of disorder, get out of control	اضطرب حبلُه
Many times as much	أضعاف أضعافِه
Many times, a hundredfold	أضعافاً مضاعفةً
Confused dreams	أضغاث الأحلام
What's more, moreover, furthermore	أضِف إلى ذلك أن
To bear s.o. a grudge, harbour ill will against s.o.	أضمر له الشر
To secrete, conceal, hide, keep secret in one's heart	أضمره في نفسه
He kept staring at him	أطال النظر إليه
He stayed a long time	أطال الوقوف

To keep s.o. waiting a long time	أطال عليه
To speak in a forward manner, be pert, saucy, insolent in speech	أطال لسانه
He pressed my hand	أطبق على يدي
Fingertips	أطراف الأصابع
The extremities of the body, the limbs	أطراف البدن
The contracting parties	الأطراف المتعاقدة
The outskirts of the city	أطراف المدينة
To throw o.s. down, prostrate o.s.	اطّرح على الأرض
To bow one's head	أطرق رأسه (برأسه)
To appease s.o.'s hunger	أطعمه من جوع
To work day and night	أطفأ جذوة يومه وأحرق فحمة ليله في العمل
To manifest its force, set in (e.g. of a disaster)	أطلّ بخطْمِهِ
The firing at s.th., the shooting of s.o.	إطلاق الرصاص على
Release of s.o.	إطلاق السراح
Opening of fire, shelling, gunning, cannonade	إطلاق النار (النيران)
His release	إطلاق سراحه
Absolutely	إطلاقاً
To give a free hand to s.o.	أطلق الإرادة لـ
To give free rein, impose no restraints, let things take their course	أطلق الحبلَ على الغارب
The medicine loosened his bowels	أطلق الدواءُ بطنَه
To fire, shoot at	أطلق الرصاص على
To incite s.o. (e.g. a crowd or mob, to boisterous demonstrations, emotional outbursts and the like)	أطلق ألسنتهم بِـ
To give free rein to s.o. or s.th., give vent to s.th.	أطلق العنان له
To open fire on, fire or shoot at	أطلق النار على

أطلق النار في	To set fire to, set s.th. on fire
أطلق النفس على سجيتها	He gave rein to his instincts
أطلق حرباً من عقالها	To unleash or start a war
أطلق رجليه إلى الريح	To run away head over heels, to beat it
أطلق زوجتَه	To repudiate, divorce one's wife
أطلق ساقيه للريح	To run away head over heels, dash off like the wind, to bolt
أطلق سبيله	To release s.o., set s.o. free, let s.o. go
أطلق سبيله لعبرته	To let one's tears flow freely
أطلق سراحه	To set s.o. at liberty, free s.o., release s.o. (from jail)
أطلق على	To apply s.th. (e.g. an expression, a designation) to
أطلق عليه اسم ...	To name or call s.th., designate s.th. as ...
أطلق لحيته	To let one's beard grow
أطلق لسانه فيه إطلاقاً شنيعاً	To indulge in defamatory remarks about s.o., backbite s.o.
أطلق له العنان	To give free rein to s.o. or s.th., give vent to s.th.
أطلق يده بِـ	To be open-handed with, bestow s.th. lavishly
أطلق يده في	To give s.o. a free hand (in, to do s.th.), give s.o. unlimited authority for
أطلقوا أيديَهُم في البلاد	They did as they pleased with the country
أطمع من أشعب	Greedier than Ash'ab
أعاد أثراً بعد عين	To ruin s.th. completely
أعادَ الأمرَ جَذَعاً	He reopened the whole affair, he reverted to the earlier status

To re-examine, reinvestigate, verify, revise s.th., go over s.th. again	أعاد النظرَ في
To rebuild a mosque	أعاد بناء مسجد
To revive or reawaken memories	أعاد ذكريات
To reprint a book	أعاد طبع الكتاب
Reconstruction	إعادة البناء
Re-formation	إعادة التكوين
Reorganisation	إعادة التنظيم
Rehabilitation	إعادة الحقوق
Restoration of the status quo	إعادة الشؤون على ما كانت عليه
Re-examination, reconsideration, revision of s.th.	إعادة النظر
Retrial of a case	إعادة النظر في دعوى
To destroy or wipe s.th. out, leaving only a trace or memory	أعاده أثراً بعد عين
To put back, lay back s.th.	أعاده إلى محله
The most outstanding of the tribe	أعاظم رجال القبيلة
From a subjective point of view or in reality	اعتباراً أو حقيقةً
With respect to, with regard to, in consideration of, considering ...	اعتباراً لِـ
From, as of, beginning ..., starting with ..., effective from ... (with foll. indication of time)	اعتباراً من
Self-confidence, self-reliance	الاعتداد بنفسه
Gratitude	اعتراف بالجميل
To block s.o.'s way	اعترض سبيله
To be grateful	اعترف بالجميل
To retire from service, from work, go into retirement	اعتزل الخدمةَ
To retire from work, go into retirement	اعتزل العملَ
To knit one's brow (pensively)	اعتصر جبينَه

To maintain silence	اعتصم بالصمت
To maintain equanimity	اعتصم برباطة الجأش
Self-confidence, self-reliance	الاعتماد على النفس
To adopt a new religion	اعتنق ديناً آخر
To be conceited, be vain	أُعجِبَ بنفسه
To paralyse s.o.'s every move	أعجزه عن الدب والمشي
To make comprehension impossible for s.o.	أعجزه عن الفهم
The time was too short for him to …	أعجله الوقتُ عن
To make one's preparations for, prepare o.s. for	أعدّ عُدَّتَه لـِ
The worst of enemies	أعدى الأعداء
He who warns is excused	أعذر من أنذر
To turn away from s.th. and to s.th.	أعرض عن إلى
Rare	أعز من بيض الأنوق
Difficult to reach, hard to get at	أعسرُ متناولاً
The genitals	الأعضاء الدقيقة
The disease defied all medical skill, gave the physicians a headache, posed a puzzling problem for the doctors	أعضل الداءُ الأطباءَ
To surrender or submit to s.o.	أعطاه بيده
To give s.o. s.th. for nothing, give s.o. s.th. as a present	أعطاه شيئاً عن ظهر يدٍ
To turn one's mind to, give one's attention to, bear in mind	أعطى (جعل) باله إلى (لـِ)
To give evidence, give one's testimony (legal)	أعطى أقواله
To give lessons	أعطى دروساً
To conclude a bargain, effect a transaction	أعطى صفقةً

To make one's bid (at an auction)	أعطى قوله
Prayers performed after the prescribed salat	أعقاب الصلوات
Further up, above	أعلاه
Boosting, furtherance, promotion or advancement of s.th.	أعلاه شأن الشيء
To declare war on s.o.	أعلن الحربَ على
Absolute maximum (of temperature)	أعلى درجةٍ في النهاية الكبرى
To play up, stress, emphasise	أعلى شأنه
To raise the prestige of s.o.	أعلى كلمتَه
Charitable deeds, pious actions	أعمال الخير
Forced labour, slave labour	أعمال السخرة
Clerical work, office work, desk work	أعمال كتابية
He caused a massacre among them, had them massacred	أعمل السيف في رقابهم
To busy the mind, think, reflect, ponder, muse	أعمل الفكرَ
That is, i.e.	أعني
God forbid! God save me from that!	أعوذ بالله
He lacked the thing, he needed it, he was in want of it	أعوزه الشيء
The disease defied all medical skill, defeated the physicians, thwarted all efforts of the doctors	أعيا الداءُ الأطباءَ
He didn't know what to do, he was at the limit of his resources, he knew no way out, he was at the end of his tether, he was at his wit's end	أعيته الحيلةُ
The earth, the ground	الأغبر
To force one's entry into a country	اغتصب أبواب البلاد
To seize or take the opportunity, avail o.s. of the opportunity	اغتنم الفرصة
To run fast, hasten, hurry	أغذَّ في السير

أغرّ محجّل	Unique, singular
أغرب في الضحك	To laugh noisily or heartily, guffaw
أغرض الغرضَ	To attain the goal
أغرق في الضحك	To laugh noisily or heartily, guffaw
اغرورقت عيناه بالدموع	His eyes were bathed in tears
أغرى العداوة بين ...	To cause or excite enmity among ...
أغضى على القذى	To bear annoyance patiently, swallow the bitter pill
أغضى عينَه	To close one's eyes
أغضاه عنه	To avoid seeing, condone
أغلب الأمر (أمره)	In most cases, mostly
أغلب	In most cases, mostly
أغلبية قدرها مائة صوت	A majority of a hundred votes
أغلظ فيه النكايةَ	To beset s.o. grievously, ride roughshod over s.o.
أغلظ له القولَ (في القول)	To bark at s.o. rudely, speak rudely, impolitely with s.o.
أُغْلِقَ على	To be ambiguous, dubious, incomprehensible to s.o.
أغمض عينيه عن	To make s.o. blind to
أغمض من عينيه	To close one's eyes, refuse to see
أُغمِيَ عليه	To faint, lose consciousness
آفاق الأرض	The remotest parts of the earth
آفاق جديدة	New horizons
أفاق من النوم	To get up from sleep
آفاقي	Coming from a distant country or region
أفانين من	All kinds of, sundry, various
افتأت برأيه	To act on one's own judgement
افتداه بالنفس	To sacrifice o.s. or s.th., risk life and property for s.o. or s.th.
افترق طرائق قِدداً	To split into many parts or groups, become divided

He was exposed	افتضح أمره
To die suddenly	اُفْتُتِتَ
Fear left him	أفرخ روعُه
To exert o.s. to the utmost, make every effort, do one's best	أفرغ جهدَه (مجهودَه)
To mould s.th. (fig.)	أفرغه في قالب
To play s.o. a dirty trick	أفسد عليه أمرَه
The hidden treasures of the earth	أفلاذ الأرض
In droves, in crowds	أفواجاً
The remotest parts of the earth, the ends of the world	أقاصي الأرض
May God regard your offence as undone	أقال الله عَثْرتَك
To discharge s.o., dismiss, depose s.o.	أقاله من المنصب
To steady one who has stumbled	أقاله من عَثْرته
The country, countryside, provinces (as opposed to the city)	الأقاليم
To furnish the unmistakable proof for, clearly prove s.th.	أقام البرهان الجليَ على
To protest, lodge a protest	أقام الحجّة
To furnish evidence	أقام الدليل على
To prove that …	أقام الدليلَ على أن …
To move heaven and earth, to make a stir	أقام الدنيا وأقعدها
To perform the liturgical rites	أقام الشعائر الدينية
To perform the ritual prayer	أقام الصلاة
To administer justice, handle the law, dispense justice	أقام العدلَ
To read the Mass for s.o.	أقام القُدّاسَ على
To provide for s.o.'s needs, support s.o.	أقام أوَدَه
To render account to s.o., give one's mind to s.o. or s.th., make s.o. or s.th. one's concern	أقام حساباً لِـ

أقام دعوى على شخص	To file a lawsuit against s.b.
أقام على	To occupy o.s. with constantly, to abide, stay, remain
أقام قضية (دعوى) على	To take legal action against s.o., sue s.o.
أقام له وزناً	To set great store by s.th., attach importance to s.th., make much of s.th.
أقام مباراة	To stage a contest
أقام مقامه	To make s.o. replace s.o. else, substitute s.o. for s.o. else
أقام نفسَه مقامَ المحامي	To pose as a protector
أقام وزناً كبيراً لِـ	To attach great importance to, set great store by
إقامة الشعائر الدينية	Performance of the religious ceremonies
إقامة العدل	Administration of justice
أقامه على	To put s.o. in charge of s.th., commission s.o. with the management of s.th.
أقامه وأقعده	To upset s.o. seriously, throw s.o. in a state of violent emotion
أقاويل	Sayings, locutions, proverbs
إقبال على	Attention for, concern for, interest in
إقبالاً وإدباراً	Back and forth, to and fro, up and down
أقبل عليه الدهر (أقبلت عليه الدنيا)	Luck is on his side, fortune smiles on him
أقبل عليه أيّما إقبال	He showed the greatest interest in it
اقتبس علماً من	To acquire knowledge from
اقتبس ناراً من	To take fire from
اقتدح النارَ	To strike fire

To commit an offence	اقترف ذنبا
A thriving economy	اقتصاد مزدهر
In order to save time	اقتصاداً في الوقت
To follow s.o.'s tracks, track s.o., to follow up, pursue s.o.	اقتفى أثره
To avail o.s. of the circumstances	اقتنص الظروفَ
To seize the opportunity	اقتنص الفرصة
To have to return empty-handed, with nothing accomplished	اقتنع من الغنيمة بالإياب
He squeezed himself between them	أقحم نفسَه بينهم
Seniority	أقدمية
To gladden, delight s.o.	أقرّ عينَه
To extend greetings to s.o.	أقرأه السلامَ
The earlier of the two dates or deadlines, i.e. death or divorce (Isl. Law)	أقرب الأجلين
It is quite probable, it is fairly correct, it comes fairly close to the truth	أقرب إلى الصواب (الصحة)
Easy to understand, more comprehensive	أقرب إلى الفهم
To swear by all that's holy	أقسم بمقدساته
To adjure or entreat s.o. to do s.th.	أقسم عليه إلا فَعَلَه
They swore by all that is right and holy	أقسموا جهد أيمانهم
To dismiss s.o. from a job	أقصاه عن الخدمة
To rob s.o.'s sleep	أقضَّ عليه المضجعَ
To be lame	أُقعِدَ
To dampen s.o.'s zeal	أقعد من همته
Absolute minimum (of temperature)	أقل درجةٍ في النهاية الصغرى
Quite insignificant, all but negligible	أقل من القليل
To be proud, bear one's head high	أقمح بأنفه

Testimonies, evidences, depositions	أقوال الشهود
What they said came quite close to the truth	أقوالهم أقرب ما تكون إلى الصواب
Too strong as to ..., too strong for ...	أقوى من أن ...
Leaders of the people	أكابر القوم
The grandees and notables	الأكابر والأعيان
The remotest areas of the earth	أكارع الأرض
Senior official	أكبر الموظفين
To contribute	اكتتب بِـ (لِـ)
To subscribe for	اكتتب لِـ
To copy s.th., make a copy	اكتتبه
To earn a living for one's family	اكتدح لِعياله
Prescription, acquisition of property or rights by uninterrupted possession of them for a certain period	اكتساب بمرور الزمان
Long-range reconnaissance	الاكتشاف البعيد المدى
At best	أكثرَ الأمر
It is very likely that ...	أكثر الظن أن ...
More and more	أكثر فأكثر
To do constantly	أكثر في
To do much, to give much or frequently	أكثر لِـ (من)
As much as possible	أكثر ما يمكن
Besides, moreover	أكثر من ذلك
More than once, several times	أكثر من مرة
The majority, most of them	الأكثرون
A greater liar than 'Urqub	أكذب من عرقوب
A greater liar than Musaylama (proverbially of a liar)	أكذب من مسيلمة

For your sake, to please you	إكراماً لخاطرك
In his honour	إكراماً له
To receive s.o. hospitably, treat s.o. with deference	أكرم (أحسن) وفادتَّه
To make immune to …	أكسَبَ مناعةً ضِدَّ …
To take usurious interest	أكل الربا
To encroach s.o.'s rights	أكل حقّه
To have independent means of subsistence	أكل خبزَ الوقف
To be old and worn out, be timeworn	أكل عليه الدهرُ وشَرِبَ
To eat off a plate	أكل في صحن
He ate (a little, some) of the food	أكل من الطعام
His skin itched	أكله جلدُه
Voracious, gluttonous	أكول
Certainly! Surely!	أكيداً
To end with, wind up with, he eventually got to the point where …	آل (انتهى) به المطاف إلى …
The long and the short of it was that …	آل الأمر إلى …
Except that …	إلا أن …
Only with great effort, with great difficulty, barely	إلا بِشِقِّ الأنفس (بشق النفس)
Oh, do look! Why, look!	ألا فانظروا
But for a few exceptions, with a few exceptions only	إلا ما قل وندر
Labour pains	آلام الوضع
Ready-made clothes	ألبسة جاهزة
Typewriter	آلة كاتبة
To entrust, commit one's cause, one's affair to	ألجأ أمرَه إلى
Mind your own business!	إلزَمْ شُغْلَكَ

ألزمه الحجة	To force proof on s.o., force s.o. to accept an argument
ألزمه الفراشَ	To confine s.o. to bed, compel s.o. to stay in bed (of a disease)
ألزمه المالَ (بالمال)	To impose the payment of a sum on s.o.
ألستَ معي في أن ... ؟	Don't you think that ...?
ألصق به تهمةً	To raise an accusation against s.o.
ألصق لوحةً	To post a placard
ألصقه بـ	To attach, paste, glue s.th. to
ألعاب القُوَى	Athletics
ألعاب رياضية	Athletics, sports
ألعاب سحرية	Sleight of hand, magic
ألعاب نارية	Fireworks
ألّف بين قلوبِهم	To reconcile people with each other
ألفاظها بحروفها	His words literally
ألقى (أطلق) الحبلَ على الغارب	To let things go, give a free hand, impose no restraint
ألقى (ضرب) به عُرْضَ الحائط	To undervalue, scorn, disdain, despise, reject s.th.
ألقى البيضَ	To lay eggs
ألقى التَّبِعَةَ على	To make s.o. or s.th responsible
ألقى الحبلَ على الغارب	To give free rein, give a free hand, impose no restraint
ألقى الحجزَ على	To confiscate s.th.
ألقى الدرس	To recite the lesson
ألقى الرعب في قلبه	To strike terror in s.o.'s heart, frighten, alarm s.o.
ألقى السلاح	To lay down one's arms, capitulate, surrender
ألقى السمع إليه	To lend one's ear to s.o., listen to s.o.
ألقى القبضَ على	To arrest s.o.

To drop bombs on s.th., bomb s.th.	ألقى القنابل على
To place the responsibility on s.o., saddle s.o. with the responsibility	ألقى المسؤولية على
To place the responsibility on s.o.	ألقى المسؤولية على عاتقه
To entrust s.o. with management, put s.o. in charge	ألقى إليه مقاليد الأمور
To pay attention to	ألقى بالاً لـِ (إلى)
To lay one's fate in s.o.'s hands, entrust s.o.'s arms	ألقى بزمامه إلى فلان
To throw o.s. into, plunge into	ألقى بنفسه في
To throw o.s. into s.o.'s arms	ألقى بنفسه في أحضانه
To make a statement about or on	ألقى بياناً عن
To surrender to s.o., give o.s. up to s.o.	ألقى بيده إلى
To make a public address to	ألقى خطاباً على
To teach sciences	ألقى علوماً
To impose s.th. on s.o., hold s.o. responsible for	ألقى على عاتقه شيئاً
To dictate to s.o., to direct, instruct s.o., give s.o. instructions	ألقى عليه القول
To apply o.s. to s.th. adjust to it, accustom o.s. to it	ألقى عليه جِرانَه
To put a question to s.o., ask s.o. a question	ألقى عليه سؤالاً
He pronounced the formula of divorce against her	ألقى عليها كلمة الطلاق
To make a speech, give a public address	ألقى كلمةً
To give a lecture, hold a class	ألقى محاضرة
To lay one's fate in s.o.'s hands, entrust s.o.'s arms	ألقى مقاليد أمره إلى فلان
Not … though?	ألم؟
Haven't I told you, though?	ألم أقل لكم؟

ألم يأن	It is high time, isn't it about time
ألمعي	Sagacious, smart, shrewd
ألهج لسانه بالشكر	To elicit profuse thanks from
ألوان الأطعمة	All kinds of food
ألوى (الراية - العلم)	To hoist (a flag)
ألوى (ه) عن	To avert s.th. from
ألوى بيده	To wave one's hand
ألوى عنان الشيء (عن)	To avert, prevent, restrain s.th. from
إلى أبعد الغايات	To the nth degree
إلى أجل غير مسمى	For an indefinite period, until further notice
إلى آخره (إلخ)	And so forth, etc.
إلى أقصى حد	To the extreme limit, to the utmost, as far as possible
إلى الخارج	Outward, to the outside, abroad
إلى الخلف	To the back, at the back
إلى اللقاء	Goodbye! So long! Au revoir!
إلى الملتقى	Goodbye! So long! Au revoir!
إلى النهاية	To the end
إلى الوراء	Backward
إلى أي حد	How far, to what degree or extent
إلى باكر	Till tomorrow
إلى ثلاثة أمثاله	Up to three times as much
إلى جانبه	To him, to his address
إلى جواره	Beside him, at his side
إلى حد	Until, up to, to the extent of
إلى حد الآن	Up to now, so far
إلى حد بعيد	To a considerable extent or degree, extensively
إلى حد كبير	To a considerable extent or degree, extensively
إلى حد ما	To a certain degree

إلى حيث	Where (direction), to where..., to the place where...
إلى حين	For some time, meanwhile, for the time being
إلى خلف الشيء	In the wake of s.th.
آلى على نفسه أن...	He promised himself that he...
إلى غير حد	Boundless, unlimited, without limits
إلى غير عَودة	Never to return again, forever, good riddance! Farewell forever!
إلى غير نهاية	Ad infinitum, to infinity
إلى قيامة الساعة	Till doomsday, forever and ever, in perpetuity, for all time to come
إلى م؟	Whereto? Which way? Where?
إلى ما شاء الله؟	Whereto? Which way? Where?
إلى ما لا نهاية له	Endlessly, ad infinitum
إلى متى؟	Till when? How long?
إلى مدى بعيد	At a great distance
إلى هنا	Here, over here, to this place, up to this point, so far,=
إلى هناك	There, over there, to that place
أليس كذلك؟	Isn't that so?
إليك عني!	Away of me!
أم القرآن	Chapter 1 of the Qur'an
أم الكتاب	Chapter 1 of the Qur'an
أما الأمر كذلك	Things being as they are, there will, no doubt
أما بعد	Now then, to proceed
أمَا حان لهم أن يفهموا؟	Haven't they understood yet...?
أما عني فلا!	As far as I am concerned, no!
أماط اللثام عن	To disclose, uncover, reveal s.th., bring s.th. to light

Places of entertainment	أماكن اللهو
Recreation centres	أماكن المتعة
Difficult terrain, rugged country	أماكن وَعِرة
To lose one's husband, become or be a widow	آمت من زوجها
To probe into s.o.'s very nature	امتحن معدِنَه
Personal belongings	الأمتعة الشخصية
To be master of s.th., rule over s.th.	امتلك نواصي الشيء
Proverbs	الأمثال السائرة
People like him, people of his kind	أمثاله
To grant s.o. another respite in this life (of God)	أمد (الله) بأجله
Life expectancy	أمد الحياة
Accomplished fact, fait accompli	الأمر المقضي
Absolute master, vested with unlimited authority	الآمر الناهي
The accomplished fact	الأمر الواقع
A wonderful, marvellous thing	أمر عجب
He ordered him to be killed	أمر فقتلوه
An insignificant, unimportant matter	أمر لا يؤبه له
An unexpected matter, s.th. one wouldn't dream of	أمر لم يَخْطِرْ ببال
S.th. or other, some affair, some business	أمر من الأمور
Strict order	أمر نافذ
To let one's eye's wander over, to pass one's glance over	أمر نظرَه على
The matter is clear as daylight	الأمر واضح وضوحَ الشمس في رابعة النهار
Day before yesterday	أمس الأول
To hold one's breath	أمسك أنفاسَه

To take s.o. by the hand	أمسك بيده
To keep, retain	أمسك على نفسه
Keep …!	أمسِكْ عليك
To keep one's tongue in check	أمسك لسانه
To hold o.s. upright	أمسك نفسَه واقفاً
To take s.o.'s hand	أمسك يده
To stop publication, fold up (newspaper)	أمسكت عن الصدور
To throw one's full support behind s.th., endorse s.th. wholeheartedly	أمضى أمرَه على
He showered him with a hail of (e.g. stones), with a flood of (e.g. abuses, threats)	أمطر بوابل من
He showered him with a hail of (e.g. stones), with a flood of (e.g. abuses, threats)	أمطر عليه وابلاً من
To shower s.o. with a flood of abuse, to hurl abuse at s.o.	أمطر عليه وابلاً من الشتم
To shower s.o. with a hail of bullets	أمطره وابلاً من الرصاص
Close examination, careful study, scrutiny	إمعان النظر
To fix one's eyes on s.th., regard s.th. attentively, examine s.th. closely, scrutinise s.th.	أمعن النظر فيه
False hope	أمل كاذب
To be safe from	أمِنَ جانبُه
Ample funds	أموال سخية
Brigadier general	أمير اللواء
It is time, the time has come	آن الأوان
Rudeness must be met with rudeness (lit. iron is cleft with iron)	إن الحديد بالحديد يُفلَحُ
If you like, if it seems all right to you	إن حسُن لديك
Truly my Lord hears the prayer	إنّ ربي لسميع الدعاء

إن شاء الله	God willing
إن ضلوعي لا تنحني على ضِغْنٍ	I harbour no grudge, I feel no resentment
إن كانت الأخرى	Otherwise
آن له أن ...	It's time for him to ...
إن لهذا الرجل شأناً	There is a man to keep an eye on, this is an important man, there is s.th. about this man!
أنا الآخر	I also, me too
أنا طوعَ بنانك	I am at your disposal, I am at your service
أنا على يقينٍ (من) أنّ ...	I am convinced, I am positive, I am certain that ...
أنا في جَناحِه	I am under his protection
أنا في عِرْضِكَ	I rely on your generosity, have mercy upon me!
أنا كمسلم	I (in my capacity) as a Muslim
آناء الليل وأطراف النهار	By day and night
أناب إلى الله	To turn repentantly to God
أناخ عليه البؤس بكلكله	To be in great distress, be in a great plight
أناطه بشرط	To make s.th. dependent (or subject to) a condition
أناطه بعهدته	To entrust s.o. with the responsibility for s.th.
انبثق الفجرُ	Dawn broke
أنت في حِلٌ من..	You're free to ..., you may readily ...
أنت في ضيافتي	You are my guest
أنت في نَفَس من أمرك	You can do as you please!
أنت ملء حياتي	You are all my life
أنت وشأنَك	Do as you like

انتحر شَنقاً	To hang o.s., commit suicide by hanging
انتحل (ه) لنفسه	To claim for o.s. (s.th.)
انتحل اسمَه	To assume s.o.'s name
انتحل الإسلامَ	To profess Islam
انتحل الأعذار	To think up excuses, make excuses, use subterfuges
انتحل الأعرابية	To claim to be a Bedouin
انتحل شخصيةَ فلان	To impersonate s.o., to pass o.s. off as s.o., purport to be
انتحى جانباً	To step back, withdraw
انتحى ناحيةً	To turn aside
انتشق الهواء	To get some fresh air
انتصب الحكَم	To sit in judgement
انتظر الشيء الكبير من ...	To expect much of ...
انتظر من ورائه كل خير	To set the greatest expectations in s.th.
انتظم صفوفاً	To line up in rows or files
انتفخ سَحرُه	His lungs became inflated (out of fear or pride)
انتفخت أوادجه	He became furious, he became inflated with pride
انتفخت مساحره	His lungs became inflated (out of fear or pride)
انتفض واقفاً	To jump up, jump to one's feet
انتقص من قدره	To disparage s.o., detract from s.o., degrade s.o.
انتقل إلى جوار ربه	To die, pass away (lit. to be transferred into the presence of the Lord)
انتقل إلى رحمة الله	To die (lit. to pass away into God's mercy)
انتقل به إلى	To shift, translocate, relocate s.th.

To go from one extreme to the other, move in extremes	انتقل من النقيض إلى نقيضه
Opportunism	انتهاز الفرص
Sacrilege	انتهاك الحرمة
Offence involving moral turpitude	انتهاك العورة
To cover the distance quickly or at tremendous speed	انتهب الطريقَ (إلى)
To follow s.o.'s example, follow s.o.'s footsteps, imitate s.o.	انتهج سبيلَه
To seize the opportunity, avail o.s. or take advantage of the opportunity	انتهز الفرصة
To use s.th. as an opportunity for …	انتهزه فرصةً لـ
The upshot was that …, the long and short of it was that …	انتهى الأمر إلى أن …
To come to the point where …, result in	انتهى إلى أن …
He got to the point where …	انتهى به الأمر إلى أن …
He had children by her	أنجب منها
To withdraw, fall back, give way	انجرّ إلى الوراء
To avert one's eyes from	أنحا بصرَهُ عن
To turn s.o. away from, to dissuade s.o. from	انحرف به عن
To be indisposed, be ill	انحرف مزاجُه
To be or become united under s.o.'s rule	انحصر تحت حكمه
Disturbance of equilibrium	انخرام في التوازن
To break into tears	انخرط في البُكاء
To enter, join an organisation, a community	انخرط في سلك
He was completely taken aback, he was alarmed, startled	انخلع قلبُه
Rarer than a white-footed crow (proverbially of s.th. rare)	أندر من الغرب الأعصم

To rush to the front	اندفع إلى الأمام
Ultimatum	إنذار نهائي (بلاغ نهائي)
He gave him notice to vacate the premises	أنذره بتسليم منزله
To be annoyed by	انزعج من
To take ashore from a vessel, land, disembark	أنزل (ه) إلى البر
To launch a ship	أنزل إلى البحر
To inflict a heavy loss on s.o.	أنزل به خسارة فادحة
Landslide	انزلاق أرضيّ
To slide on the snow	انزلق على الثلج
He gave him the same status as	أنزله منزلة فلان
They took them in as guests	أنزلوهم ضيوفاً عليهم
To like s.o.'s company	أنِسَ به
He saw that he was a capable man	آنس فيه الكفاية
To like to listen to s.o.	أنِسَ لحديثه
Contrition, penitence, repentance	انسحاق القلب
To be in deep thought, be absent-minded, allow one's thoughts to wander	انسرح يفكّر
To leave s.o. (in grief, sorrow, fear and the like)	انسرى عنه
To be or become happy, rejoice	انشرح خاطره
To be gladdened, be pleased, be cheered, be happy, rejoice	انشرح صدرُه
To be a schismatic	انشق عن
They fell out (with one another), broke with one another	انشقت عصاهم
He exploded (with anger), he blew his top	انشقت مرارتُه
He burst with anger	انشقت مرارته غيظاً
He left to do his work	انصرف إلى شأنه

انصرف إلى نفسه	To withdraw by o.s., isolate o.s.
انصرف يفعل	To set about to do s.th., proceed to do s.th.
انضوى (إلى) تحت لوائه	To rally, flock around or under s.o.'s banner
انطلق لسانه على	To utter words against
انطلق لغايته	To head or set out for one's destination
انطلق مسرعاً	He went quickly, rushed away, dashed off
انطلق وجهه	His face brightened, became cheerful
انطلق يجري	He set out in a hurry
انطوى على نفسه	To withdraw within o.s., be self-centred, be introverted
أنظُر بعدَه	See below
أنظُر ظهرَه	See reverse, please turn over
أنعم الله صاحبَك	Good morning
أنعم النظر في	To look closely at, scrutinise s.th., become engrossed in
انفتحت ميازيب السماء	The heavens opened their gates
انفتل من الباب	To slip out the door
انفرط عقدُهم	They broke up, they parted company, they dissolved
انفسحت لي الأوقات	I had plenty of time
انفطر بالبكاء	To break into tears
انقباض الصدر	Depression, low spirits, gloom
انقباض القلب	Dejectedness, despondency, depression
انقبض صدرُه	To be dejected, dispirited, depressed
انقطاع التيار	Power shutdown

To take the offensive	انقلب إلى الهجوم
To be turned topsy-turvy	انقلب ظهراً لبطن
Devotion, dedication, occupation, pursuit of	انكاب على
Self-denial, selflessness, unselfishness	إنكار الذات
Ingratitude towards s.o.	إنكار لجميله
To throw o.s. at s.o.'s feet	انكب على قدميه
To throw o.s. down	انكب على وجهه
To deny o.s.	أنكر ذاتَه
To harbour self-doubts	أنكر نفسَه
I pretended not to see him	أنكرتُ أني أراه
Dejectedness, despondency, contrition	انكسار القلب
He broke his leg	انكسرت ساقه
To collect one's thoughts, gather one's strength, concentrate	انكمش على نفسه
He is not made for that, he doesn't belong there, it is not in his line	إنه ليس من تلك الحَلْبَةِ
He is a wonderful friend indeed!	إنه نِعمَ الخليلُ
Searchlight	أنوار كشافة
It is high time, isn't it about time	أنَى له أن
To insult s.o. to his face	أهانه في وجهه
Watch out for your own interests! Take care of your own affairs! Mind your own business!	اِهْتَبِلْ هَبَلَكَ
To be elated by s.th.	اهتز إليه قلبه
To tremble with joy	اهتز فرحاً
To be shaken in every joint	اهتزت جنباتُه
To appease s.o.'s hunger	اهجأ جوعه
To run fast	اهطع في العدو

أهل الخير	Decent folk
أهل الرأي	Experts
أهل الشرك	The polytheists, the idolators
أهل الكتاب	The People of the Book, the Christians and Jews
أهل اللغة	Philologists, lexicographers
أهل المدَر والوَبَر	The tent-dwellers and the city-dwellers, the nomads and the sedentary population
أهل النظر	Theorists, speculative thinkers
أهل الوجاهة	The notables
أهل أهلها	You are the right person for it
أهل زمانه	His contemporaries
أهلك الحرث والنسل	To destroy lock, stock and barrel
أهمل شأنه	He neglected him
أهون الشرين	The lesser evil
أهوى بيده إلى	To stretch out one's hand for, reach out for
أو بالأحرى	Or to tell the truth, put more exactly, to be exact, rather
أو تشك في ذلك	You wouldn't doubt it, would you?
أو على الأصح	Or more properly speaking
أو قُل	Or rather, or say even …
أوابد الدنيا	The wonders of the world
أواسط الشهر	In the middle of the month
أواصر الولاء	Bonds of friendship
أوجس خيفةً	To have a sensation of fear
أوجس فيه الملل	To feel that s.o. is bored, sense s.o.'s boredom
أوحِي إليَّ	It occurred to me, I was inspired
أود أن يفعل ذلك	I should like him to do this
أودعه السجنَ	To throw s.o. in prison

To destroy s.o.'s life	أودى بحياته
To ruin s.o.'s health, sap s.o.'s strength	أودى بصحته
To incur great expenses	أوسع النفقة
More patient	أوسع صدراً
Broader, wider	أوسع مدى
To treat s.o. with the greatest reverence, bestow ample favours upon s.o.	أوسعه برّاً
To heap abuse at s.o.	أوسعه شتماً
To give s.o. a sound beating, wallop s.o.	أوسعه ضرباً
To be about to do s.th.	أوشك على (أن)
He urged him to take care of	أوصاه خيراً بِـ
To give everyone his due	أوصل كل ذي حق بحقه
Living conditions	أوضاع حياتية
To stir up s.o. against, arouse bitter feeling in s.o. against	أوغر صدره على
To walk briskly, advance quickly	أوغل في السير
To exaggerate, draw a longbow	أوغل في الكلام
Luckier, more fortunate	أوفر حظاً
To draw to a close	أوفى على الانتهاء
From time to time	أوقاتاً أوقاتاً
To set s.th. on fire	أوقد فيه النار
To strike terror in s.o.'s heart, frighten	أوقع الرعب في قلبه
To inflict a punishment on	أوقع عقوبةً على
To let s.o. walk into an ambush	أوقعه في كمين
To concentrate on	أوقف اهتمامه على
To grant a reprieve, arrest a judgement (law)	أوقف تنفيذ الحكم
To obstruct traffic	أوقف حركة المرور
To relieve s.o. of his post, remove s.o. from office	أوقفه عن العمل

The first of its kind	الأول من نوعه
To have confidence in s.o.	أولاه ثقته
To do s.o. a favour	أولاه معروفاً
People of deep sight	أولو الأبصار
The influential people, the competent people, those concerned with the matter	أولو الشأن
Sometimes, at times	آونة – أخرى
What does it matter? What of it?	أي بأس؟
Why should one feel restrained in ...?	أي حرج في؟
What business of yours is this? What's that to you?	أي شأن لك في هذا؟
Whoever it may be	أي من كان
Anyone	أي واحد
Whoever he (or she) is, no matter who he (or she) is	أيّاً كان (أيّةً كانت)
Take care not to ...	إياك أن ...
The rainless days, the dry season	الأيام الشحائح
For several consecutive days, for some time	أياماً موصولة
To carry out s.o.'s orders	ائتمر بأمره
In conformity with, in accordance with, according to	إيجاباً لـ
Manpower, workmen, hands	الأيدي العاملة
As a sign that the conversation is (was) ended	إيذاناً بانتهاء الحديث
I swear by God!	أيمن الله (أيم الله)!
What has the ground to do with the Pleiades? (proverbially of things of disproportionate value)	أين الثَّرى من الثُّرَيَّا؟
Worlds separate us from (fig.)	أين نحن من
What is this compared with that!	أين هذا من ذاك!
What a difference there is between us!	أين هو مني!

ب

باء بالخيبة	To fail
باء بالفشل	To fail
باب الصدر	Front door
الباب مفتوح على مصراعيه	The door is wide open
بأبي أنت وأمي	You are as dear to me as my own father and mother
بات في حكم المؤكد	It is now as good as certain
بات من المقرّر	It has become a sure thing, is now certain
باتحاد	In unison, with combined efforts
باتفاق الآراء	Unanimously
بأجمعه	In its entirety, to its full extent
باختصار	In a few words, briefly, in short
بادأه بالكلام	To accost s.o., speak first to s.o.
بادر إلى	To do s.th. promptly, hasten to do s.th.
بادر إلى إنجاز الوعد	To set out to fulfil a promise
بادرة خير	A good or generous impulse
بادره بِـ	To fall upon s.o. with, assail, surprise s.o. with s.th.
بادره بكلام غليظ	To snap rudely at s.o.
بادى بالعداوة	To show open hostility
البادئ ذكرُه	The person or thing mentioned at the outset, the first mentioned
بادئ ذي بدء	Right from the outset
بإذن الله	God willing
بإذنك	With your permission

بارت البنت	The girl could not get a husband (remained a spinster)
بارك الله فيك	God bless you!
باستمرار	Continually, constantly
باستهزاء	Mockingly, derisively
باض بالمكان وفرّخ	To be born and grow up in a place, to establish itself and spread (plague)
باطلاً	Falsely, in vain
باع بالوكس	To sell at a loss
باعتبار الشيء	With respect to, with regard to, in consideration of, considering, in view of (s.th.)
باعتبار أن ...	Considering (the fact) that, with regard to the fact that, in view of the fact that, provided that, with the proviso that ...,
باعتباره	As, in terms of, in the capacity of
باعد بين أجفانه	To stare wide-eyed
باعد بين فلان وبين الشيء	To prevent s.o. from attaining s.th.
بأعلى صوت	Very loud, at the top of one's voice
بأقرب ما يمكن	As soon as possible, in the shortest time possible
بأكمله	Entirely, wholly
باكورة الفواكه	Early fruit
بالإجماع	Unanimously
بالإجمال	On the whole, in general
بالإحالة على	With reference to
بالإحكام	Accurately, precisely, exactly
بالاختصار	In a few words, briefly, in short
بالاشتراك (مع)	Jointly, in concurrence, together

بالأصالة عن نفسه	Spontaneously, of one's own accord, personally
بالإضافة إلى	In comparison with, in relation to, with respect to, regarding, in addition to, beside
بالإضافة إلى ذلك	Moreover, furthermore, besides
بالإكراه	By force
بالإيجاز (إيجازاً)	In short, concisely
بالباع والذراع	With might and main
بالبداهة	Spontaneously
بالتأكيد	Most certainly!
بالتالي	Then, later, consequently
بالتبع	Successively
بالتَّبِعَية	Subsequently, therefore
بالتحليل	In detail
بالتفرقة	In detail, in portions
بالتفريق	In detail, in portions
بالتفصيل	In detail, elaborately
بالتناوب	Successively, one after another, in rotation
بالتوصيل	To order, on commission
بالتي هي أحسن	In a friendly manner, amicably, with kindness
بالجُرم المشهود	In the act, red-handed, flagrante delicto
بالجملة	Wholly, on the whole
بإلحاح (في إلحاح)	Insistently, earnestly, urgently
بالحرف	Verbatim
بالحرف الواحد	Verbatim
بالحُسنى	Be fair means, in a friendly manner
بالحصر	Strictly speaking
بالحق	Truly, actually

By chance, accidentally, as chance will have it, haphazardly	بالصدفة
Necessarily	بالضرورة
By nature, by natural disposition, naturally! Of course! Certainly!	بالطبع
Across, in breadth	بالعرض
Incidentally, by chance	بالعَرَضِ
On the contrary, conversely	بالعكس
With the naked eye	بالعين المجرّدة
Of highest perfection	بالغ في الإحكام
Forcibly, by force	بالغصب
In the void (of the target) = in the bull's-eye	بالفارغ
Indeed	بالفعل
In the vicinity of, near, close to	بالقرب من
By fate and divine decree	بالقضاء والقدر (قضاءً وقدراً)
By force, forcibly, inherently	بالقوة
By word and deed	بالقول والعمل
In comparison with, (as) compared to	بالقياس إلى
Almost, nearly	بالكاد
Written	بالكتابة
Sufficiently, enough	بالكفاية
On the whole, in the aggregate, taken altogether, in bulk	بالكل
Orally, verbally	بالكلام
On the whole, in the aggregate	بالكلية
Indirect, not clear and unequivocal	بالكناية
Orally, verbally	باللسان (لساناً)
By God!	بالله
For God's sake, I implore, I beg of you	بالله عليك

In the same manner, equally.	بالمِثل
At all, absolutely, entirely, (with neg.) not at all, never, by no means	بالمرة
In (all) fairness, with appropriate courtesy, amicably	بالمعروف
In detail	بالمفردات
By retail	بالمفرّق
In the literal sense, literally, unequivocally, clearly	بالمفهوم
By the job, by the contract	بالمقاولة
Topsy-turvy, upside down, inside out, the other way round, vice versa	بالمقلوب
In turns, one after another	بالمناوبة
According to the text, explicitly, unequivocally	بالمنطوق
Hence, consequently	بالنتيجة
Concerning, with regard to	بالنظر إلى
In cash, for cash, cash down	بالنقد
Alternately, one by one, by turns	بالنَّوبَة
acting, deputy, by proxy	بالنيابة
By telephone	بالهاتف
Duly, dutifully	بالواجب
Indirectly	بالواسطة
Obliquely	بالورب
With one's own eyes	بأم العين
With one's own eyes	بأم عينيه
To manifest itself clearly and unmistakably	بان بالكاشف
To be separated from	بان من
Accurately, regularly	بانتظام

Fringed, trimmed with fringes	بأهداب
Merely, simply	ببساطة
Slowly	بِبُطْءٍ
Definitely, once and for all	بتًّا
Definitely, positively, decidedly	البتَّة
Definitely, positively, decidedly	بتَّة
Freely	بتصرف
In other words, expressed otherwise	بتعبير آخر
Intentionally, deliberately, wilfully, on purpose	بتعمد
In the full sense of the word	بتمام معنى الكلمة
With the years, as time goes on	بتوالي السنين
To plant or lay mines	بث الألغام
To peer around	بث العيونَ
To transmit a programme, broadcast	بث برنامجاً
With unwavering courage	بجأش رابط
Side by side with, in addition to, aside from	بجانب (إلى جانب)
At his side, next to him (it)	بجانبه
Earnestly, seriously	بجد
The heart of the matter, the actual state of affairs, the true facts	بَجْدَةُ الأمر
In a new and unusual fashion	بجدة وطرافة
At any price, regardless of the sacrifice involved (lit. at the cost of having one's nose cut off)	بِجدع الأنف
With one stroke of the pen	بجَرَّةِ قلم
Plainly, visibly	بجلاء
With great difficulty	بجهد جهيد
Life of ease and comfort, prosperity, affluence	بحبوحة العيش
Merely, exclusively, nothing but …	بحتاً

بحث (يسعى إلى) حتفه بظِلْفه	He brings about his own destruction, digs his own grave
بحث المسألة طرداً وعكساً	To study a problem from all sides, in all its aspects
بحد ذات	As such, in itself
بحذافيره (ها)	All of it, without exception
بِحَسَبِ (على حَسَبِ)	According to, in accordance with, depending on
بِحَسَبِ الظروف	According to circumstances, depending on the circumstances
بحسبك مقنعاً أن ...	It will be enough to convince you if ...
بحضوره	In his presence
بِحَقٍّ	As to, as for, regarding ...
بِحَقٍّ	Rightly
بحق السماء	By the truth of heaven!
بحكم	By virtue of, pursuant to
بحيث	Inasmuch as, in such a manner that ..., (he found himself) at a point or degree where ...
بحيث أن ...	In such a manner that ...
بحيث لا	Insofar as ... not, provided that ... not
بخاصة	Especially, in particular
بَخَسَ قيمته	To lessen the value of s.th.
بخصوص	With respect to, as regards, concerning
بخط اليد	Handwritten
بخلاف	Apart from, aside from
بدا عليه أنه ...	One could see that he ...
بدا للعيان	To come to light, come in sight, be before one's eyes

بداءة بدء	Right at the outset, at the very beginning
بَدَالَ ما (مِن)	Instead of (being, doing, etc.)
بداهةً	All by itself, spontaneously
بدر تمام	Full moon
بدع من	S.th. else than, unlike, different from
بَدعاً وعَوداً	Repeatedly
بدَل التمثيل	Allowance for professional expenditure
بدون استحقاق	Undeservedly
بدون الالتفات	Inattentive(ly)
بدون الالتفات إلى	Inconsiderate of, without consideration for
بدون انقطاع (من غير انقطاع)	Incessantly, constantly, continually, without interruption
بدون شيء من الجهد	Without any effort at all
بدون كتابة	Unwritten, oral
بدون وجه حق	Without legitimate claim, without being in the least entitled, in an entirely unlawful manner
بديع الصَّنع	Of wonderful workmanship
بذريعة أن ...	The pretence that ...
بذل الطاعةَ لِ	To obey s.o., defer to s.o.
بذل الغالي والرخيص في سبيل	To spare no effort, go to any length, pay any price for or in order to
بذل المساعي	To make efforts
بذل النفس والتنفيس	To make every conceivable sacrifice, give up all one's possessions
بذل بالذات	Self-sacrifice
بذل جَهْدَهُ	To take pains

To exert efforts, to take pains	بذل قصاراه
To exert every conceivable effort to, go to great lengths, go out of one's way, leave no stone unturned	بذل قصارى الجهد لـ
To spare no effort, go to any length, give everything, pay any price for or in order to	بذل كُلَّ غالٍ
To grant every assistance	بذل كل مساعدة
To sacrifice one's honour	بذل ماء وجهه
To exert efforts, to take pains	بذل مجهوداً
To make every effort, to go to great lengths	بذل مجهوداتِه
To give a word of advice	بذل نصيحة
To do one's utmost, do one's best, to go to great pains	بذل وُسْعَه
Filial piety	البر بالوالدين
Outside, out	برّاً
He acquitted the man	برّأ ساحة الرجل
By land and sea	برّاً وبحراً
Patently, openly and plainly	براحاً
With distinction	برتبة شرف
The matter has come out, has become generally known	برح الخفاء
To justify o.s. by	برّر وجهه بِ
To advance to the realm of fact, i.e. to become a reality	برز إلى حيّز المفعول
To stand out against, contrast with	برز أمامَ
A little while	بُرهَةً
Innocent	برئ من
Under the leadership of	بزعامة
The civilised world	بِسَاطُ المعمور
Because of, on account of, due to, by	بسبب

Because of that, for that reason, therefore	بسبب ذلك
By means of, through, by	بسبيل (عن سبيل)
Appropriately, appositely	بسداد
To your health! Cheerio! Skoal!	بسركم
To lay the table	بسط المائدة
To spread one's arms	بسط ذراعيه
To hold out a helping hand to s.o., ease the way to vindication for s.o.	بسط له مِهادَ العُذْرِ
To extend a helping hand to s.o.	بسط له يد المساعدة لِـ
Amply, abundantly	بسَعة (عن سَعة)
Regarding, with regard or respect to,	بشأن
To indulge in the happy hope that ...	بشّر نفسَه بِـ
On the condition that ...	بشرط
With (the greatest) difficulty, barely	بشق النفس (بشق الأنفس)(لا ... إلا)
Increasingly	بشكل متزايد
Opposite, in front of	بصدد (على صدد)
Currently busy with s.th., he is at present occupied with a matter	بصدد أمر
Regardless of, irrespective of, notwithstanding, to say nothing of	بصرف النظر عن
Regardless of, irrespective of	بصرف النظر عن (بقطع النظر عن)
As, in the capacity of	بصفة
Unmistakably	بصفة قاطعة
In his capacity of minister, as a minister	بصفته وزيراً
Fingerprint	بصمة الأصابع

Aloud	بصوت عالٍ
Audibly	بصوت مسموع
Softly, in a low voice, under one's breath	بصوت واطئ
Obviously, evidently	بصورة جلية
Especially, particularly	بصورة خاصة
Generally, in general	بصورة عامة
Irrevocably	بصورة مبرمة
Perceptibly, tangibly	بصورة محسوسة
Increasingly, on a larger scale	بصورة مكبَّرة
Noticeably, markedly	بصورة ملحوظة
Temporarily, provisionally	بصورة موقتة
Proficient in, acquainted with s.th.	بصير بِـ
In a decided form, in no uncertain terms	بصيغة حاسمة
Combustible merchandise	بضائع تقبل الالتهاب
By the very nature of the case, ipso facto, as a matter of course	بطبيعة الحال
With, at, on the part or side of	بطرف
By chance, accidentally, as chance will have it, haphazardly	بطريق الصدفة
Sole of the foot	بطن القدم
Palm of the hand	بطن الكف
Upside down	بطناً لظهرٍ
He suffers from diarrhoea	بطنه لَيِّن
Within, in a (given) period of	بظرف (في ظرف)
Behind s.o.'s back, insidiously, treacherously, stealthily, secretly	بظهر الغيب
In other words, expressed otherwise	بعبارة أخرى
To fill s.o. with trembling fear	بعث إليه هَزَّة الخوف
To breathe life into s.th.	بعث روح الحياة في

بعثه من الموت	To resurrect from death
بعد إذ	After
بعد الآن	From now on, henceforth, in the future
بُعْدُ الشُّقَّة	Large or wide distance
بُعدُ الصوت	Fame, celebrity
بعد الظهر	In the afternoon, p.m.
بُعدُ العهد	The fact that s.th. is long past, that s.th. belongs to the remote past
بعد اللُّتَيَّا والتي	After lengthy discussions, after much ado
بعد النظر	Farsightedness, foresight
بعد أن (من بعد ما)	After
بعد أيام من هذه الحوادث	A few days after these events
بعد بُرهتين	In a short time
بَعُدَ به عن	He kept him away from
بعد ذلك	Afterwards, later on, besides, moreover
بعد ساعة أخرى	After still another hour
بَعْدُ صغير	He is only a small boy, he is still young
بعد غد	Day after tomorrow
بعد فوات الوقت	Too late
بعد قليل	A little later, sometime later on
بعَد كونه ...	Aside from the fact that he is ...
بعد لأي	After great difficulties, in the end, finally, after all
بعد ما	After
بُعداً لِـ	Away with ...!
البعض	Several, some people
بعض الأحيان	Occasionally
بعضَ الشيء	To a certain extent, a little, somewhat

One in the other, within one another	بعضه في بعض
One another, each other, mutually	بعضهم بعضاً
Of far-reaching consequence	بعيد الأثر
Long term, long lasting	بعيد الأجل
Ancient, remote in time, going way back in history	بعيد التاريخ
Far-aiming, far-aspiring, very ambitious	بعيد الشأو
Far away, distant, remote	بعيد الشُّقَّة
Deep, profound, unfathomable	بعيد الغور
Far-reaching	بعيد المدى
Hardly attainable, hard to get at, Unattainable	بعيد المنال
Farsighted	بعيد النظر (طويل النظر)
In person, personally, exactly the same, the very same thing	بعينه
None other than he, precisely the one	بعينه
With his own eyes	بِعَيْنَي رأسه
There was a light shower	بغشت السماء
Aside from, not to speak of, let alone, irrespective of, notwithstanding	بغض النظر عن
Without	بغير
Completely unrestrained, out of control	بغير ضابط ولا رادع
Illogical	بغير قياس
Impatiently	بفارغ الصبر
Thanks to, owing to, due to	بفضل
Out of, because of, due to	بفعل
As far as possible, as far as it is feasible	بقدر (على قدر) المستطاع
Commensurate with, in proportion to	بقدر (على قدر)

بقدر الإمكان	As much as possible, in the best way possible, to the best of one's abilities
بقدر الإمكان (على قدر الإمكان)	As much as possible, as far as possible
بقدر المستطاع	As far as possible, as much as possible, in the best way possible, to the best of one's abilities
بقدر ما	In the same measure, to the same extent as, as much as
بقطع النظر عن	Irrespective of, regardless of, without regard to
بقلمه	Written by him
بقوة وجلاء	(to speak) loud and clear
بَقِيَ مكتوفَ الأيدي أمام ...	To stand helpless before ...
بِقِيام	Undertaking of
بقيت دار لقمان على حالها	Everything has remained as before
بقيد الحياة (على قيد الحياة)	(still) alive, living
بكامل الاحتراز	With all reservation
بكامله	Altogether, in its entirety
بكثرة	Plentifully, abundantly, a lot
بكثير	Far, by far
بكّر عن الموعد	To come earlier than the appointed time
بكّر في (بِـ)	To do s.th. early, prematurely, ahead of its time
بكل أسف	Unfortunately
بكل جوارحه	With might and main, with all his strength
بكل ما تتسع له الكلمةُ من معنى	In the widest sense of the word
بكل معنى الكلمة	In the full sense of the word
بكلمة أخرى	In other words

In its entire being, completely, totally, entirely, wholly	بكليته
How much? How much (is it)?	بِكم
In its full scope, completely, entirely, wholly, totally	بكماله
My early return	بُكُوري في العَود
To recover from an illness	بلّ بَلُّ من مرض
Without	بلا
Informa(lly), without (standing on) ceremony	بلا تكليف
Incontestably, indisputably	بلا جدال
Of no avail, useless, futile, in vain	بلا جدوى
Boundless, unlimited, without limits	بلا حد
Unhesitatingly, without restraint or fear	بلا حرج
Without limit or bounds	بلا حساب
Thoughtlessly, inadvertently	بلا حيطة
Unnecessary	بلا داع
With no strings attached, unconditional (obedience, surrender, etc.)	بلا شرط أو قيد
Without doubt, doubtless, undoubtedly, certainly, positively	بلا شك
Without interruption	بلا فاصل
Without any reservation, with no strings attached, unconditional	بلا قيد ولا شرط
Indisputably, incontrovertibly, undeniably	بلا نزاع
Unendingly	بلا نهاية
Ultimatum	بلاغ أخير
Slander, defamation	بلاغ كاذب
Mentally confused, absent-minded	بلُبٍّ شارد
In his real form	بلحمه وشحمه

Close to him (or it)	بلصقه
Gently	بلطف
To catch one's breath, have a break, take a little rest (lit. to swallow one's saliva)	بلع ريقَه
To grant s.o. a short rest	بلّعه (أبلعه) ريقه
To attain full maturity, come of age	بلغ أشُدَّهُ
To reach the highest level of	بلغ أعلى درجة من
To attain its highest degree	بلغ أقصى حدودَه
The matter became serious	بلغ الأمرُ مبلغَ الجد
The matter reached a climax, things came to a head	بلغ السيلُ الزُّبَى
To carry off the prize, hit the bull's-eye	بلغ الشأو البعيد
To reach its peak, attain its climax	بلغ أوْجَهَ
He began to reel so violently that . . .	بلغ به الترنح أن ...
His ingratitude went so far that he . . .	بلغ به الجحودُ أن ...
To cause s.o. to arrive at, lead s.o. to, to get s.o. or s.th. to the point where	بلغ به إلى
It reached such a pass, it went so far that . . .	بلغ حدًّا أن ...
To fulfil a mission	بلّغ رسالةً
To attain the highest goal, achieve ultimate results	بلغ سدرة المنتهى
To undergo tremendous progress	بلغ شأواً بعيداً في الرُّقي
To get as far in s.th. as s.o. else, match s.o. in s.th.	بلغ شأوَهُ في
To attain a high degree of s.th.	بلغ في الشيء مبلغاً
To be sexually mature, attain manhood, come of age	بلغ مبلغ الرجال
To attain great age, to be far advanced in years	بلغ من العمر عُتِيّاً

بلغ منتهاه	To reach its climax, come to a head, to reach its highest degree
بلغ منه كلّ مبلغ	To work havoc on s.o.
بَلِّغْهُ سَلَامِي	Give him my best regards!
بلهجة العاتب	In a reproachful tone, reproachingly
بم	With what? Wherewith?
بما أنّ	In view of the fact that, inasmuch as
بما فيه	Including, inclusive
بمثابة	Like, as, tantamount to, having the same function as
بمثل ما	In the same manner as
بمجامع عينيه	(To look at s.o.) with complete concentration, intently
بمجرّد ما	As soon as, at the very moment when
بمحض اختياره	Entirely of his own accord
بمَحْضَرٍ منه	In s.o.'s presence
بمزيد الارتياح	With extreme satisfaction
بمزيد الأسف	With greatest regret
بمعرفة	By, through (after the passive)
بمعروف	With appropriate courtesy, amicably
بمَعْزِل عن	Separated, secluded, isolated from
بمعية فلان (في معية فلان)	In the company of so-and-so
بمعية هذا	Herein enclosed, herewith
بمفرده	By o.s., alone, apart, singly
بمقتضى	According to, in accordance to, in conformity with
بمقدار ما	To the same extent or degree as, as much as
بمكان كذا وكذا	At such and such a place

بملء الفم	In a loud voice
بملء حوانيهم	(They shouted) at the top of their lungs, with all their might
بملء فيه	With a ring of deep conviction ('say', 'declare', 'exclaim'), loudly at the top of one's voice ('shout', 'cry' etc.)
بِمنتهى الشدة	With extreme force
بِمَنِّه تعالى	By the grace of God
بمواجهته	In his presence
بموجب (على موجب)	According to, on the basis of, by virtue of
بناء على ذلك	Accordingly, thus
بنات الصدر	Worries, anxieties, apprehensions
بنت الكَرْم	Wine
بنصه	Verbatim
بنصّه وفصّه	In the very words, ipsissima verba, literally, precisely
بنفسه	He himself, personally, in person
بنو ماء السماء	The Arabs
بنوع خاص	In particular, especially
بنى العزمَ على	To determine or be firmly determined to do s.th.
بنى بها	To consummate a marriage
بنى عزمَه على	To determine or be firmly determined to do s.th.
بُنِي على	To be based, be built, rest on
بَهْجَة الأنظار	Delight of the eyes, welcome sight
بهذا	Hereby, herewith
بهذا الاعتبار	From this standpoint, from this viewpoint
بهذا الخصوص	In this connection, in this matter, in this respect, concerning this
بهذا المقدار	To a certain extent or degree

In this connection, in this occasion	بهذه المناسبة
By this means	بهذه الواسطة
With unflagging zeal	بِهِمَّة لا تَنِي
Calmly, quietly	بهودء
To take a place, settle down, live or stay at a place	بوّأ مكاناً
Means of, through	بواسطة
By means of that	بواسطة ذلك
The secret depths of the earth	بواطن الأرض
The factors, circumstances or reasons at the bottom of s.th.	بواطن الأمر
First signs, heralds, harbingers (fig.)	بواكير
To make s.o. take a position or place	بوّأه مكاناً
Especially, in particular	بوجه (على وجه) خاص
Approximately, roughly, nearly	بوجه (على وجه) التقريب
On the whole, by and large, in general	بوجه الإجمال
Approximately, roughly about	بوجه التقريب، بالتقريب، على التقريب
In general, generally	بوجه العموم
Some way or other, somehow, to a certain extent	بوجه ما
Briefly stated, in a few words, in a nutshell!	بوجيز العبارة
By means of, through	بوساطة
Clearly, plainly	بوضوح
At once, right away, immediately	بوقته
He was acknowledged with homage as caliph	بُويِعَ له بالخلافة
By day and by night	بياضَ يومه وسوادَ ليله
The main point, the essence, the core, the gist, the climax of s.th. (lit. the principal verse of the ode)	بيت القصيدة

بيّت في الصف	To fail (pupil)
بَيْدَ أن	Although, whereas, yet, however, but, though
بيّض الله وجهَه	May God make him happy!
بيّض وجهَه	To whitewash, exculpate, justify o.s.
بَيَّضَ وجهَه	To make s.o. appear blameless, to whitewash, vindicate
بيضة الإسلام	The pale of Islam
بيضة البلد	A man held in high esteem in his community
بيضة الخِدْرِ	A chaste respectable woman
بين أحضان	Amid, among, in the presence of s.o.
بين أحنائها	In her bosom
بين أظهرهم	In their midst, among them
بين الآونة والأخرى	From time to time
بين الفينة والفينة	From time to time, now and then, once in a while, sometimes
بين أمرين	To have two possibilities
بين أيدينا	At our disposal
بين تلافيفه	In it, inside it, around in it
بين ثنايا	In, inside, among, between
بين جنبات الغرفة	The whole room
بين جنبيه	Inside it, within
بين جُنْحَى الكَرَى	When everyone's asleep
بين جوانحي	In my bosom, at heart
بين حوافيه	Within it, therein
بين حين	From time to time, now and then, once in a while
بين حين وآخر	From time to time, now and then, once in a while
بين ذراعيه	In his arms
بَين عشية وضحاها	Overnight, from one day to the next, all of a sudden

Once in a while, now and then, from time to time	بين فترة وأخرى
In parentheses	بين قوسين
Alternately, intermittently, by fits and starts, by jerks	بين كر وفر
Overnight	بين ليلة وضحاها
In square brackets	بين معقفين
Before his eyes	بين ناظريه
In front of	بين يدي
In front of him, in his presence, in his power	بين يديه
We are through with one another once and for all	بيني وبينك فصل الخطاب

ت

By God!	تالله
To turn to God in repentance	تاب إلى الله
Falling to the responsibility of, under the jurisdiction of	تابع (راجع) بالنظر لِـ
To continue on one's way	تابع سيرَه
To be late (i.e. arrive after the agreed time), miss a deadline	تأخر عن الموعد
Sometimes – sometimes, at times – at other times	تارة – أخرى
To radiate with joy	تألق سعادةً
Absent-minded	تاله العقل
Compunctions, contrition, repentance	تأنيب الضمير
May evil befall him! May he perish!	تبّاً له
To suggest itself strongly, be obvious	تبادر إلى الذهن
To be immediately understood	تبادر إلى الفهم
It occurred to me all of a sudden that …	تبادر إلى ذهني أن …
Exchange of shots	تبادُل إطلاق النار
Exchange of views	تبادل الآراء
Telepathy	تبادل الخواطر
Exchange of greetings	تبادل السلام
The first shimmer of aurora, the first glimpse of dawn	تباشير الفجر
One by one, one after the other	تِباعاً
To get mixed up (with)	التبس بِـ
To be obscure, equivocal, ambiguous for s.o.	التبس على
To talk freely, without formality	تبسّط في الحديث

He smiled maliciously	تبسّم في خبث
To attend classes regularly	تبع الدروسَ
In accordance with, pursuant to	تبعاً لِـ
To come to power, take over	تبوّأ الحكمَ
To take on a position, take over a post	تبوّأ منصباً
To ascend the throne	تبوّأ العرش
To occupy a place	تبوّأ مركزاً
To hold a position	تبوّأ مقاماً
To gain ground, become generally accepted	تبوّأ مكاناً
Making the mouth water, appetising	تتحلّب له الأفواه
The prices fluctuate	تتذبذب الأسعار
His confidence is wavering	تتزعزع ثقته
To work as an apprentice under s.o.	تتلمذ على يده
A smile flits over his face	تَتِيهُ على وجهه ابتسامةٌ
They were deep in conversation	تجاذبوا أطراف الحديث
God has taken your son unto Himself	تجبّر الله بِإبنك
Repulsion of ideologies, attacks, enemies	تجبيه لِـ
To gather information for s.o., to spy for s.o.	تجسّس له أخباراً
Wage freeze	تجميد الرواتب
Metaphorically	تجوُّزاً
Affiliation with, joining of, entrance to (office, school, etc.)	التحاق بِـ
To bring one another before the judge	تحاكم إلى الحاكم
To brace o.s., to pull o.s. together	تحامل على نفسه
Under the seal of secrecy	تحت (في) طي الكتمان

تحت (في) متناول يده	Available, at s.o.'s disposal, within reach, at hand
تحت إبطه	Ready at hand, pat (e.g. answer), at one's fingertips (e.g. knowledge)
تحت إشراف	Under the patronage or superintendence of, under the auspices of
تحت أعيننا	Before our eyes
تحت الاختبار	On probation, on trial
تحت التحضير	In preparation
تحت التسديد	Outstanding, due, unpaid, unsettled
تحت التسوية	Due, outstanding, unsettled
تحت التشطيب	Under construction, near completion, available shortly
تحت التمرين	Undergoing preparatory training, engaged on probation
تحت الحفظ	In custody, under guard
تحت الخلاء	Under the open sky, outdoors, in the open air
تحت السداد	Due, outstanding, unsettled, unpaid (com.)
تحت الشبهة	Suspicious, suspect
تحت الشعور	Subconscious
تحت الطبع	In press, in print
تحت القيد	Under construction
تحت المقياس	Substandard
تحت النظر	Under consideration, being dealt with
تحت اليد	At hand, in hand, available, handy
تحت إمرته	Under his command
تحت أمرك	At your service! At your disposal!

At s.o.'s disposal	تحت تصرفه
To be at s.o.'s mercy	تحت رحمته
For them to hear	تحت سمعهم
Under the motto ...	تحت شعار ...
Under the pressure of public opinion	تحت ضغط الرأي العام
Under penalty of death	تحت طائلة الموت
At s.o.'s disposal	تحت طلبه
Under the protection or patronage of, under the auspices of	تحت ظل
In wrathful agitation, infuriated	تحت عامل الغضب
Under the title of	تحت عنوان
Under the oppressive burden of s.th.	تحت كلكله (كلاكله)
To be under the protection of so-and-so	تحت نظر فلان
Under his authority, under his power	تحت يده
To defy death, invite death	تحدّى الموتَ
To arouse, challenge, stimulate s.o.'s intellect	تحدّى ذكاءَه
To brave the buffetings of fate	تحدّى عادياتِ الزمان
This made things difficult for people	تحرّج به الناسُ
To feel depressed by, feel annoyed at	تحرّج صدرُه من
To be overcome with longing	تحرّق شوقاً
Tautology	تحصيل الحاصل
All eyes are upon him, he is the centre of attention	تَحُفُّ به العيونُ
He is obviously a good person	تحفُّ به شمائلُ الطِّيبَةِ
To go into government service	التحق بالحكومة
Precise pronunciation	تحقيق النطق

التحقيق أن ...	It is a matter of fact that, it is certain that ...
تحلّب ريقي	My mouth was watering
التحليل النفسي	Psychoanalysis
تحوّل كلَّ حيلة	To use every conceivable trick
تَحْيَةً لذكراه	In remembrance of him
تحيّر في أمره	To be confused, baffled, bewildered
تحيّرت في مآقيه الدموع	His eyes were brimming with tears
تحيّن الفرصةَ	To wait for an opportunity, bide one's time
تخبّط في سيره	To wander about blindly
تختّم بالذهب	To wear a golden ring
تخرّج في	To graduate in or from
تخرّج من	To graduate in or from
تخطّى البحارَ	To cross the seas
تخطّى به إلى الأمام	To promote, advance s.th.
تخطّى وثباً من فوق ...	To hurdle over ...
تخفيف العبء عن كاهله	Unburdening, disencumbrance of s.o. or s.th.
تخلّع في الشراب	To be addicted to drinking, drink heavily
تخلّف عن العودة	Not to return
تخلّف عن المجيء	To fail to arrive
تخلّى عن دينه	To renounce one's religion
تخليداً لذكراه	In memoriam ...
تخميناً	Approximately, roughly
تخيّل فيه الخيرَ	To have an inkling of s.o.'s good qualities, think well of s.o.
تدابير أمنيّة	Security measures
تدابير زجريّة	Injunctive measures
تدابير لازمة	Necessary measures

To correct the mistake	تدارك الخطأ
To rectify the situation	تدارك الموقف
To discuss s.th.	تداول في شيء
To consider a matter	تدبّر أمراً
To manage his affairs	تدبّر أمره
Housekeeping	تدبير منزلي
Mismanagement	تدبير: سوء التدبير
Military intervention	تدخُّل عسكريّ
To interfere in the matter	تدخّل في الأمر
Meddling in internal affairs	تدخُّل في الشؤون الداخليّة
To meddle in other people's business	تدخّل في شؤون الآخرين
To interfere in a dispute	تدخّل في نزاع
To practise teaching	تدرّب على التدريس
To rehearse a piece of music	تدرّب على قطعة موسيقيّة
To steadily climb the ladder of success	تدرّج في سلم النجاح
Intensive training	تدريب مكثّف
Military training	تدريبات عسكريّة
Central heating	تدفئة مركزيّة
To threaten to fall down	تدلّى للسقوط
Degeneration of morals	تدهور الأخلاق
An economic downturn	تدهور الأوضاع الاقتصاديّة
Intellectual decay	تدهور فكريّ
To deliberate on	تذاكر حول
To exercise patience	تذرّع بالصبر
To use s.th. as a pretext, to use s.th. as an excuse	تذرّع بحجّة شيء
Popular discontent	تذمّر شعبيّ
To complain about s.th.	تذمّر من شيء
To grumble at s.b.	تذمّر منه

Community spirit	ترابط اجتماعي
An economic downturn	تراجع اقتصاديّ
The prices are dropping	تراجع الأسعار
To revoke measures	تراجع عن إجراءات
To reverse a judgement	تراجع عن الحكم
To reconsider his decision	تراجع عن قراره
A drop in income	تراجع في الدخل
Instant messaging	تراسل فوريّ
To plead in s.b.'s defence	ترافع عن شخص
The accumulation of debts	تراكم الديون
He has heard that	ترامى إلى سمعه
To wait for an opportunity	تربّص الفرصة
A strict upbringing	تربية صارمة
Autobiography	ترجمة ذاتية
He asked God to have mercy on his mother	ترحّم على أمه
Deportation of an immigrant	ترحيل مهاجر
To visit the café frequently	تردّد على المقهى
To hesitate	تردّد في
To look down on s.o.	ترفّع عن شخص
To be above s.th.	ترفّع عن شيء
To anticipate the arrival of s.o.	ترقّب قدوم شخص
To be promoted to	ترقّى إلى
To give free rein to s.o. or s.th.	ترك (ألقى) حبلَه على غاربه
To give free rein, impose no restraints, let things take their course	ترك الحبلَ على الغارب
To give free rein to s.o. or s.th.	ترك حبلَه على غاربه
To leave one place for (another)	ترك مكاناً إلى
I left him without regret, I was only too glad to leave him	تركته غير آسفٍ
To leave s.th. aside	تركه جانباً

تركه على حاله	To leave s.th. or s.o. unchanged, leave s.th. or s.o. alone
تركه في ذمته	To leave s.th. in s.o.'s care, leave s.th. to s.o.
تركه وشَأنَه	To leave s.o. to his own devices, leave s.o. alone
تركه يفعل	To let s.o. do s.th.
ترنّحت الأعطاف	They were carried away, became ecstatic
التزاحم على المناصب	To scramble for jobs or positions
التزام	Engagement, commitment
تزامن مع	To coincide with
تزحلق على الجليد	To ice-skate, to ski
التزاماً	By contract, by the job
تزوجها على الكتاب والسنة	To marry her according to the Quran and Sunna
تزوّد بالوقود	To refuel
التزويد بالمعلومات	Newsfeed, briefing
تزوير العملة	Counterfeiting
تزوير الوثائق	Falsification of documents
تساءل هل (عن)	To ask o.s. (about) whether
تساقط الثلوج	Snowfall
تساقط حُطَاماً	To go to ruin, disintegrate
تساقط على نفسه	To break down, collapse
تسبّب إلى	To seek reasons or motives for s.th., to account, give an explanation for
تسبّب عن	To arise, result from
تسبّب في	To be the reason or cause, be at the bottom of, be to blame
تسقّط الأخبارَ	To gather information
تسلّم مقاليد الحكم	To take over (the reins of) government, seize power

To beg	تَسَوَّل
They had their arms linked	تشابكت أذرعُهم
To imitate, copy s.o., s.th.	تشبّه بِـ
Encouragement to	تشجيع على
To speak affectedly	تشدّق بالكلام
To be meticulous in one's work, do one's work painstakingly	تشرّط في عمَلِه
It is (was) an honour to me	تَشَرَّفَنا
To branch off from, to result from	تشعّب عن
To take on the shape of s.o., assume the form of s.th.	تشكّل بشكله
To nose about for news	تشمّم الأخبارَ
Partisanship, partiality, bias for	تشيُّع لِـ
To have social intercourse, associate with, become friends	تصاحب مع
The vicissitudes of fate	تصاريف الدهر
To be wet with perspiration, break into a sweat	تصبّب عَرَقاً
May you be well tomorrow morning!	تُصبِح على خير!
To separate from, part from	تصدّع عن
Agreement to	تصديق على
To proceed arbitrarily in or at	تصرّف تصرفاً كيفياً في
The vicissitudes of time	تصرُّفات الزمن
Settlement, wind-up or management of affairs	تصريف الشؤون
Settlement of accounts	تصفية الحسابات
Applause	تصفيق الاستحسان
To warm o.s., seek warmth by the fire	تصلَّى بالنار
Elevations, undulations of the ground	تضاريس الأرض

Wrinkles of the face	تضاريس الوجه
Inflation	تضخُّم نقدي
Tightening of the rope	تضييق الخِناق
To bear one's head high (with pride)	تطاول برأسه
To take on, assume or receive s.o.'s peculiar character, bear s.o.'s stamp or impress	تطبّع بطباعه
To look off into the distance	تطلّع إلى بعيد
Her face broke into a radiant smile	تطلّق وجهها بابتسامة
To perform a good deed voluntarily	تطوّع خيراً
Road construction	تعبيد الطرق
To fail, meet with failure	تعثّر بأذيال الخيبة
To demand a quick reply from s.o.	تعجّله الجوابَ
Census	تعداد الأنفس
To come to blows with s.o., lay hands upon s.o.	تعدّى عليه بالضرب
Infraction, violation, breach (e.g. of laws)	تعديات
The disease defied all medical skill, gave the physicians a headache, posed a puzzling problem for the doctors	تعضّل الداءُ الأطباءَ
To put on a coat, wrap o.s. in a coat or cloak	تعطّف بالعطاف
To be or become unemployed	تعطّل عن العمل
To express o.s. with difficulty	تعقّد لسانه
To adhere, cling to s.th.	تعلّق بأهداب الشيء
To be fond of s.o., be affectionately attached to s.o.	تعلّق بحبه
To make a pretext, plead s.th. as an excuse	تعلّل بعلة
Intentionally, deliberately, wilfully, on purpose	تعمُّداً

تغرغرت عينه بالدمع	His eyes were bathed in tears
تغطرس في مشيته	To display a haughty bearing, swagger, strut
تغلّب عليه الصحة	To be fairly
تغلّب عليه الكآبة	He is in low spirits most of the time, melancholy prevails in him
تغلّب عليه النعاس	He was overcome by drowsiness
تُفًّا لك	Phew! Fie on you!
التفت حوله	To look around, glance about
تفرقوا طرائق قددًا	To split into many parts or groups, break up, dissolve
تفزّع من نومه	To be roused from one's sleep
تفصيلًا	In detail, elaborately, minutely
تفصيليًا	Separately, singly, one at a time
تفويض مطلق	General power of attorney
تقادم الزمن	Much time has gone by (since)
تقادم العهد (الزمن)	Progression or lapse of time
تقادم عهده	It happened long ago, it belongs to the past
تقاذفت به الأمواج	To be tossed about by the waves
تقارضوا الثناءَ	They competed in the recital of eulogies
تقاطيع الوجه	Features, lineaments of the face
تقدّم به	To further, advance, promote s.th.
تقدّم خطوةً فخطوة	To proceed step by step
تقدّم للامتحان	To submit o.s. to an examination
تقدّم منه	To approach s.o.
تقدّم نحوه	To step up to s.o.
تقدّمت به السنُّ	To get older, be advanced in years
تقديرًا	By implication, implicitly
تقديرًا لهذا	In appreciation of this

Police report	تقرير الشرطة
Self-determination	تقرير المصير
They took turns in dealing him painful blows, they gave him a severe beating	تقسموه ضرباً وجيعاً
Dissension, variance, disunion	تقسيم الكلمة
To follow s.o.'s tracks	تقصّص أثرَه
Negligence, dereliction of	تقصير في
To make a picture	التقط صورةً
Relations between … are broken off, they no longer have anything in common	تقطّعت الأسباب بين
To be at one's wit's end, be at the end of one's tether	تقطّعت به الأسباب
To be at the end of one's resources, be utterly helpless	تقطّعت به الحبالُ
To not desire s.th.	تقعّد عن
Change of weather	تقلّب جوي
To live in utmost misery	تقلّب على رمضاء البؤس
To have at one's disposal (s.th.)	تقلّب في
To lead a life of ease and comfort, live in prosperity	تقلّب في اعطاف العيش الناعم
To lead a life of ease and comfort	تقلّب في النعمة
He held numerous offices	تقلّب في وظائف عديدة
His prestige or authority faded, diminished, dwindled away	تقلّص (قلص) ظلّه
His prestige declined, it dwindled, faded	تقلّص ظلّه
Birth control	تقليل النسل
Manicure	تقليم الأظافير
To talk foolishly	تقوّل الأقاويلَ
To fabricate lies, spread rumours	تقوّل على
Gregorian calendar	التقويم الحريجوري

Chronology	تقويم زمني
Birth control	تقييد النسل
Cost of living	تكاليف المعيشة
To be angry, annoyed, displeased	تكدّر من
Repeatedly, quite often, frequently	تكراراً
In his honour	تكريماً له
The matter turned out to be of no consequence	تكشّف الأمر عن لا شيء
To be opened up (so as to reveal s.th.)	تكشّف عن شيء
To show o.s. utterly helpless	تكشّف عن منتهى العجز
To undertake, take upon o.s.	تكفّل بـ
To pounce, rush in, assail s.o.	تكلّب على
To force a laugh	تكلّف الضحك
To spend, to cost s.o. such and such	تكلّفه على
Legal capacity	تكليف
To predict, presage, prophesy	تكهّن بـ
To go well (with)	تلائم مع
His face became gloomy	تلبّد وجهه
The sky became overcast with clouds	تلبّدت السماء بالغيوم
To look around, glance around	تلفّت حوله
He looked to the right and left	تلفّت يَمَنَةً ويَسَرَةً
To agree wholeheartedly to s.th., submit willingly to s.th.	تلقاه بالتسليم والقبول
To take orders (commands and the like)	تلقّى الأوامر
Studies at (e.g. university)	تَلَقِّي العلوم في
To study at the university	تلقّى العلوم في الجامعة
To receive an order, have orders (soldier)	تلقّى أمراً
To take lessons in	تلقّى دروساً في

تلكّأ في	To dawdle, hesitate, tarry in s.th.
تلكّأ في الاداء	To be in default, fail to meet one's financial obligations
تلميحاً	By way of suggestion, indirectly
تماثل للشفاء (إلى الشفاء)	To be on the way to recovery
تمالك نفسَه	To gain control (over a feeling)
تمثّل بين يديه	To appear before s.o.
تمحّل له العذر	To use a pretext, make an excuse
التمسته في مظانه	I looked for him where I expected to find him, where he presumably was
تمسّك بأهداب الشيء	To adhere, cling to s.th.
تمسّك بأهدابه	To be most devoted to s.o., be at s.o.'s beck and call, be under s.o.'s thumb
تمسّك برأيه	To stick to one's opinion
تمشّى جيئة وذهاباً	To walk back and forth, pace up and down
تمهّل في خُطاه	To slacken one's pace
تمهّل يقول ...	He said slowly ...
تمهيداً لِـ	In order to facilitate, in preparation of, for the purpose of
تميّز غيظاً	To burst with anger
تنازع البقاء	Struggle for existence
تنازل عن العرش لِـ	To abdicate in favour of
تنازل عن منصب	To resign from office
تنافس حيوي	Struggle for existence
تناقل الكلامَ	To talk with one another, have a talk
تناقلت الجرائدُ الخبرَ	The report was taken up by the entire press
تناقلته الألسن	To pass from mouth to mouth, be on everybody's lips, be the talk of the town
تناقلته الأيدي	To pass on from hand to hand, change hands

To race along at a tearing pace	تناهب الأرضَ عدواً
To come to s.o.'s hearing, to s.o.'s knowledge	تناهى إلى أسماعهم
He has suffered one misfortune after another	تناوبته الخطوب
To regain consciousness	تنبّه لنفسه
To nose around for news, sniff out the news	تنسّم الخبرَ
Interior decoration	تنسيق داخلي
To refuse to take the responsibility, evade or shirk the responsibility	تنصّل من التَّبِعة (المسؤولية)
You are wasting your time	تنفخ في الرماد
To have painful sighs	تنفّس الحسرات المؤلمة
To sigh deeply, to breathe a sigh of relief	تنفّس الصُّعَدَاء
To be at one's last gasp, be dying	تنفّس النفسَ الأخير
To breathe one's last, die	تنفّس عن الحياة
To tell s.o. a fib	تنفّق بكِذبَةٍ على
To be versed in rhetoric	تنقّل في منازل البلاغة
To make s.o. deviate or swerve from	تنكّب به عن
Appendicitis	التهاب الزائدة
To exchange greetings, greet or salute each other	تهادى التحية
False accusation	تهمة باطلة
Unevenness of the terrain	التواء الأرض
To disappear from sight	توارى عن الأنظار
He is richly endowed with youth and good looks	توافر فيه الشباب والجمال
Nervousness	توتُّر الأعصاب
Relations were strained	توتّرت العلاقات
To regard s.th. as an evil omen	توجّس شرّاً من

To stand alone in one's opinion	توحّد برأيه
To give s.o. particular attention, to single out s.o. for one's special care	توحّده بعنايته
Unification, unanimity	توحيد الكلمة
To follow a method, proceed systematically	توخّى طريقه
To pursue an object, have an aim in mind	توخّى غايةً
To be embroiled, be entangled, become involved	تورّط في
To incur great expenses	توسّع في النفقة
So as to succeed by this means in, in order to get to the point where ...	توسُّلاً إلى ...
To see promising signs in s.o.	توسّم فيه خيراً
Lowering of the voice	توطئة الصوت
Safeguarding peace	توطيد السِّلم
To work as an official with the government	توظّف في الحكومة
Investment	توظيف الأموال
God has taken him unto Himself	توفّاه الله
He fulfils the conditions	توفّرت فيه الشروط
He has the necessary qualities	توفّرت فيه الصفات اللازمة
He was overcome by despair	تولّاه اليأسُ
To be in power, to seize power	تولّى الحكمَ
To be in control, to seize the reins of power, assume power	تولّى زمام الأمر

ث

To regain consciousness	ثاب إلى نفسه
To recover one's sense	ثاب إليه رُشْدُه
Staunch, undismayed, fearless	ثابت الجأش
Determined, firmly resolved	ثابت العزم
To fly into a rage, become furious, flare up	ثار ثائرُه
To revolt, rebel, rise against	ثار على
To be triggered, break out	ثار في وجهه
Shrewd, sagacious, sharp-witted	ثاقب الفكر
Sharp-eyed	ثاقب النظر
For the second time, once more, again	ثانياً
Maintenance of s.th., adherence to	ثَبَاتاً على
To fix one's eyes on, gaze at	ثبّت بصرَه به
To stand a critical test	ثبت على مِحَكِّ النظر
To hold one's own against s.o., assert o.s. against s.o.	ثبت في وجهه
To gain a foothold	ثبّت قدميه
To exist definitely, be certain, proven	ثبت وجودُه
The official determination of the beginning of a lunar month	ثبوت الشهر
Confidence, self-esteem	الثقة بالنفس
To train, educate s.o.	ثقّف عُودَه
To burden the budget	ثقّل كاهل الميزان
To load, burden, encumber s.o. or s.th.	ثقّل كاهلَه
Hard of hearing	ثقي الأذن
Unpleasant, disagreeable (person)	ثقيل الدم
Dull (person)	ثقيل الروح

Hard of hearing	ثقيل السمع
Insufferable, repugnant, unpleasant, disagreeable (person)	ثقيل الظل
Slow-witted, slow of understanding	ثقيل الفهم
He is a burden to them	ثقيل عليهم
To topple a throne, overthrow	ثَلَّ عرشاً
Thrice as much, threefold	ثلاثة أضعافه
Triangular	ثُلاثي الزوايا
It snowed, was snowing	ثَلَجَتِ السماء
Defamation	ثَلْمُ الصِّيت
A gap that cannot be closed, an irreparable loss	ثلمةٌ لا تُسَدُّ
There, there is	ثَمَّ (ثَمَّةَ)
He turned his glance on him	ثنى طرفَه إليه
He galloped off	ثَنَى عِنَانَ فَرَسِهِ
From time to time	ثِنْيَا بعد ثِنْي
Embellished garments	ثياب مزركشة
May God reward him	ثيّبه الله

ج

جاء القوم قضُّهم	All the people came
جاء القوم قضيضُهم (بقضيضهم)	All the people came
جاء ذكرُه	The discussion turned to him, people started to talk about him
جاء عقبه	He came closely after him
جاء على قدر	He arrived just at the right time
جاء في عقبه	He came closely after him
جاء بعقبه	He came closely after him
جاء من بغداد	He has come from Baghdad
جاء من نفسه	He came of his own accord
جاء والشمس طالعة	He arrived at sunset
جاء وحده	He came alone
جاءت نوبته	It was his turn
جاءني هو نفسه (بنفسه)	He himself came to me, he came personally to see me
جات يده في	He laid his hands on, he committed defalcations of
جاد بنفسه	To sacrifice o.s., to give up the ghost
جادت السماء	Heavens granted rain
جادت عيناه بالدمع	Tears welled from his eyes
جاذب أطراف الحديث	To talk, converse, have a conversation
جاذبه الحبلَ	To vie with s.o., to be able to compete with, s.o. be a match for s.o.
جاذبه الكلامَ	He engaged him in conversation, involved him in a discussion
جاذبه أطراف الحديث (حديثاً)	He engaged him in conversation, involved him in a discussion

جارت به الطريقُ	The way led him astray, he got off the wrong path
جازت عليه الحِيلَةُ	He fell for the trick, the trick worked with him
جازف بنفسه	To risk one's life
جازف به في	To plunge s.o. into (some adventure)
جال الدمع في عينيه	His eyes swam in tears
جال بباله	To run through or go on in s.o.'s mind, to preoccupy s.o.
جال برأسه	To run through or go on in s.o.'s mind, to preoccupy s.o.
جانب الفم	The corners of the mouth
جانب كبير من	A great deal of, a large portion of
جانبٌ من	A certain degree of, a good deal of
جاهد في سبيل الشيء	To fight for s.th.
جاهد في سبيل الله	To wage jihad
جاوز الثلاثين من العمر	He is past thirty, he is thirty plus
جاؤوا بأجمعهم	All of them came
جبّار الخطوة	Taking huge strides
جبّار العزمة	Of strong determination
جبر خاطرَه	To console, comfort, oblige s.o.
جُبِل على	To be born for, be naturally disposed to, have a propensity for
جثم على صدره	To weigh heavily on s.o.'s soul (problem, difficulty)
جثم في كسر بيته	To live in seclusion, stay in one's four walls
جحد جميلَه	To be ungrateful to s.o.
الجد الأعلى	Ancestor
جدّ في سيره	He strode quickly on his way
جدّ في طريقه	He strode quickly on his way, strained forward in a hurry

جدّاً	Very, much
جداء عن	Advantage, gain for s.o.
جدول الأعمال	Agenda
الجديدان	Day and night
جدير بالذكر	Worth mentioning
جذبه إلى حظيرته	To bring s.o. under one's influence
جرّ النارَ إلى قُرْصِهِ	To secure advantages for o.s., feather one's nest
جرّ جريرةً	To commit an outrage, a crime against
جرّ قدميه	To drag one's feet, have a dragging gait
جرّ قُيُوداً	To be in shackles, go shackled
جرّب الأيّامَ	To gather experience
جرّب نفسَهُ في	To try one's hand at
جرت الأمور في أعنَّتها	Things took a normal course, developed as scheduled
جرت العادة بـ	To be customary, usual, common or current, be the vogue, be a common phenomenon, have become common practice
جرت بذلك عادتهم	That was their habit, that's what they used to do
جرجر خطاه	To drag one's feet, shuffle along
جرّد السَّيْفَ	To draw, unsheathe the sword
جرّد من ملابسه	To undress s.o.
جرّد نفسَه من	To free o.s. from, rid o.s. of, give up s.th.
جرّده من السلاح	To disarm s.o.
جَرِضَ بريقه	He choked on his saliva (because of excitement, alarm or grief)
جرى (قام) على قدم وساق	To become fully effective, be in full progress, be in full swing

To do s.th. customarily, be in the habit of doing s.th.	جرى بالعادة على
To be in force, be valid, be commonly observed (law, custom)	جرى به العملُ
He ran after her	جرى خلفَها
To make s.o.'s mouth water	جرّى ريقَه
To circulate, make the rounds (rumour)	جرى على الألسن
To follow a plan	جرى على خطة
To come to s.o.'s pen	جرى على قلمِهِ
To be on everyone's lips	جرى على كل لسان
To follow s.o. loyally	جرى في غبارِه
To articulate, pronounce, utter, express s.th.	جرى لسانَه بِـ
He had a talk with	جرى له حديث مع
To take the same course as	جرى مجراه
It had become second nature to him	جرى منه الشيء مجرى الدم
In accordance with, according to	جرياً على
Capital crime	جريمة عظمى
At random, haphazardly	جُزَافاً
God bless you for it!	جزاك الله خيراً
He returned to him good for evil	جزاه جزاء سِنِمَّارَ
Of sound, unerring judgement	جزل الرأي
Partly	جزئيّاً
The particular and general aspects, the minor and the major issues	الجزئيات والكليات
To probe, sound out, try to find out s.th.	جسّ نبضَ الشيءِ
To feel s.o.'s pulse	جَسَّ نبضَه
To direct one's attention to..., have in view	جعل (وضع) ه نُصبَ عينيه

جعل زَوبَعَةً في فنجان	To cause a tempest in a teapot
جعل في صورة	To represent s.th. as, or in the form of s.th.
جعل كل شيء فداءه	He sacrificed or gave up everything for it
جَعَلَتْ عصمتَها في يدها	She made herself independent, she remained independent
جُعلتُ فداك	Oh, could I but sacrifice myself for you! (lit. may I be made your ransom)
جعله بمنزلة	To place s.o. on equal footing with
جعله على طرف الثُّمام	He made it readily understandable, he presented it plausibly for all
جعله في متناوَل يده	To bring or put s.th. within s.o.'s reach
جعله في متناوله	To bring s.th. within s.o.'s reach, make s.th. attainable, available to s.o.
جعله قاعاً صفصفاً	To devastate s.th., lay s.th. waste
جعله لقمة سائغة لـ	To make s.o. an easy prey of
جعله مضغةً في الأفواه	To make s.o. the talk of the town, send tongues wagging about s.o.
جعله هدفاً لـ	To make s.o. the target or object of, expose s.o. to s.th.
جعله يفعل	To induce s.o. to do
جفوة بين	Tense or unfriendly relation, rupture
جُلُّ الأمة	The majority of the people
جَلَّ ألوانَه	To bring the different aspects of s.th., point to s.th., make s.th. stand out
جل شأنه	The Sublime (of God)
جَلَّ عن الحصر	To be innumerable
جُلُّ ما فيه	Its main contents

جلب النارَ لقُرْصِهِ	To feather one's own nest, have an eye out for one's own interest, know on which side one's bread is buttered
جَلَبَهُ معه	To bring s.th. along, take s.th. along with o.s.
جلس (قعد) القرصاء	To squat on one's heels
جلس على النار	He was sitting by the fire
جلس على قتاد	He sat on a bed of thorns
جُلَّهُ	Most of it
جلياً	Obviously, evidently
جلية الأمر	The true state of affairs
جليس الأطفال	Babysitter
جليسُه	The man who was at the party with him
جليل الخطر	Momentous
جَمُّ الأثر	Effective
جَمٌّ غَفِير	Large crowd, throng
جماعاتٍ وأفراداً	In groups and individually
الجماهير	The masses
جمة الكائنات	Everything in existence
جمح به خيالُه	His imagination ran away with him
جمدت نفسُه على	To be indifferent towards, put up with, acquiesce to
جمدت يدُه	To be tight-fisted
جمع (توحيد الكلمة)	Union, unanimity, joining of forces
جمع أطراف الشيء	To give a survey or outline of s.th., summarise, sum up s.th.
جمع أطراف الشيء	To summarise, sum up s.th, give a survey of s.th.

جمع البراعة من أطرافها	To be a highly efficient man, be highly qualified, to do an excellent job
جمع الشمل	Union, integration
جمع القرآنَ	To learn or know the entire Quran by heart
جمع الكثرة	Plural of multitude (gram.)
جمع شَمْلَ القطيع	To round up the herd
جمع كَفَّه	To clench one's hand into a fist
جمعوا كلمتَهم على	They decidedly unanimously to, they were unanimous about
جُملةً	On the whole, in general
جملة معترضة	Parenthetical clause, parenthesis
جملةً وتفصيلاً	On the whole and in detail
جمهرة الناس	The populace
جموع الشعب	Masses of people, crowds
جميع الناس (الجميع)	All men, all mankind, all people, the public at large
جميعاً	Altogether, entirely
جميل التكوين	Well-shaped, shapely
جُنَّ جُنُونُهُ	To get madly excited, become frantic
جنباً إلى جنب	Side by side
الجنس اللطيف	The fair sex
الجنون فنون	Insanity has many varieties, manifests itself in many ways
جنى ثمرات الأرض على أنها نعمة الآلهة	He reaped the fruits of the earth (accepting them) as a boon bestowed by the grace of the gods
جنى جنايةً	To commit a crime, an offence
جنى ذنباً	To commit a crime, an offence

جنى ربحا	To make a profit
جنيه وكسور	A little over a pound
الجهات	The outskirts, provinces
جهاز الالتقاط	Receiver (radio)
الجهة المختصة	The competent authority
جُهْدَ الطاقة	As much as possible
جُهْدَ إِمْكانه	As much as he can
جَهَدَ جَهْدَهُ	To do (try) one's utmost, make every conceivable effort
جُهْدَ طاقتِه	As much as he can
جُهدَ ما	To the limits of what …
جُهدي	As far as I can
جهراً	Publicly, loudly (in prayer)
جوانب من حياته	Episodes out of his life
جيّد الحَبْكِ	Well and tightly woven, well-made
جيّد جدّاً	Very good (exam grade)
جيّداً	Well, thoroughly
جيش عَرِم	Huge army

ح

Altogether, all in a medley	حابلهم ونابلهم
Urgent need	حاجة ماسة
It is urgently needed	الحاجة ماسة إليه
Insurmountable barrier	حاجز منيع
To be confused, baffled, bewildered	حار في أمره
To be careful, be on one's guard	حاسب على نفسه
Sense of touch	حاسة اللمس
Bare-headed, hatless	حاسر الرأس
Far be it that you did it	حاش لله أن تفعل
Far be it from you that you …	حاشا لك أن …
God forbid!	حاشا لله
Far be it that I do it	حاشاي أن أفعل
Briefly, in short	الحاصل
The present, at present, now	الحاضر
	في الحاضر
Quick-witted	حاضر الفكر
quick-witted	حاضر النكتة
Incentive, stimulus, motive	حافز على
Full of, replete with, abundant, rich in content (history), much frequented (by visitors, etc.)	حافل بِ
To make s.th. inaccessible to s.o., impossible for s.o., to obstruct s.o.'s way to s.th.	حال بين فلان وبين الأمر
To deny o.s. any sympathy, to resist compassion	حال بين نفسه وبين الإشفاق
To withdraw from a contract	حال عن عهد
Presently, right way, now, at present	حالاً

State of emergency	حالة الطوارئ
Living standard	الحالة المعيشية
Whereas	حالةَ أن
State of mind, mood	حالة نفسية
At present, actually	حالياً
He was suspected, suspicion fell on him	حامتِ الشبهةُ ضدَّه
Standard bearer, flagman	حامل العَلَم
The right time has come, now is the time	حان الوقت
The time has come for him to …	حان له أن …
I happened to turn around to, it just happened that my eyes fell on	حانت مِنِّي التفاتَةٌ إلى
Weary of life, dispirited, dejected	حانق على الحياة
Misogynist	حانق على النساء
Confused, baffled	حائر في أمره
Curiosity, inquisitiveness	حب الاستطلاع
Self-love	حب الذات
Ostentatiousness, love of pomp	حب الظهور
Patriotism	حب الوطن
In the desire to	حباً في
Out of curiosity	حباً في الاستطلاع
Out of love for	حباً لـ
For your sake and in your honour	حباً وكرامةً لك
Jets of water	حبال الماء
It would be nice, or he would do well, if he did it	حبذا الحالُ لو فعل
How nice it would be if …	حبذا لو …
Mere ink on paper, of no effect (e.g. an agreement, a treaty)	جِبرٌ على ورق
To make s.o. catch his breath, take s.o.'s breath away	حبس عليه أنفاسَه

He was committed to prison under hard labour	حُبِس مع الشغل
To devote o.s. entirely to	حبس نفسَه على
To take (s.th.) out from under s.o.'s power	حبس يدَه عن
Umbilical cord	الحبل السُّرِّي
Jugular vein	حبل الوريد
Amicably	حُبِّياً
Until when?	حتَّامَ؟
Decidedly, inevitably	حتماً
Until now, hitherto, so far	حتى الآن
To the last breath	حتى النَّفَس الأخير
Even if	حتى لو
Till when? How long?	حتى متى؟
How far? To which point?	حتى متى؟
Not even, and be it only	حتى ولا
To hurry, to hasten	حثَّ الطريقَ
To quicken one's pace	حثَّ خُطاه
To break into a run	حثَّ قدمَيْه
To think well of s.o., have a good opinion of s.o.	حجا به خيراً
Limestone	حجارة كِلسِيَّة
To block s.o.'s view	حجب الرؤية عن شخص
Cornerstone	حجر الناصية
Quarantine	حِجْر صِحِّي
Stumbling block	حجر عُثْرة
Thought-ban, mind control	الحِجر على الأفكار
Precious stone	حجر كريم
To postpone a case until sentencing	حجزه للحكم

Minimum	الحدّ الأدنى
The minimum wage	الحدّ الأدنى للأجور
The maximum	الحد الأعلى
The maximum	الحد الأقصى
Utmost limit, last step	حد النهاية
Prevention (of s.th.), restriction	الحد من
To instigate s.th.	حدا بِ
Their conversation led them to	حدا بهم الحديثُ إلى
An unpleasant event	حدث مزعج
He said to himself, told himself that …	حدّث نفسَه أن …
To talk o.s. into s.th.	حدّث نفسَه بِ
His innermost feeling told him	حدّثته نفسُه
His heart, his innermost feeling told him	حدّثه قلبُه
To stare	حدّج ببصره (بنظره)
To dart sharp glances, to scrutinise	حدّد بصرَه
To rattle off, express quickly (an utterance, a thought)	حدر حدراً
To fix one's glance on	حدّق النظر
New-built	حديث البناء
Young	حديث السن
Of recent date, new	حديث العهد
Recent, late, new, young	حديث العهد
Inexperienced at s.th., new at s.th.	حديث العهد بِ
Newly-wed	حديث العهد بالزواج
Newborn	حديث العهد بالولادة
New-fashioned, modern	حديث النمط
Conversation drifts from one topic to another	الحديث شجون

حديث عهد بِـ	Having adopted or acquired (s.th.) recently, inexperienced at (s.th.), new at (s.th.)
حديث عهد بعرس	Newly-wed
حديث نبوي	Prophetic tradition
حديثاً	Recently, lately
حذار أن (من)	Beware of doing ..., watch out for! Be careful of!
حَذْوَ القُذَّة بالقُذة	Exactly identical, deceptively alike
حَذْوَكَ النَّعْلَ بِالنعل	In a completely identical manner, like two peas in a pod
حرام عليك	You mustn't do that!
حرب العِصَابات	Guerrilla war(fare)
حرب ضَرُوسٌ	Fierce, murderous war
الحرث والنسل	The civilisation of man
حِرْصاً على	In the desire for, out of concern for
حرفاً بحرف	Word for word
حرّفه عن موضعه	To distort the sense of s.th., rob s.th. of its true meaning
حرَق أسنانَه	To gnash one's teeth
حَرَقَ الأُرَّمَ (غَضباً)	To gnash one's teeth (in anger)
حرق قلبَه (قلوبَهم)	To vex, exasperate s.o.
حرّك العواطفَ	To affect the feelings, be touching
حرّك ساكنَه	To rouse s.o., agitate s.o.
حرّك مشاعرَه	To excite, thrill s.o.
حركات لاإراديّة	Involuntary movements
حركة كشفية	Boy scout movement
حرّمه على نفسه	To deny o.s. s.th., abstain, refrain from s.th.
حري بالتصديق	Credible, believable
حَرِيٌّ بالذكر	Worth mentioning, considerable
حرّيّة الرأي	Freedom of opinion

حزّب الأمرُ	The matter became serious
حزَبَهُ حازبٌ	He met with a mishap
حزم أمرَه	To take matters firmly in hand
حزّم متاعَه	To pack one's things, tie up one's effects
حَسَبَ الأصول	Properly, in conformity with regulations
حَسَبَ الظاهر	In outward appearance, externally, outwardly
حسب ألفَ حسابَ لـ	To have a thousand apprehensions about …
حسب اللزوم	As required, as the occasion demands
حسب حساباً لـ	To attach importance to s.o. or s.th.
حسب حسابَه	To take s.th. or s.o. into account or into consideration, count on s.th. or s.o.
حسباني أن …	I expect that …
حسبُك (بحسبك) درهم	One dirham is enough for you
حسبك أن …	It suffices to say that, you know enough when you hear that, you need only …
حسبما	According to what, depending on how …
حسبما اتفق	As chance will have it
حسبما أذكر	As far as I remember
حسبما يحلو له	At his discretion, as he pleases
حَسَر البَصَر	Near-sightedness, myopia
حسُن استعدادُه لـ	He was all willing to …
حسن الأداء	Good rendition (of a work of art, of a musical composition)
حُسْنُ التصرف	Discretion
حسن التعبير	Euphemism

Good behaviour	حسن السلوك
Good fortune, lucky star, good luck	حسن الطالع
Good opinion, favourable judgement	حسن الظن
Good opinion	حسن الظن
Of good ancestry, of good stock	حسن العِزوة
Good intention, good will	حسن القصد (النية)
Well-built	حَسَن القَمَّة
Good intention, good will, honesty	حسن النية
To have a good opinion of s.o., think well of s.o.	حَسُنَ ظنُّهُ به
Well, splendidly	حَسَناً
To have good intentions	حسنت نيته في
To push one's way through the crowd	حشر نفسَه بين الناس
Racehorse	حصان السباق
Thoroughbred horse	حصان كريم
To result, take place	حصل
To happen, occur to s.o.	حصل لـ
Stronghold (fig. e.g. of radicalism)	الحصن الحصين
To immunise	حصّن ضِدَّ
Obtainment of	حصول على
To take part, participate in a meeting	حضر مجلساً
Presence of mind	حضور الذهن
To dismount, encamp	حطّ الرحالَ
Reduction, decrease of s.th.	حطّ من
To depreciate the value of s.th.	حطّ من قدره
To depreciate the value of s.th.	حطّ من قيمته
The vanities of the world	حُطَامُ الدنيا

To support s.o., back s.o. up	حطب في حبله
Enjoying (s.o.'s interest, attention), favoured by s.th.	حظي بِـ
To wipe one's winds on s.th.	حفّ يديه بِـ
Gravedigger	حفّار القبور
To prepare a pitfall, prepare an ambush	حفر حُفَرَةً
To dig trenches	حفر خنادق
To memorise the Quran	حفظ القرآن
To be loyal to s.o., keep faith with s.o.	حفظ الوفاءَ لِـ
To keep one's word	حفظ كلمتَه
To keep s.o. in fond remembrance	حفظ له جميلاً
May God protect him!	حفظه الله
Right of granting pardon	حق العفو عن العقوبة
Right of veto	حق النقض
Absolute certainty	حق اليقين
You are wrong	الحق عليك
It is your duty	حق عليك
He deserved it (punishment)	حق عليه
You are right	الحق معك
Plain truth	حق ناصع
Really, indeed, in truth	حقّاً
For quite a time, for some time	حِقْبَةٌ من الزمان
To look closely, to study, examine	حقّق النظرَ
To inject s.th. in the veins	حقن العروقَ بِـ
To give s.o. an injection	حقنه إبرةً
What he can claim, what is his due	حقُّه
In reality, in effect, literally	حقيقةً
The whole truth, nothing but the truth	الحقيقة كل الحقيقة
Accomplished fact	حقيقة مقررة

حلّ في صدره	It impressed him, affected him, touched s.th. inside him
الحكم المطلق	Absolute power, authoritarian regime
حكم بإدانته	To convict s.o.
الحكم بالإعدام	Death sentence
حكم ببراءته	To acquit s.o.
حكم بصحته	To determine that s.th. is right
حكم تجهيل الرجل	He decided that the man should be declared *jāhil*, i.e. not responsible for his actions
حكم ذاتيّ	Self-determination
حكم على أن ...	He judged or decided that ...
حُكِم عليه بالإعدام	He was sentenced to death
حكم فيه بتحريم	He decreed it to be forbidden, that it should be considered unlawful
الحكم نافذ فيه	The sentence will be carried out, has legal force
حكم نهائي	Final decision, final judgement
حكماً	Virtually, legally
حكومة موقتة	Provisional government
حكومة نيابية	Representative government
حل أوصاله (قطع أوصاله)	To dismember, dissect s.th.
حلّ ثالثاً	He came in third place
حلّ في منصب	To take over or hold an office
حل محل التقدير لديه	To enjoy s.o.'s high esteem
حل محل الشيء	To take the place of s.o. or s.th., replace, substitute
حل محل فلان	To replace, substitute
حلّ محلَّه	To be in the right place
حلّ من نفوس القراء محلَّ الاستحسان	To meet with readers' approval

Middle solution, compromise	حل وسط
He enjoyed the thing	حلا له الشيءُ
It pleased him that, he was delighted that …	حلا له أن …
Euphoria	حلاوة الروح
He has seen good and bad days	حلب الدهرَ أشطرَه
Racetrack	حلبة (ميدان) السباق
She held a place in his heart	حلّت في قلبه محلاً
To swear by all that's holy	حلف بالطلاق
To swear by God	حلف بالله
To take an oath	حلف يميناً
A gathering of remembrance, meditation, a Sufi circle	حَلْقَةُ الذكر
Vicious circle, *circulus vitiosus*	حلقة مُفرَغة
Daydream	حُلْم اليقظة
Amusing or entertaining thing	حلو الحديث
The decision was already made	حُمّ القدرُ
To decree s.th. (said of God)	حمّ الله
That is his destiny	حُمّ له ذلك
Thanks to God	الحمد لله
To know the Quran by heart	حمل القرآن
To involve, comprise, contain	حمل بين طيّاته
To launch an attack	حمل حملةً على
To pull o.s. together, brace o.s.	حمل على نفسه
To be an upholder of an idea	حمل فكرةً
To feel annoyed, feel blue	حمل في نفسه
To hold a title	حمل لقباً
Advertising campaign	حملة دعائيّة
To bring around, win over s.o. to one's opinion, convince	حمله على رأيه
To misinterpret, misconstrue s.th.	حمله على غير محمله

حمله على محمل …	To take s.th. to mean, interpret or construe s.th. in the sense of, as if it were …
حمله محملَ الجد	To take s.th. seriously
حمّله وزرَه	To make s.o. bear the responsibility for s.th., make s.o. answerable for s.th.
حمى الوطيس	Fierce fighting broke out
حُمَيّاً	Heat, agitation, excitement
الحمية القومية	Chauvinism
حميلة على	A burden to, completely dependent upon
حَنِثَ بيمينه	To break one's oath
حَنِثَ في يمينه	To break one's oath
حنّن قلبَه	To move, fill with compassion s.o.'s heart
حنى رأسَه	To bow one's head down
حوالي	Around, about, approximately
حوّل الدَفَّة	To change the course
حوّل بصرَهُ عن	To avert one's gaze from
حوّل نظرةً إلى	To direct a glance towards
حوله	Around him, about him
حوّم به الفكرُ في أودية شتى	His thoughts trailed off, he was thinking of s.th. else
حي الضمير	Conscientious, scrupulous
حياة التشريد	The unsettled life, life of a vagabond
حياة زوجيّة	Married life, marriage
حيّاك الله	God preserve your life!
حيث أن …	Since, due to the fact that …
حيث كان	Wherever it be, in any case
حيثما اتفق	Anywhere, wherever it may be, at random

What a pity! Too bad!	حَيْفٌ عليه
When I had come to this point in my reminiscences	حين بلغت بذكرياتي هذا المبلغ
For some time, once, one day	حِيناً
From time to time, now and then, once in a while	حيناً بعد حين
At that time, then, that day	حينذاك
While, when, as	حينما
At that time, then, that day	حينئذ
Mammal	حيوان لبون
Predatory animal, beast of prey	حيوان مفترس
The rodents	الحيوانات القاضمة

خ

The end of the matter, the final issue, the upshot of it	خاتمة المطاف
Outside	خارجاً
Outside of, apart from	خارجاً عن
Supernatural	خارق الطبيعة
Extraordinary	خارق للعادة
The specific and the general, high and low, all people, everybody	الخاص والعام
The upper class	الخاصة
The most select elite	خاصة الخاصة
High and low, all men, all, everybody	الخاصة والعامة
Especially for that reason	خاصةً وأنّ
To rush into battle	خاض المعركةَ
To delve into exegesis	خاض في علم التفسير
To address s.o. on an intimate first-name basis	خاطبه بالكاف
To call s.o. up	خاطبه بالهاتف
To risk one's life	خاطر بنفسه
To fear s.o., be afraid of s.o.	خاف (رهب, هاب) جانبَه
To lower one's voice	خافت بصوته
To lower one's voice	خافت بكلامه
East and West	الخافقان
Devoid of	خالٍ من
Unoccupied, uninhabited	خال من السكان
Unemployed	خال من العمل
Useless	خال من الفائدة
To be uppermost in s.o.'s heart	خالج قلبَه

To glance furtively at s.o.	خالسه النظرَ
To befall, attack s.o. (pain, etc.)	خالط نفسَه
Unrestrained, uninhibited, debauchee	خالع العِذار
Empty-handed	خالي الوطاب
Vacant, free, empty-handed	خالي الوفاض
To break a contract, a trust	خان أمانةً
He didn't have enough money, his pocket had a hole in it	خان جَيبُه
To deceive one's wife	خان زوجتَه
To break a contract, a trust	خان عهداً
Success eluded him	خانه التوفيق
Completely devastated	خاوٍ على عروشه
Empty-handed, without a catch	خاوي الوِفاض
Alarmed by, apprehensive of	خائف على (من)
To sink in sand	خبّ في الرمل
That which is hidden in the earth, natural resources	خبايا الأرض
To stamp the ground (of animals)	خبط الأرضَ
To knock on the door	خبط البابَ
He struck out blindly at them (with a cane)	خبط فيهم خبطَ عشواء
God made him impervious (to guidance)	ختم الله على قلبه
To damage s.o.'s reputation	خدش سمعتَه
To mislead, dupe s.o.	خدعه عن نفسه
To till or cultivate the soil	خدم الأرض
To be at s.o.'s beck and call	خدم ركابَ فلان
To serve s.o.'s interest	خدم مصالح فلان
For the sake of truth, in the interest of truth	خدمة للحقيقة
He rendered him many services	خدمه خدمات كثيرة

خذ على يمينك	Turn to the right!
خرَّ بين يديه	He prostrated himself before him
خرَّ تحت قدميه	He fell at his feet
خرَّ على الأرض	To fall to the ground
خرج عليه بِـ	To come up to s.o. with, confront s.o. with
خرج عن	To be an exception to (a principle)
خرج عن الخط	To be derailed, run off the track
خرج عن طوره	To lose one's self-control
خرج من عنق زجاجة	To get out of a tight spot
خرج من ميدان العمل	To be put out of service or commission
خرج منه ظافراً غانماً	To overcome s.th. successfully
خرج منه في عافية	To recover nicely from s.th.
خرجت الجماهير عن بكرتها	The crowd went forth as one man
خرَقَ العادة	To go beyond what is ordinary or customary
خُرْقٌ في الرأي	Stupidity
خُرم الإبرة	Eye of a needle
خروج على القاعدة	Violation of a rule
خروج عن القياس	Abnormality, irregularity
خزَقه في الأرض	To drive, ram s.th. to the ground
خزَمَ أنفه	To make s.o. subservient to one's will (lit. insert the nose ring for the bridle)
خسارة مذلّة	A humiliating defeat
خسف الله به الأرضَ	God made him sink into the ground, God made the ground swallow him up
خَسِئْتَ	Beat it! Scram!
خَشَعَ ببصرِه	To lower one's eyes

Coarse to the touch, rough	خَشِنُ الجس
Uncouth	خشن الخُلْق
Thick-shelled	خشن القِشرة
Coarse to the touch, rough, wrinkled	خَشِن اللمس
Out of fear that …	خشيةً أن …
For fear of	خشيةً من
To take possession of	خص به نفسَه
To mention s.b. explicitly	خصّ شخصاً بالذكر
To make special mention of s.o. or s.th.	خصّه بالذكر
To devote one's attention to s.o.	خصّه بعنايتِه
To take possession of	خصّه لنفسه
Especially, particularly, specifically	خُصوصاً
Especially for that reason	خصوصاً وأنّ
To tame s.o., hold s.o. in check, curb s.o.'s power	خَضَدَ شوكتَه
To till the earth, to sow the land	خضّر الأرضَ
Geographical longitude, meridian	خط الطول
Degree of latitude	خط العرض
To draw a line	خطّ خَطّاً
Line of defence	خطّ دفاع
To draw a line	خطّ سطراً
Erroneously, by mistake	خطأً
To take large strides (fig. to make extraordinary progress)	خطا خطوات واسعة
Misprint	خطأ مطبعي
To betroth one's daughter to s.o.	خطب بنتَه لِ
To preach, deliver a sermon	خطب في الناس
He courted her love	خطب مودّتَها
He courted her love	خطب وُدَّها
To propose to a girl (said of the man)	خطبها

خطر الأمر على (في) باله	The matter came to his mind, occurred to him, he recalled the matter
خطر الأمر على قلبه	The matter came to his mind, occurred to him, he recalled the matter
خطر بباله	It occurred to him, it came to his mind
خطرٌ على	Danger, peril, menace to
خطر له خاطر	He had an idea
خطف البصرَ	To dazzle the eyes
خطفة من خطفات الشعور	An impulse, a sudden emotion
خطّه الشيبُ	His hair turned grey
خُطىً	Step, pace, stride
خطير الشأن	Of great importance
خفّضَ السرعةَ	To reduce one's speed, slow down
خفض جَنَاحَهُ لـ	To show o.s. open-minded, responsive, accessible to
خفّضَ صوتَه	He lowered his voice
خَفِّضْ عليك	Take it easy!
خَفِّضْ عليك جَأْشَكَ	Calm down! Relax!
خفض له جانبَه	To meet s.o. on fair terms, to be affable or gracious
خفّف الآلام عنه	To soothe s.o.'s pains
خَفِّفْ عنك	Cheer up! Take it easy!
خَفِّفْ من سرعتك	Slow down!
خفف من غُلوائه	To curb s.o.'s enthusiasm, dampen s.o.'s ardour
خَفَقَات القلب	Heartbeats
خُفية	Secretly, covertly, without anyone's noticing

Without his knowledge	خُفيةً عنه
Likeable, nice (of a person)	خفيف الظل
Having a sparse beard	خفيف العارضين
Stop this nonsense!	خلٍّ عنك هذا الهُرَاء
Desist from such desires!	خلٍّ عنك هذه الميولَ
Except, save, with the exception of	خلا
To commune with o.s., search one's heart	خلا إلى نفسه
His mind is at rest, he has no worries	خلا بالُه
To forsake, desert s.o.	خَلا به
To have free scope, have freedom of action	خلا له الجو
His way was unobstructed, he had clear sailing	خلا له وجهة الطريق
Contrary to	خلافاً لـ
Other, the like	خلافُه (غيره)
Others (than those mentioned)	خلافُهم
During, between, through	خِلَال
To bewitch, enchant s.o.'s mind	خلبه عقلَه
To rest	خَلَدَ إلى الراحة
To lie down to sleep	خَلَدَ إلى النوم
By stealth, surreptitiously, unobtrusively, unnoticeably	خُلْسَةً
To restore one's right	خَلَّصَ حقَّه
To be free from	خَلَّصَ من
To confuse s.o.'s thinking	خلط عليه تفكيرَه
To talk confusedly	خلط في كلامه
In confusion	خلط ملط
To disown one's son	خلع ابنَه
To refuse obedience	خلع البيعةَ

خلع الطاعة	To refuse obedience
خلع ثِيابَه	To undress
خلع عِذارَه	To throw off all restraint, drop all pretences of shame
خلع على نفسه حقَّ	To arrogate to o.s. the right of
خلع عليه خِلعَةً	To bestow a robe of honour upon s.o.
خلعه من العرش	To dethrone s.o.
خلفَ	Behind, after
خلّف وراءه	To leave s.th. behind
خِلْقَةً	By nature
خلّى بين فلا وبين الشيء	To let s.o. have his own way with or in
خلّى سبيلَه	To let s.o. off, release s.o.
خَلِيُ البال	Happy-go-lucky
خليط من	Blend of
خليق أن ...	It is only natural for him that he ...
خليق بِ	Suitable for s.th.
خليق بهذا أن يكون مؤلماً	It is only natural that this is painful
الخمر جماع الإثم	Wine is the vessel of sin
خمسة أمتار في عشرة	Five meters by ten (width and length)
خمسة في ثلاثة	Five times three
خَمَلَ ذِكرُه	To have fallen into oblivion, be forgotten
خوارق المصادفات	Miraculous coincidences
الخوافق	The four quarters of the world
خُولِطَ في عقله	To be or become disordered in mind
خَوَى مما حَوَى	To have become empty (e.g. purse)
خيار الناس	The best of all people, the best people
الخيال الخلّاق	Creative imagination

Creative imagination	الخيال المبتكر
Slightest doubt	خيال شك
Infidelity	خيانة زوجيّة
To dash s.o.'s hopes	خيّب آماله
The best of all people, the best people	خير الناس
The very best	الخير كل الخير
It is better for you	خير لك
Rope, cord	خيط القُنَّب
A spark of hope, a thread of hope	خيط أمل
He imagined, thought that, it seemed to him that ...	خُيِّلَ إليه (له) أن ...

د

Curable disease	داء يقبل الشفاءَ
To do s.th. consistently	دأب على شيء
Orphanage	دار الأيتام
Mint	دار السكة
The hereafter	دار القرار
Court of justice, tribunal	دار القضاء
Library	دار الكتب
Medina	دار الهجرة
The whole house	الدار جَمْعَاء
War broke out	دارت رحى الحرب
To suffer adversities	دارت عليه الدوائر
An Islamic preacher	داعيّة إسلاميّ
A peace activist	داعيّة سلام
To defend one's opinion	دافع عن رأيّه
To defend someone	دافع عن شخص
To defend his interest	دافع عن مصالحه
A powerful incentive	دافع قويّ
Encyclopedia	دائرة المعارف
Electoral district	دائرة انتخابيّة
An official authority	دائرة رسميّة
Doubt crept into him	دبّ الشك في نفسه
The enemy tanks	دبّابات العدوّ
To write a poem	دبّج قصيدة
To arrange matters	دبّر الأمور
To conduct the course of business	دبّر الشؤون
To hatch a plot	دبّر خطّة

To hatch a plot	دبّر كميناً
Sound of footsteps	دبيب أقدام
To arm s.o. to the teeth	دجّجه بالسلاح
Monthly income	دخل شهريّ
To involve oneself in the war	دخل الحرب
To enter a new world	دخل عالما جديدا
To come to the point	دخل في الموضوع
To belong to, to fall under	دخل في باب
To belong to the past, be no longer existent	دخل في خبر كان
To become effective, come into force	دخل في طور (دور) التنفيذ
Steady income	دخل قار
Low income	دخل محدود (بسيط)
He entered through the gates	دخل من الباب
Prayer time has started	دخل وقت الصلاة
Free admission	دخول مجّانيّ
Foreigner, outsider	دخيل القوم
A drama taken from real life	درامة مستخرجة من صُلب الحياة
Melting point	درجة الانصهار
Freezing point	درجة الجمد
University degree	درجة جامعيّة
Centigrade (thermometer)	درجة مئوية
To conspire	دسّ السَمّ في الدسَم
To slip s.o. poison	دسّ السّمّ لشخص
To inaugurate a university	دشّن جامعة
Desist! Stop!	دع عنك
Not to speak of, let alone …	دع من …
To advocate for Islam	دعا إلى الإسلام
To call for peace	دعا إلى السلام
He called him to account	دعاه إلى الحساب
To be run over by a car	دعسته سيّارة

دعك من هذا	Stop that! Cut it out!
دعم حكوميّ	A government subsidy
دعم ماليّ	Financial support
دعنا من هذا	Let's not talk about it! Enough of that!
دعنا نذهب	Let's go!
دعني وشأني	Let me alone!
دعوى عسكريّة	Military proceedings
دعوى مدنيّة	Civil proceedings, civil action, civil suit
دفاع جوّيّ	Air defence
دفاع ذاتيّ	Self-defence
دفاع عن المصالح	Defending one's interest
الدفاع عن بيضة الدين	Defence of the faith
الدفاع عن بيضة الوطن	Defence of the country
الدفاع عن حوزة مصر	The defence of Egyptian territory
دفع أجرا	To pay wages
دفع الحساب	To pay the bill
دفع بالتقسيط	Payment in instalment
دفع بمنكبيه الهواء	To race along, dash along
دفع ثمن جريمته	To pay for one's crime
دفع مسبّق	Advance payment
دفعة قويّة في الاتجاه الصّحيح	A step in the right direction
دفعة واحدة	All at once
دفوع شكليّة	Formal plea
دقّ يداً بيدٍ	To clap one's hands
دقائق الأمور	The niceties
دقة الشعور	Sensitivity, sensibility
دقيق الشعور	Sensitive
دقيق الصنع	Finely worked

To ruin s.th. completely, run s.th. into the ground	دكّه إلى الحضيض
To indicate s.th.	دلّ على شيء
To spoil his children	دلّل أطفاله
Phone directory	دليل الهاتف
Irrefutable evidence	دليل دامغ
Circumstantial evidence	دليل ظرفي
Cogent proof, conclusive evidence	دليل قاطع
Conclusive evidence	دليل ناطق
Conclusive proof, cogent evidence	دليل ناهض
Gentle, mild-tempered	دمث الأخلاق
To destroy weapons	دمّر أسلحة
To demolish the house	دمّر البيت
To be completely destroyed, be wiped off the map	دُمِّرَ عَن آخره
Of bad character	دَنِس الثياب
Incessantly, without interruption	دواماً واستمراراً
A downward spiral of violence	دوّامة العنف
Government circles	دوائر الحكومة
Places of entertainment, amusement centres	دُور اللهو
Blood circulation	دوران الدم
Monthly cycle	الدورة الشهريّة
Election round	دورة انتخابيّة
Training, internship	دورة تدريبيّة
Legislative session	دورة تشريعيّة
A round of talks	دورة مشاورات
The sister states	الدول الشقيقة
The authoritarian states	الدول ذات الحكم المطلق
Donor country	دولة مانحة
Host country	دولة مضيفة

Without delay	دون إبطاء
Far from being true	دون الواقع بكثير
Without delay	دون تأخير
Of no use, of no avail, useless, futile	دون طائل
In the twinkling (blink) of an eye, in a moment, in a flash, instantly	دون لمح البصر
Without resistance	دون مقاومة
Irrespective of, regardless of	دون نظر إلى
Unconscious	دون وعي
The blast of the explosion	دويّ الانفجار
The rumbling of thunder	دويّ الرعد
The rumbling of cannons	دويّ المدافع
The holy places	الديار المقدّسة

ذ

ذا الحين	Just now, right now
ذاب حياءً	To die of shame
ذاب غمّاً	To die of grief
ذات الصدر	Chest complaint, bottom of the heart, secret thoughts
ذات مرةٍ	Once, one time, one day
ذاد عن حياضه	To assume the defence of s.o.
ذاد عن وطنه	To defend one's country
ذاع صيته	To become famous
ذاكرة جماعيّة	Collective memory
ذائع الصيت	Famous, celebrated, well-known
ذب عن حياض الدين	To defend the faith
ذرّ الرماد في عيون شخص	To pull the wool over s.b.'s eyes, to deceive s.b. with a smokescreen
الذراعي العسكريّ	The armed wing
ذرّة رمل	A grain of sand
ذرف دموعا	To shed tears
ذُروة النشوة	Orgasm
ذعر شديد	Strong fear
ذكاء اصطناعيّ	Artificial intelligence
ذكاء حادّ	A keen intellect
ذكر الشيء على سبيل المثال	To quote s.th. as an example
ذكّر شخصاً بشيء	To remind s.b. of s.th.
ذكر شخصاً بالخير	To mention s.b. favourably
ذكره بالخير	To retain a good impression of s.o., to speak well of s.o.
ذكرى مئويّة	Centenary

ذلك شأنه	That is his habit
ذلك من الأهمية بمكان	That is of considerable importance
ذمّتُهُ بَرَاءٌ مِن ...	He is innocent of ...
ذهاباً وإياباً	There and back, back and forth, up and down
ذهب أدراج الرياح	To be in vain
ذهب (مضى) على وجهه	To go one's own way, to go one's way
ذهب بعيداً	To go far away, go to distant lands
ذهب به هباء	To ruin, thwart s.th., to scatter s.th. in all directions
ذهب جفاءً	To be in vain, be of no avail, pass uselessly
ذهب جيئةً وذهاباً	To pace the floor, walk up and down
ذهب سُدىً	To be in vain, futile, useless
ذهب صيحةً في واد	To die unheard
ذهب ضحيّته	To fall victim to, become a victim of s.th. or s.o.
ذهب كعبُهم	Their days of glory are past
ذهب لبعض شأنه	He attended to a task, he went to do s.th.
ذهب للقاء ربّه	He passed away
ذهب هباء منثوراً	To go up in smoke, fall through, come to nought, dissolve into nothing
ذهب هدراً	To melt away uselessly, futilely, be spent in vain, be wasted
ذهبوا أيدي سَبَا	To be scattered in all directions, they were scattered to the four winds
ذهوب ومآب	Coming and going
ذو الاقطاع	Liege lord, feudal lord

ذو الشأن ذات الشأن	The responsible man, the man in charge, the man directly concerned with the matter
ذو المعاش	Pensioner
ذو النفوذ	Influential
ذو بأس	Courageous, brave, intrepid
ذو بال	Significant, important
ذو ثلاثة أبعاد	Three-dimensional
ذو حدّين	Double-edged
ذو حَسَب ونَسَب	Of noble descent
ذو حظٍّ من	Endowed with
ذو خطر	Dangerous, perilous, important
ذو سعة	Wealthy
ذو شأن	Significant, important
ذو عُدَواءَ	Rough, rugged, adverse, inconvenient, bad, poor
ذو عقل	Intelligent
ذو علاقة بِـ	Connected with, related to
ذو قيمة	Valuable
ذو لسانين	Deceitful, double-tongued, insincere, two-faced
ذو مال	Wealthy, rich
ذو معنى	Significant, meaningful, telling
ذو مغزى	Significant
ذو ملاحظة	Considerable, notable
ذو نَفَس	Enough to shake the thirst
ذوق رفيع	To have a good taste
ذوو الشبهات	Dubious persons, people of ill repute
ذوو قدر	People of distinction, important people
ذَوُوا الشأن	The influential people, the competent people, those concerned with the matter

ر

The Muslim league	الرابطة الاسلامية
Gross salary	راتب إجمالي
Net wage	راتب صافٍ
Eternal rest	راحة أبديّة
The submit of the mountain	رأس الجبل
New year	رأس السنة
Capital	رأس مال
Nuclear head	رأس نوويّ
Head over heels, topsy-turvy, upside down	رأساً على عقب
Glad to have saved one's skin (lit. content with returning without booty)	راضٍ من الغنيمة بالإياب
To comply with the decision	راعى القرار
To respect s.o.'s wishes, to have regard for s.o.'s feelings	راعى خاطرَه
To respect s.b.'s feelings	راعى شعور شخص
Eager to buy	راغب الشراء
To take pity on s.b.	رأف بشخص
To accompany s.o.	رافق شخصا
All the best	رافقتك السلامة
To bet that ...	راهن على أنّ ...
To gamble on one's life	راهن على حياته
To bet on s.th.	راهن على شيء
Under the circumstances	راهن: الظروف الراهنة
The present	راهن: الوضع الراهن

رأى النورَ	To come into being (see the light of day), come into the world, be born
رأى رأي العين	To find out, or see, with one's own eyes
رأى من قواضي الذمة أن ...	To regard it as one's duty to ...
الرأي العام	Public opinion
الرأي والمبنى	Content and form
رأيته على حقيقته	I saw its true nature, as it really is
رائحة زكيّة	Fragrance
ربّ الأسرة	The head of the family
رُبّ قائل قال	Many people say
ربّة المنزل	The lady of the house
ربح إجمالي	Gross profit
ربح دعوى	To win a lawsuit
ربط جأشَهُ	To remain calm, composed, be undismayed, to keep one's self-control
ربط على قلبه	To fortify s.o., give s.o. patience
ربط لسانه	To silence s.o.
ربطة العنق	Tie, necktie
الربع الخالي	The Empty Quarter
الربيع العربي	The Arab Spring
ربيع عمره	The prime of his life
الرتابة اليوميّة	The monotony of daily life
رتّب أفكاره	To collect one's thoughts
رتّب حساباته	To be prepared for s.th. or to do s.th.
رتبة عسكريّة	A military rank
رتّبت أمورها	To order one's affairs
رث الهيئة	Of shabby appearance
رجال الإطفاء	Firemen, the fire department

رجال السخرة	Serfs, bondsmen
رجال الكَهنُوت	The clergy, the ministry
رجال عِدَّة	Many men
الرجال كلهم	All men
رجع (عاد) بصفقة المغبون	To return empty-handed, to lose the game
رجع (عاد) على عقبيه	To retrace one's steps, turn back, to turn on one's heels
رجع (فاء) إلى صوابه	To regain one's reason, get back to one's senses, become reasonable again
رجع الصوت	Echo, reverberation
رجع إلى حافرته	To revert to its original state or origin
رجع إلى صوابه	To come round
رجع بخُفَّيْ حُنَيْن	To return with empty hands, without having achieved one's mission
رجع عن قراره	To go back on a decision
رجع في كلامه	To go back on his word
رجعت به الذاكرة إلى	He recalled, remembered
رجعوا (عادوا) على أعقابهم	They turned back
رجل عالي الكعب	A distinguished, capable, successful man
رجل كهذا	Such a man, a man like this
رجل من قريش	A man of the Quraysh tribe
رجل هذا شأنُه	A man whose situation is this, a man who can be described as, a man in this situation
رجل واسع الحيلة	A resourceful, ingenious man
رحاب الكون	Vastness of outer space
رحابة الفناء	Hospitable reception, generous entertainment

Generous, liberal	رحب الباع
Roomy, spacious	رحب الجوانب
Generous, magnanimous, open-minded	رحب الصدر
Broad-minded	رَحْبُ العَطَن
To greet or welcome the guest	رحّب بالضيف
Expedition	رحلة استطلاعية
Flight	رحلة جوّيّة
Study tour	رحلة دراسيّة
Business trip	رحلة عمل
They set out all together or with bag and baggage	رحلوا بِقَلِيَّتِهِم
God bless his soul	رحمه الله
To be permitted to return	رُخِّص له بالعودة
Driving licence	رخصة قيادة
To straighten s.th. out, set a matter right	رَدَّ (أعاد) أمراً إلى نصابه
Rehabilitation	ردّ الاعتبار
To return the greeting	ردّ السلام
To bring the rear to the fore, i.e. to reverse conditions, make up for a deficiency	رد العجز على الصدر
Reaction	ردّ الفعل
Retaliation	ردّ انتقامي
Positive response	ردّ إيجابي
To answer in the affirmative, say yes	ردَّ بالإيجابِ
To respond quickly	ردّ بسرعة
To reject a charge	ردّ تهمة
To answer	ردّ جوابا
To respond to something	ردّ على شيء
To pay s.o. back twofold, bring double retaliation on s.o.	رد له الصاع صاعين

To return the echo	ردّد الصدى
To reconsider	ردّد النظر في
To reduce s.o. to the lowest level or status	ردّه أسفل سافلين
To drive s.o. back to where he came from	رده على عقبيه
To drive s.o. back to where he came from	ردهم على أعقابهم
Of ill repute	رديئ السمعة
A slight drizzle	رذاذ خفيف
God blessed him with a boy	رزقه الله طفلاً
A divine mission	رسالة سماويّة
A verbal letter	رسالة شفويّة
Lampoon	رسالة طاعنة
A written letter	رسالة كتابيّة
A text message	رسالة نصيّة
Registration fee	رسم التقييد
Illustrative figure	رسم بياني
Detailed drawing	رسم تفصيلي
Cartoon	رسم كاريكاتوريّ
A royal decree	رسم ملكيّ
School fees	رسوم الدراسة
Import duties	رسوم جمركيّة
Registration fees, booking fees	رسوم قيدية
Animated cartoons	رسوم متحرّكة
A spatter of rain	رشاش من المطر
To filter water	رشّح الماء
To throw stones	رشق بالحجارة
A stray bullet	رصاصة طائشة
A rubber bullet	رصاصة مطّاطيّة
To spy on the enemy	رصد العدوّ

To earmark a sum of money	رصد مبلغاً
An outstanding balance	رصيد معلّق
Platform	رصيف المحطّة
Bottle-feeding	رضاعة اصطناعيّة
Breastfeeding	رضاعة طبيعيّة
Relative humidity	رطوبة نسبيّة
To have a dislike of s.th.	رغب عن
A fervent wish	رغبة عارمة
A zest for life	رغبة في الحياة
His desire is directed towards ...	رغبة معلقة بِـ
Impulse	رغبة ملحّة
In defiance of him, to spite him, in spite of himself	رغم أنفه
In spite of himself	رغماً عن أنفه
To flutter one's eyelids	رفّت عيناه
A firm refusal	رفض قاطع
An outright refusal	رفض مطلق
Correction, rectification, clarification	رفع الالتباس
Rectification, correction	رفع الإيهام
To disclose, unveil s.th. (also a monument)	رفع الستار عن الشيء
To let s.th. take its course, give free rein to s.th. (also to a feeling)	رفع الصِّمَام
To hoist the flag	رفع العلم
To invigorate the spirit	رفع المعنويّات
To express one's sympathy, offer one's condolences	رفع تعزيته
To lift a sanction	رفع حصاراً
To file a lawsuit	رفع دعوى
To sue someone	رفع دعوى ضد

To institute legal proceedings	رفع دعوى قضائيّة
To upgrade s.th.	رفع من مكانته
We have exalted some of them above the others	رفعنا بعضهم فوق بعض
To class s.o. with, put s.o. on the same level with …	رفعه إلى مصافِ …
To find recreation	رقّه عن نفسه
High-ranking	رفيع الشأن
High-ranking	رفيع المستوى
A childhood friend	رفيق الطفولة
Life partner	رفيق العمر
Classmate, schoolmate, a school friend	رفيق المدرسة
Strict censorship	رقابة صارمة
Border check	الرقابة على الحدود
Censorship of the press	رقابة على الصحف
To have a pessimistic outlook, look on the dark side of everything	رقب بمنظار أسود
Delicacy of feeling	رقّة الشعور
Gentleness, mild temper	رقّة المزاج
To pass away	رقد رقدته الأخيرة
Costume ball	رقص متنكر
Record	رقم قياسي
To promote s.b.	رقّى شخصاً
Friendly	رقيق الجانب
To put together the machines	ركّب الأجهزة
To expose o.s. to danger	ركب الخطر
To construct a sentence	ركّب جملة
To speed along like the wind	ركب ذنب الريح
To concentrate on	ركّز على

To park the car	ركن السيّارة
To rest, take it easy	ركن إلى الراحة
Economic stagnation	ركود اقتصاديّ
Volcanic ash	رماد بركانيّ
A symbol of peace	رمز للسلام
To throw s.th. in the air	رمى به في الفضاء
To shoot at s.o.	رمى شخصاً
To accuse s.o.	رمى شخصاً بتهمة
To shoot and hit, shoot dead on the spot	رمى فأصمى
At your service	رهن إشارتك
At s.o.'s beck and call, at s.o.'s disposal	رهنَ إشارته
To pawn s.th.	رهن شيئاً
Bonds of friendship	روابط الصداقة
The distribution of goods	رواج البضائع
To spread a message	روّج خبراً
To propagate s.th.	روّج شيئاً
Team spirit	روح جماعيّة
Morale	روح معنويّة
Their mind thirsts most of all for knowledge	روحهم أشد ما تكون تعطشاً إلى العلم
To train an animal	روّض حيواناً
The rapture which holds me completely enthralled, which pervades my heart through and through	الروعة التي تأخذني من جميع أقطاري
Tiptoes	رؤوس الأصابع
To narrate a story	روى قصة
Viewing the crescent (esp. in Ramadan to determine the beginning of the lunar month)	رؤية الهلال

A vision of the future	رؤية مستقبليّة
Gradually	رويداً رويداً
A cold wind	رياح باردة
An Olympic sport	رياضة أولمبيّة
An individual sport	رياضة فرديّة
A cross-wind	ريح جانبيّة
Monsoon	ريح موسميّة
The prime of one's life	ريعان الشباب
Chief of staff	رئيس أركان
Chief of protocol, master of ceremonies	رئيس التشريفات
High priest	رئيس الكهنة (كبير الكهنة)
Chief prosecutor	رئيس النيابة
Prime minister	رئيس الوزراء
Head of state	رئيس دولة

ز

Crammed, overflowing	زاخر الجنبات
To make things worse, aggravate or complicate the situation	زاد الطينَ بلة
His prestige has risen	زاد شأنه
To make a thing worse	زاد ضِغْثاً على إبَّالةٍ
To increase one's knowledge	زاد علماً
To make things worse, aggravate or complicate the situation	زاد في الطين بلةً
To visit s.o. at intervals	زاره غِبّاً
To combine two jobs	زاوج بين عملين
An acute angle	زاوية حادّة
He was thrown into prison	زج به في السجن
To get o.s. embroiled in an issue	زجّ نفسه في قضية
To scold s.o.	زجر شخصاً
To discourage, to restrain s.o. from s.th.	زجر شخصاً عن شيء
To force s.o. out of their position	زحزح شخصاً من مكانه
The vanities of this world	زخارف الدنيا
Flowers of speech, rhetorical flourishes	زخارف لفظية
To be full of, to teem with, to burst with	زخر بِ
Florid speech	زخرف الكلام
Ecological farming	الزراعة البيئية
Organic farming	الزراعة العضوية
Heart transplantation	زراعة القلب
To put a smile on his face	زرع البسمة (الفرحة) على وجهه
To sow fear	زرع الخوف في
To sow seeds of discord	زرع بذور الفتنة

الزرع والضرع	Agriculture and stock farming
زرفاتٍ ووُحداناً	In groups and alone
زرّق عين شخص	To give s.o. a black eye
زعامة سياسية	Political leadership
زعزع استقرار البلد	To destabilise the country
زعم لنفسه	To claim for o.s.
زعيم الحزب	The party leader
زعيم ديني	Religious leader
زفّ الخبر إلى	He conveyed the good news to
زفزفت الريح	The wind whistled
زقزقة العصافير	The chirping of birds
زكاة الفطر	Obligatory alms at the end of the month of Ramadan
زكّى المال	To pay alms
زكيّ الرائحة	Sweet-smelling
زلزلت الأرض	The earth convulsed
زمام الأمور	Reins of power
زمن الفطحل	Primeval times, pre-Adamic period
زميل في الدراسة	Fellow student, classmate
زميل في العمل	Co-worker
زواج شرعيّ	A lawful marriage
زوبعة في فنجان	A storm in a teacup
زوجة الأب	Stepmother
زوّد المخابرات بمعلومات	Provide intelligence with information
زوّدهم بالطعام	To supply them with food
زيّ مدنيّ	Civilian clothes
زيّ موحّد	A uniform
زيادة الإنتاج	An increase in production
زيادة طفيفة	A slight increase

A substantial increase	زيادة هائلة
State visit, official visit	زيارة رسميّة
Playboy, womaniser	زير نساء
To embellish s.th.	زيّن شيئًا
Make-up	زينة الوجه

س

ساء به ظناً	To have a low opinion of s.o., think ill of s.o.
ساء طالعه	He fell on evil days, he met with evil fortune
سابح في أفكاره	Lost in thought
سابق لأوانه	Premature
سابقا	Formerly, previously
سابقاً – لاحقاً	Previously – later on, at first – subsequently
ساجله الحديث	To draw s.o. into a conversation, have a talk with s.o.
ساحة القتال	Battlefield
سار على غير هدى	To wander aimlessly
سار في خُطاه	To walk, or follow, in s.o.'s footsteps
سار يخطو في فناء الغرفة	He walked about the room
سارح الفكر	Distracted, absent-minded
سارق النظرَ إليه (سارقه النظر)	To steal a glance at s.o., glance furtively at s.o.
سارق النومَ	To take a short nap
سارّه في أذنه	To whisper in s.o.'s ear
ساري المفعول	In force, effective, valid
الساعة الثانية إلا الثلث	Twenty to two (time)
الساعة الثانية إلا ربعاً	A quarter to two (time)
ساعده الأيمن	His right hand, he is indispensable to him
ساكن الجِنان	Deceased person (lit. inhabitant of paradise)
سال لعابُه على ...	His mouth watered for ...
سأله ألا	To implore, adjure s.o. that he ...

To ask s.o.'s opinion, consult s.o.	سأله رأيه
To ask s.o. a question	سأله سؤالاً
To enquire of s.o. about s.o. else	سأله عن أخباره
To humiliate, degrade s.o.	سامه خَسْفاً
Arms race	سباق التسلح
Regatta, boat race	سباق القوارب
Main reason	سبب أكبر
Compelling reason	سبب قهري
Cause and effect	السبب والمسبَّب
Sound reason	سبب وجيه
To praise, glorify God, by saying سبحان الله ('praise the Lord!')	سبّح الله
To sing s.o.'s praise	سبّح بحمده
The sublimity, or the august splendour, of God's countenance	سُبْحَات وجه الله
God is far above, God is beyond …	سبحان الله عن …
To fertilise the land	سبّخ الأرض
To probe the depth of s.th., get to the bottom of s.th., study s.th. thoroughly	سبر أغوار الشيء
Liberal, open-handed, generous	سَبِط اليدين
Premeditation, wilfulness (jur.)	سَبْقُ الإصْرارِ
He had been previously sentenced to …	سبق الحكمُ عليه
One has to accept the accomplished fact, there is (was) nothing we can (could) do about it, it was already too late (lit. the sword anticipated censure)	سبق السيفُ العَذَلَ
We have previously (already) said that …	سبق لنا القول أن …
He had already done it	سبق له أن فعله

سبق له أن قابله	He had already met him before
سبق لي (أن)	It happened to me before, I experienced before that
سبقة القلم	Slip of the pen, *lapsus calami*
سبقه على	To surpass, beat s.o.
سبقه لسانه	To burst out impulsively (with an utterance)
سبك ودقة	Accuracy, precision
ستر الظواهرَ	To keep up appearances
سجّل إصابة	To score s.th. (e.g. a hit)
سجّل على نفسه أن	To go on record for (doing or being s.th.)
سجّله بمداد	To inscribe s.th. with golden letters
سجله في الشرائط المسجلة	To record s.th., to capture
سحابة أربعة قرون	In the course of four centuries
سحابة النهار (اليوم)	All day long
سحب العملَ به على	To extend the applicability of s.th. to
سحّت السماء	It rained cats and dogs
سحقاً له	Away with him! To hell with him!
سخّم بصدره	To irritate s.o., make s.o. angry
سخِي النفسِ عن الشيء	Only too glad to relinquish or give up s.th.
سدّ النواقص	To remove or remedy deficiencies
سدّ ثُغرةً	To fill a gap, close a breach
سدّ ثُلْمَةً	To fill a gap
سدّ حاجتَه	To meet s.o.'s needs
سدّ خلةً	To remedy a shortcoming
سدّ رمقه	To keep s.o. or o.s. barely alive, eke out an existence, to allay s.o.'s hunger

To fill a gap	سدّ فراغاً
To fill s.o.'s place, replace s.o.	سدّ مسده
To satisfy or fulfil s.o.'s claims	سدّ مطامعه
Level-headedness	سداد الرأي
To guide s.o.'s steps	سدّد خطاه
To pay or settle a debt	سدّد ديناً
To cover a deficit	سدّد عجزاً
To direct s.th. to, point, aim at	سدّده إلى
To guide s.o. to	سدّده نحو
Watchword, password	سر الليل
A very great secret	السر كل السر
Secretly, privately	سراً
Secretly and publicly	سراً وعلانية
Quickly, in a hurry	سراعاً
Swarm of bees	سرب من النحل
To comb one's hair, to do one's hair	سرّح شعره
To dispel s.o.'s worries	سرّح غمومَه
To set one's eyes on	سرّح نظره إلى
To do as one likes, proceed arbitrarily, to do as one pleases	سَرِحَ ومَرِحَ
How quickly …!, before long, soon, in no time (with foll. verb)	سُرْعَانَ ما …
Credulity	سُرعةُ التصديق
Presence of mind	سرعة الخاطر
We have travelled all day long	سرنا سحابة يومنا
The leaders of the people	سروات القوم
To pervade s.o.'s soul, of a feeling	سَرَى إلى نفسه
To traverse one's nightly course	سرى سُراه
To rid s.o. of worries, and the like, dispel s.o.'s worries	سرّى عنه
To be valid, be effective, be in force	سرى مفعولَه

سُرِّي عنه (عن نفسه)	To leave s.o. (grief, sorrow, fear and the like)
سريع التأثر	Easily impressed, impressible, sensitive
سريع التصديق	Credulous
سريع التقلب	Very changeable, very fickle, capricious
سريع التنقل	Mobile, manoeuvrable, easily manageable
سريع الخُطَى	Walking rapidly, taking long strides
سريع الزوال	Ephemeral, fleeting, transient
سريع الطلْق (الطلقات)	Quick-firing, rapid fire
سريع العَطَب	Fragile
سريعاً	Fast, quickly, speedily, promptly
سطح البحر	Sea level
سطح مائل	Inclined plain
سطحيات	Externals, superficialities
سعة الصدر	Patient
سَعدانة الباب	Doorknob
سعر التسليف	Rate of interest
سعر الخصم	Discount rate, bank rate
سعر القطع (مُعَدَّل)	Bank rate, discount rate
سعر القطعة	Price by the piece
سعى بِـ (عند، إلى)	To discredit s.o. with, to slander s.o.
سعى به إلى ...	To lead s.o. or s.th. to ...
سعى في الأرض فساداً	To spread evil, cause universal harm and damage
سعى في خراب الشيء	To work at the ruin of s.th., undermine s.th.
سعى لحَتْفِهِ بظِلْفِهِ	To bring about one's own destruction, dig one's own grave

To get or achieve s.th., to run after s.th.	سعى وراء
Of blessed memory, the late ...	سعيد الذكر ...
Poor, inferior stuff	سفساف الأمور
Bloodshed	سفك الدماء
Lowly people, riff-raff	سِفلة الناس
The height of stupidity	سفةٌ ما بعده سفه
To make a fool of o.s.	سفّه نفسه
To expose s.o., show s.o. up, make a fool of s.o.	سفه وجهَه
Waste, scrap, refuse	سقط المتاع
They had word from him that he ...	سقط إليهم عنه أنه ...
To drop s.o. or s.th.	سقط به
He was born in, his birthplace was ...	سقط رأسُهُ في ...
To be killed in battle	سقط صريعاً
To fail an examination, flunk	سقط في الامتحان
To stand aghast, be embarrassed, be bewildered	سُقِطَ في يده
To be dropped from membership	سقط من العضوية
To drop in s.o's estimation	سقط من عينه
Rainfall	سقوط الأمطار
Loss of hair	سقوط الشعر
To temper steel	سقى الفولاذ
Railroad	سكة الحديد
Heart failure	سكة قلبية
His anger abated	سكت عنه الغضب
Agony of death	سكرة الموت
Graveness, sedateness, seriousness	سكون الطائر
It's a double-edged sword	سلاح ذو حدّين
Firearms	سلاح ناري
May peace be upon you!	السلام عليكم

سَلَّة المهملات	Wastepaper basket
سَلِس القِياد	Docile, manageable, pliant
سلسلة النسب	Family tree, genealogy, pedigree
السلف الصالح	The worthy ancestors, the venerable forefathers
سلك الهواء	Aviation
سلك طريق الصواب والحق	To act in exactly the right manner, pursue the right course
سلوك مزعج	Irritating behaviour
سليم الطوية	Guileless, artless
سليم النواحي	Sound in body
سمّ ذعاف	Deadly poison
سَم قاضٍ	Deadly poison
السمعُ والطاعةُ	I hear and obey! At your service! Very well!
سمعاً لا بَلْغاً	God forbid! May it be heard but not fulfilled!
سمعاً وطاعةً	At your service! I hear and obey!
سن التمييز	Age of discretion
سن اليأس	The climacteric
سِنَة من النوم	A short nap
سهل الاستعمال	Easy to handle
سهل المراس	Tractable, manageable, compliant
سهل المنال	Easy to get, attainable
سهل واسع	Vast (sweeping) plain
سوء الاستعمال	Abuse, misuse
سوء التفاهم	Discord, dissension
سوء الحالة	Predicament, plight
سوء الخُلُق	Ill nature
سوء الظن	Low opinion

Misapprehension, misunderstanding	سوء الفهم
Evil intention, nefarious motive	سوء القصد
Malice	سوء النية
Antecedents, previous convictions	سوابق
The great mass, the great majority, the major portion (of the people)	السواد الأعظم
Eyeball	سواد العين
The question which is on everyone's lips	السؤال الذي تلوكه الألسنة
To expose s.o. make a fool of s.o., dishonour s.o.	سوّد (سقّه) وجهه
The innermost of the heart, the bottom of the heart	سويداء القلب
Ill-disposed, ill-natured, evil by nature	سيء الطبع
Defence policy	سياسة دفاعيّة
His wife (formal style)	السيدة قرينته
People will say …	سيقول قوم أن …
Tremendous flood	سيل عُرَام
Ill-starred, ill-fated, unfortunate, unlucky, hapless person	سيئ الطالع

ش

To stint, withhold	شاحح بـ
To stint, withhold	شاحح على
Educated, trained (e.g. linguistically)	شاد في اللغة
Of deviant character	شاذ الأخلاق
Eccentric, extravagant	شاذ الأطوار
Eccentric, extravagant	شاذ الطبع
Absent-minded, distracted	شارد الفكر
With a blank stare, gazing into the void	شارد النظر (النظرات)
To share s.o.'s opinion	شاركه رأيَه
To share s.o.'s sorrow, offer s.o. condolences (on the death of s.o. else)	شاطره أحزانَه (لـ)
To share s.o.'s views, s.o.'s joy	شاطره آراءه (فرحَه)
To share s.o.'s joy	شاطره أسباب المسرة
To spread, divulge, publicise, circulate s.th., make s.th. known, bring s.th. to the public notice	شاع به
To be generally attributable, generally applicable to s.th.	شاع في
To rebel against, mutiny	شاغب على
Plaintiff, complainant	شاكٍ
Armed to the teeth, bristling with arms	شاكٍ (في) السلاح
He went away, departed, he died, he is dead	شالت نَعامَتُه
To the north and south	شاماً ويَمَناً
Northwards and southwards	شاماً ويَمَناً

Arrogant, haughty	شامخ الأنف
After the manner of a foreigner, like a foreigner	شأن الغريب
To detract from s.o.'s good reputation	شان سُمعَتَهُ
Please yourself! Do as you like!	شأنَك
Do as you please! Just as you wish!	شأنَك وما تريد
As he used to do in ...	شأنه في ...
In this matter he fares just as, he is in this respect, in the same situation as ...	شأنه في ذلك شأنُ ...
As he used to deal with people who ...	شأنه مع من ...
Eyewitness	شاهد عيان (العيان)
Eyewitness	شاهد عين
Witness for the defence	شاهد نفي
The earth	الشاهدة
They saw it with their own eyes	شاهدوه بأم أعينهم
To take counsel with o.s., reflect, bethink o.s.	شاور نفسَه
In general use, generally accepted	شائع الاستعمال
Widely known, widespread, common	شائع الذيوع
It is rumoured that ...	الشائع أن ...
To be over initial stages	شب عن الطوق
To flirt (with a woman)	شبّب بها
War broke out	شبّت نيران الحرب
A foot of ground	شبر من الأرض
To imitate s.o. or s.th. religiously, to follow s.th. literally	شبرا بشبر وذراعا بذراع
Inch by inch	شبراً فشبراً
He linked his arm with her arm	شبك ذراعه بذراعها

Cobweb, spider web	شبكة العنكبوت
Barbed wire, entanglement	شبكة شائكة
To be doubtful, dubious, uncertain, obscure to s.o.	شُبِّهَ على
To disperse or break up the gathering of people, dissolve their unity	شتّ شملَهم
What a difference between … and …! How different they are!	شتان بين … و …
How different they are!	شتان ما بينهما
What a difference between the two of them! How different they are!	شتّى بينهما
To stint, economise with or in s.th.	شحّ بِـ
To stint, economise with or in s.th.	شحّ على
Tight-fisted, niggardly, miserly, avaricious, stingy	شحيح بِـ
Stingy, tight-fisted, niggardly, miserly, avaricious	شحيح على
Person whose case is under consideration	الشخص المنظور في أمره
To rise, ascend	شخص النجم
To stare, gaze, to start out, leave, depart to see s.o., for a place, journey to s.o., to a place	شخص إلى
To fix one's eyes, one's glance on, glance, stare, gaze	شخص بصرَه إلى
A real person, a man who actually exists	شخص بعينه
To appear to s.o.	شخص لِـ
To diagnose a disease	شخّص مرضاً
An eminent person	شخصية مرموقة
To drag s.o., pull s.o., by the ear	شدّ أذنه

To help, support, back s.o. up	شدّ أزرَه
To be energetic, courageous, vigorous	شدّ أزرُه
To stay, sojourn, reside	شدّ أطنابَه
To start out, depart leave	شد الرحال إلى
To tighten the reins, master the situation	شدّ الزمام
He pulled himself together	شدّ بعضه إلى بعض
To strengthen s.o.'s determination	شدّ عزائمه
To aid, assist s.o., stand by s.o., bolster, support	شدّ عَضُدَه
To saddle an animal	شدّ على
He started out on the journey (lit. he saddled his female riding camel)	شدّ على راحلته
To put emphasis on a word, stress	شدّ على كلمة
To clasp s.o.'s hands	شدّ على يديه
To reproach s.o. severely	شدّ عليه النكيرَ
To insist on s.th.	شدّ في
To help, support, encourage, back up	شد من أزره
To strengthen s.o.'s determination	شدّ من عزمه
To seek s.o.'s protection (in adversity and misfortune)	شدّ نفسَه بظهره
To tie s.o. up, shackle s.o., fetter s.o.	شدَّ وِثَاقَه
To cling onto s.th.	شدَّ يدَه على
To know a little Arabic, have a smattering of Arabic	شدا شيئاً من العربية
To demand s.th. emphatically or inexorably	شدّد في طلبه
He was strengthened in his determination	شُدِّد من عزيمته
To fasten, tie, bind	شدّه إلى (على)
To pull, drag	شدّه من

شديد (صعب) المِراس	Intractable, unruly
شديد الاعتناء	Very attentive, very careful
شديد الانفجار	Highly explosive
شديد البأس	Courageous, brave, intrepid
شديد الشكيمة	Obstinate, unbending, relentless, stubborn
شديد اللهجة	Strongly worded, vehement in language, sharp in tone
شديد الوطأة (على)	Cruel (to), having a deadly effect (on)
شُذَاذ الآفاق	The foreigners, the strangers
شرب الدخان	To smoke
شَرِبَ في حبه	To drink to s.o.'s health, toast s.o.
شرب نخبَه	To drink to s.o.'s health, toast s.o.
شرح الصدرَ	To cause joy, evoke a gay mood, make happy
شرح خاطرَه	To gladden, delight s.o.
شرح صدرَه لِـ	To open, lay open s.o.'s heart to or for the acceptance of
شرد به الفكرُ	He became lost in thought
شَرَدَ ذِهْنُهُ	To be absent-minded
شرطاً أن ...	On the condition that, provided that ...
شرطه على	To impose s.th. as a condition on s.o., to stipulate s.th.
شرع في	To go, enter s.th., to begin, commence
شرع مشروعاً	To devise a plan
شرع يفعل	To do s.th. (with foll. imperf.)
شرعاً وفرعاً	With full right, with good cause, justly
شرعاً وقانوناً	According to religious and secular law
شرعه على	To point a weapon at s.o.

شرعه لِـ	To introduce, enact, prescribe to s.o. laws
شَرِقَ بدمعه	To choke on one's tears
شرقاً	Eastwards
شرود الفكر	Absent-mindedness, distractedness
شروع في (بـ)	Commencement, inception
شروع في سرقة (قتل)	Attempted theft (murder)
شَرَى المتاعبَ	To bring upon o.s., to ask for troubles, inconveniences
شريط القياس	Tape measure
شطّ عن (الموضوع)	To deviate from, digress from the topic
شطّ في	To go to extremes, go too far in
شطّب دعوى	To drop, nonsuit a case
شطحات الخيال	Unbridled excesses of the imagination, extravagant fantasy
شطر بصرُه	To be squint-eyed
الشعور المشترك	Community spirit, communality, solidarity
الشعور بالذات	Self-consciousness
الشعور بالنفس	Self-consciousness
شغبه على	To provoke discord, dissension or controversy
شُغِفَ به حباً	To love s.o. or s.th. passionately, be madly in love with s.o., be infatuated with or enamoured of s.o., be extremely fond of s.th.
شغل البالَ	To disquiet, discomfit, make uneasy, trouble, disturb
شغل الوقتَ لِـ	To devote time to
شغل اليد (عمل اليد)	Manual work
شغل به عن	To be distracted by s.th. from

شُغْل شاغِل	That which is uppermost in one's mind, chief or foremost concern, s.th. which preoccupies s.o.'s mind or distracts s.o.
شغل نفسَه بِـ	To occupy o.s., busy o.s. with, work at, attend to
شغل يد	Handmade
شغل يدوي	Handwork, manual labour
شفهياً	Orally
شفى غُلَّتَه (غليلَه)	To quench one's thirst, gratify one's desire, satisfy one's thirst for revenge
شفى غيظَه من	To vent one's anger on s.o., take it out on s.o.
شق السكونَ	To break the silence
شقّ العصا	To dissent, secede from the community, to part from the community
شق سبيلاً	To cut, or open, a way for o.s.
شق شارعاً (طريقاً)	To build a street (a road)
شق طريقاً جديداً	To open up, or enter upon, a new path (fig.)
شق طريقه	To force one's way, plough ahead
شق عصا الطاعة	To rebel, revolt, renounce allegiance
شق عصا القوم	To sow discord among people
شق على	To be burdensome, unbearable for s.o.
شقّت جيبَها	To tear the front of the garment as a sign of mourning (woman)
شقشق بالحديث عن	To chat, chatter about s.th.
شقشقة اللسان	(Silly) prattle
شقشقة النهار	Daybreak, peep of dawn

To tear, rip, cleave s.th.	شقّه
I thank you! Thanks!	شكراً لك
He thanked him profusely	شكره شكراً جزيلاً
Formally, in form	شكلاً
To overwhelm s.o., bring s.o. down	شَلَّ حركته
To get a breath of fresh air, take a walk	شَمَّ النسيم
To get a breath of fresh air	شَمَّ الهواء
To the left, northwards, to the north	شمالاً
North-east	شمالاً بشرق
To be arrogant, haughty, proud, supercilious	شَمِخَ بأنْفِهِ
To buckle down to a job, rally all one's forces, put one's shoulder to the wheel	شمّر عن ساعد الجِد
To bare the upper arm (by rolling up the sleeve), get to work	شمّر عن ساعده
To embark upon s.th., buckle down to s.th.	شمّر للأمر
To make off, make a getaway, beat it	شمّع الفتلة
To bestow one's care on s.o., take s.o. under one's wing	شمِل بعنايته
To launch an attack on, to attack s.o. or s.th.	شنّ غارةً على
To swear by God	شهد بالله
To notarise	شهد قانونياً
To level a gun	شهر البندقية (على)
To declare war on s.o.	شهرَ الحربَ عليه
Irregularities of the language, linguistic anomalies	شوراد اللغة
War heroes	شُوس الحرب

شوكةٌ في خاصرته	A thorn in his side
شوّه وجهَ الحقيقة	To distort the truth
شوّه وجهَ الوظيفة	To disgrace one's profession or office
شؤون الحياة	Worldly affair
الشيء الكثير	The most, most of it
شيء بحاله	A thing in itself, independent thing
شيء تقشعر منه الجلود	A blood-curdling thing, a horrible, ghastly thing
الشيءُ كالثُّمامة	It is a trifle, a piece of cake, easy to accomplish
شيء لا يُشتهى	An undesirable thing
شيء لا يطاق	S.th. unbearable, s.th. intolerable
شيء لا يقبل أخذاً ولا ردّاً	An indisputable matter
شيء من	Some, a little, a certain (amount of), a considerable
شيء من القَلَق	Some uneasiness, some anxiety
شيء من النشاط	Some activity
شيء يأخذ القلوب	S.th. which captivates the heart, a fascinating, thrilling thing
شيء يُبْهِرُ الأبصارَ	A dazzling, overwhelming thing
شيء يفوق الوصف	A thing beyond description, an indescribable thing
شيء يندَى له الجبينُ	An embarrassing or shocking thing, a disgraceful thing
شيخ البلد	Village chief
شُيِّعَتِ الجنازةُ	The deceased was escorted to his final resting place, the funeral took place
شيئاً بعد شيء	Bit by bit, one after the other, by and by, gradually, step by step
شيئاً فشيئاً	Bit by bit, one after the other, by and by, gradually, step by step

ص

By all means, under all circumstances	صاب أم أقلع
To utter a cry	صاح صيحة
Ruler, master, overlord, sovereign	صاحب الأمر
His Majesty	صاحب الجلالة
The Almighty	صاحب الحول والطَّول
His Eminence (mufti)	صاحب السماحة
His Royal Highness	صاحب السمو المَلَكِي
The one concerned	صاحب الشأن
Artisan, craftsman, expert, specialist	صاحب الصنعة
His Majesty	صاحب العظمة
Employer	صاحب العمل
Title of the Coptic Patriarch	صاحب الغبطة
The sheikhs, professors of Al-Azhar	صاحب الفضيلة
The originator of the idea, father to the thought	صاحب الفكرة
The noun to which a circumstantial phrase refers	صاحب حال
Worker of miracles	صاحب كرامات
To meet with approval	صادف الاستحسان
To come in handily, be convenient, be opportune	صادف محلَّه
To substantiate, confirm	صادق على
To lead, bring s.o. or s.th. to	صار به إلى
To become necessary, indispensable	صار ضربةً لازب
To fall to s.o.'s lot, befall s.o.	صار لـ
Tit for tat	صاعاً بصاعٍ
To work on gold and silver, practise the art of goldsmithing	صاغ الذهب والفضة

صاف الزمان أم شتا	At all times, under all circumstances
صافح سمعَه	To reach s.o.'s ear
صافي النية	Sincere, candid, open-hearted, frank
صالح السير	Passable, practicable (road)
صالَحَ بين	To foster peace between
صالح لـ	Valid for, applicable to
صالح للعمل	Fit for action, ready for use, serviceable
صَبَّ الغَارَةَ	To commit an assault
صَبَّ عَلَيْهِ بَلَاءً	To impose a trial upon s.o.
صباح اليوم	This morning
صباحَ ومساءَ	In the morning and in the evening, mornings and evenings
صباحاً	In the morning
صباحك بالخير	Good morning!
صبغه صبغةً أخرى	To transform, change s.o.
صح عزمه (صحت عزيمته) على	He was firmly resolved to, his mind was made up to
صَحَّ على	To hold good, apply, be true
صحّ عن	To result or follow definitely from
صح في الأذهان	To appear right, adequate, reasonable
صح لِـ	To be a fact, turn out for, work out well for s.o., to fall to s.o. or to s.o.'s share
صحا (يصحو) إلى	To become alert, become aware of s.th.
صحا (يصحو) من	To recover (from intoxication), sober up, wake up (from sleep)
صُحبةَ هذا	Herein enclosed

صحن الدار	Courtyard, patio
صحيح أنه ...	Ture, he was (he is), it is true ...
الصحيفة البيضاء	Honourable, name, honour
صَدَّ عن	To turn away from, to stay away, remain aloof from s.th.
صِدَام وِجداني	Mental breakdown
صُدِرَ	To have a chest complaint
صدر الإسلام	Early period of Islam, early Islam
صدر الدار	One who occupies the highest position in the house, who plays first fiddle in the house
صدر المكان	The foremost part of a room
صدر النطق السامي بـ	It was decreed by order of His Majesty that ...
صدر النهار	Daybreak, beginning of the day
صدر إلى	To go out to
صدر رحب	Generosity, magnanimity, broad-mindedness
صدر عن (من)	To emanate, arise, stem from
صدر عن إرادته	To act on one's own volition
صدر عن الجد	To set about seriously, get to work earnestly
صدراً من الزمان	Quite a stretch of time, for some time
صُدِعَ	To have or get a headache
صدع بالحق	To come out openly with the truth
صدع بأمر	To execute an order, comply with an order
صَدَّعَ خاطرَه	To molest, harass, trouble s.o., bother s.o.
صدف عن	To turn away from, avoid s.o. or s.th.

صُدْفَةً	By chance, by coincidence, accidentally
صَدِّقْ أَوْ كَذِّبْ	Believe it or not (as an affirmative parenthesis)
صدّق بِـ	To believe in
صدق على	To prove to be true, turn out to be correct, to fit exactly s.o. or s.th.
صدّق على	To consent, assent, agree to s.th.
صدق في وعده	To keep, or fulfil, one's promise
صدق وعدُه	To keep, or fulfil, one's promise
صدق (ه) عن	To tell the truth about
صدقاً	Truly, really, in truth
صدقه الحب	To love s.o. sincerely, truly
صدقه النصيحةَ	To advise s.o. sincerely
صَرَّ الفلوسَ في	To shove, put money into a purse
صرّح بِـ	To announce, declare state
صرّح عن بِـ	To let s.th. be known
صرّح لِـ (بِـ)	To allow, grant, permit
صرخ بِـ	To call s.o.
صرخ صرخةً	To cry out, let out a cry
صرخ على	To call out, shout to s.o.
صرخ في وجهه	To yell, bellow, roar at s.o.
صَرَفَ النَّظَرَ عن	To avert one's glance from, pay no attention to s.th., leave s.th. out of consideration
صرف إلى	To direct s.th. (e.g. one's eyes, one's attention) to
صرف على	To spend, expend money, to defray the cost of s.th., pay for s.th.
صرف عن	To turn away, avert
صرف في	To pass, spend, devote time at s.th., doing s.th.

Misfortunes, adversities	صروف الدهر
Addicted to the bottle	صريع الشراب
Overcome by sleep	صريع الكرى
Hard to bear, oppressive	صعب الاحتمال
Hard to please, fastidious	صعب الإرضاء
Unruly, ungovernable	صعب القياد
Obstinate, stubborn, recalcitrant, headstrong	صعب المراس
Unattainable	صعب المنال
To have deep sighs	صعّد الزفرات
To make s.o. ascend, lead s.o. up to	صعد به إلى
To put on a contemptuous mien	صعّر خدّه
To stop dead in one's tracks, stand as if thunderstruck	صَعِقَ في مكانه
Simple-minded people, simple souls	صغار الأحلام
Young	صغير السن
Mean-spirited, base, servile, toadying, cringing, grovelling, base-minded	صغير النفس
Blood group	صف الدم
To apply o.s. to s.th. with clear intent, devote o.s. wholeheartedly to, be exclusively ready for (heart, mind)	صفا لـِ
Clearness of conscience	صفاء السريرة
Eternal attributes such as knowledge, power and volition	صفات أزلية من العلم والقدرة والإرادة
Manacle, handcuff	صفاد اليدين
Egg yolk	صَفَار البيضة
To remove the water, pour off the water (e.g. in cooking)	صفّاه من الماء

صفايا	Leader's share of the loot, lion's share of the booty
صِفْرُ اليدين	Empty-handed
صفرت يده من الشيء	To have lost s.th.
صفقة خاسرة	Poor deal, bad bargain
صفقة رابحة	Favourable deal, good bargain
صفقة واحدة	All at once, wholly, entirely, altogether
صفوة العيش	An easy, comfortable life
صفّى مسألةً	To settle, straighten out a question, a problem
صفّى مشكلةً	To settle, straighten out a question, a problem
صفيق الوجه	Impudent, insolent, brazen
صقل الأذهان	Mental training
صكّ سمعَه	To strike s.o.'s ear (noise), to roar in s.o.'s ear
صكّت به الآذان	His ears were ringing or tingling
صلابة العُود	Sternness, obstinacy, inflexibility
صُلْب الرأي	Obstinate, stubborn, opinionated
صُلْب الرقبة	Stubborn
صُلْب العُود	Of robust physique, husky, stubborn, relentless, strongly built
صُلْب المَكسِر	Hard to break, robust
صَلُحَ لِـ	To be usable, useful, suitable or appropriate
صَلُحَ مَعَ	To fit s.th., apply to s.o. or s.th.
صلّى الله عليه وسلّم	Peace be upon him (of the Prophet)
صلّى بالناس	To lead people in prayer
صلّى على	To pray for, (of God) to bless s.o.
صليب معقوف	Swastika

To defy, brave, withstand, stand up to, resist, oppose, hold out	صمد في وجهه
Skilful, skilled, dexterous, deft	صنّاع اليد
Rubbish bin	صندوق القُمامة
Handwork	صنع اليد
To do s.o. a favour	صنع إليه معروفاً
To do s.th. to s.o.	صنع به
To do s.o. a favour	صنع به جميلاً
To do s.o. a dirty trick	صنع به صنيعاً قبيحاً
In kind (as opposed to in cash)	صِنفاً
Rightly, justly	صواباً
Personal interests	صوالح شخصية
To be severely afflicted by	صُودِمَ بِـ
It appeared to him it seemed to him	صُوِّرَ له
Total picture, overall picture	صورة جامعة
Photograph	صورة شمسية
True copy	صورة طِبقَ الأصل
Enlargement, blow-up (photo)	صورة مكبّرة
True copy, exact replica	صورته طِبقَ الأصل
Battle cry, war cry	صيحة الحرب
You have let the opportunity go by, you missed your chance	الصيف ضَيَّعَتِ اللَّبَنَ

ض

Sunlit	ضاحٍ للشمس
Cheerful, gay, sunny	ضاحك السن
To go up in smoke, fall through	ضاع هباء منثوراً
Not to be up to s.th., be unable to do or accomplish s.th., not be able to stand or bear s.th., be fed up with, be tired of, feel uneasy about, be oppressed by	ضاق ذَرْعاً بـ ضاق عنه ذرعاً
To be unable to stand s.b. or s.th.	ضاق ذرعا بشخص
To be annoyed, angry	ضاق صدره
To be at a loss, be at one's wit's end	ضاقت به الأرض
He was at his wit's end, to be at loss, be at the end of one's tether	ضاقت به السبيل
Life depressed her, she had a bad time, she was bad off	ضاقت بها الحياة
To be incapable of, to be too poor to	ضاقت يده عن
Goal of persistent search, object of a long-cherished wish	ضالَّة منشودة
Straitened circumstances	ضائقة العيش
Self-control, self-command	ضَبْطُ النَّفْسِ
To determine precisely the spelling and pronunciation of a word, vowelise a word	ضبط كلمةً
To grin from ear to ear	ضحك بملء (ملء) شدقيه
To show a toothy smile, to grin from ear to ear	ضحك عن دُرٍّ مُنَضَّدٍ
To laugh in s.o.'s face	ضحك في ذقنه
Forced or embarrassed laugh	ضحكة صفراء

Forced laugh	ضحكة متكلفة
To sacrifice life and property (lit. the soul and that which is precious)	ضحّى بالنفس والنفيس
To sacrifice o.s.	ضحّى بنفسه
To kill two birds with one stone	ضرب (أصاب) (واحد) عصفورين بحجر
To rack one's brain in search of a way out, to daydream	ضرب أخماساً لأسداسٍ
To rack one's brain in search of a way out, to daydream	ضرب أخماسَه في أسداسه
To settle down, take up permanent residence in a place	ضرب أطنابَه على
To take root, prevail (at a place)	ضرب أطنابَه في
To impart words of wisdom, point out morals	ضرب الأمثال
To knock on the door	ضرب الباب
To ring the bell	ضرب الجرس
To break a record	ضرب الرقم القياسي
To give a military salute	ضرب السلام
Shooting, firing, shelling, gunning, bombardment	ضَرْبُ النَّارِ
To blush	ضرب إلى الحمرة
To become established, take root	ضرب بجرانِه
To let one's head sink to the chest	ضرب برأسه على صدره
To take an active part in	ضرب بسهم مصيب في
To participate in, share s.th.	ضرب بسهم ونصيب في
To turn one's glance to	ضرب بنظره إلى
To throw s.o. or s.th. to the ground	ضرب به الأرضَ
To not give a hoot for s.th., to disdain, despise, reject s.th., to throw s.th. overboard	ضرب به عرض الحائط

ضرب بوجه صاحبه	To boomerang, fall back on the originator
ضرب بويةً على	To paint, or daub s.th.
ضرب بين (الناس)	To separate people
ضرب بيني وبينه الأيام	Fate separated me from him, drew us apart
ضرب حقناً	To administer a syringe, give an injection
ضرب خطاً	To draw a line
ضرب خيمةً	To pitch a tent
ضُرِبَ ضربة لازب	To meet with grave misfortune, be stricken by disaster
ضرب ضريبة على	To impose a tax on s.o.
ضرب طوباً	To make brick
ضرب عدداً في آخر	To multiply a number by another
ضرب على الوَتَر الحسَّاس	To touch on a sensitive spot, get to the heart of the matter
ضرب على كلمة	To efface, strike or erase a word
ضرب عن	To turn away from, leave, forsake, abandon
ضرب عنقَهُ	To behead, decapitate s.o., have s.o.'s head cut off
ضرب عنه صفحاً	To turn away s.o. or s.th., to disregard, ignore s.o or s.th., pay no attention to, pass over s.o., snub
ضرب في	To rove, roam about, travel
ضرب في الخيال	To be in the clouds, be unrealistic, to want the impossible
ضرب في حديد بارد	To take a futile step, to beat the air
ضرب فيه بعِرقٍ	To have a share in s.th., participate in s.th., to do in vain, to sweat over nothing

To imitate s.th.	ضرب قالَبَه
To fix a date for s.o.	ضرب له أجلاً
To point out a model for s.o.	ضرب له مثلاً
To give an example, to quote as an example	ضرب مثلاً
To apply a proverb to	ضرب مثلاً لِـ
To agree on time or place of meeting, make an appointment	ضرب موعداً
To mint money	ضرب نقوداً
To touch on the very essence of a matter	ضرب وجةَ الأمر وعينَه
Mortal blows, crushing blows	ضربات قواصم
Sunstroke, heatstroke	ضربة الشمس
Penalty kick (football)	ضربة جزاء
Fatal blow, death blow	ضربة قاضية
Decisive blow	ضربة قاضية (على)
She decided to stay seven days	ضربت لنفسها سبعة أيام
To affect s.o. to the very core, touch s.o. most deeply	ضربه في الصميم
He hit him at his most vulnerable spot	ضربه في مقاتله
To slap s.o.'s face	ضربه كفاً
To set s.th. on fire, set fire to s.th.	ضرّم النَّارَ في
Necessity knows no laws	الضرورات تبيح المحظورات
Necessity is the mother of invention	الضرورة تفتق الحيلة
Exigencies, requirements of the situation	ضروريات الأحوال
Necessities of life	ضروريات الحياة
Admissions tax	ضريبة الملاهي
Senility, dotage	ضعضعة الكبر
Weakness of will	ضعْف الإرادة
Sexual impotence	ضعْف التناسل

Weak-willed	ضعيف الإرادة
Dim-witted, feeble-minded	ضعيف العقل
Faint-hearted, pusillanimous, recreant, cowardly	ضعيف القلب
To pull the trigger	ضغط على الزناد
Her effort was in vain	ضل سعيها
To delude o.s.	ضلل نفسَه
To close the ranks	ضم الصفوف
He embraced his wife	ضم إليه زوجتَه
To combine, encompass, comprise s.th.	ضم بين أعطافه
He beat it, he made off	ضمَّ جراميزَه
Combination	ضم قرينة إلى قرينة
To be absolutely certain of s.th.	ضَمِنَ لنفسه شيئاً
Inclusively, implicitly, tacitly	ضِمْنًا
To press s.o. to one's bosom, embrace s.o.	ضمه إلى صدره
To comprise, hold, contain s.th.	ضمّه بين جنباته
Sunlight, sunshine	ضوء الشمس
Moonlight	ضوء القمر
Daylight	ضوء النهار
Loss of time	ضياع الوقت
To forfeit one's right	ضيَّع حقَّه
To tighten the blockade	ضيِّق الحصارَ
Illiberal, ungenerous, impatient, annoyed	ضيِّق الخلق
To tighten the grip around s.o.'s throat	ضيِّق الخِناقَ على
Vexed, annoyed, angry	ضيِّق الصدر (بِـ)
Narrow-minded, dull-witted, hidebound	ضيِّق العقل
Crampedness, lack of space	ضيِق المقام

Confined, limited, restricted, narrow scope	ضيّق النطاق
Poverty, destitution	ضِيق ذات اليد
To restrain o.s., take restrictions upon o.s.	ضيّق على نفسه

ط

To be agreeable, be good, to please, be to s.o.'s liking	طاب لِـ
Good night, may your night be pleasant	طابت ليلتكم
He was gay, cheerful, in good spirits, he felt happy	طابت نفسه
He had a liking for it, it was to his taste	طابت نفسه إليه
Fingerprint	طابع الأصابع
To snatch away, carry away, carry off	طار بِـ
To let one's imagination wander to	طار بخياله إلى
To make s.o. unconscious	طار بصوابه
To drive s.o. out of his mind	طار بِلُبِّهِ
To be angry, blow one's top	طار طائرُه
To lose one's mind, go crazy	طار عقلُه
To be beside o.s. with joy, be overjoyed	طار فرحاً
His mind became confused, he became all mixed up, bewildered or perplexed	طار فؤاده (روحَه) شَعاعاً
His fame spread among people, he became well known	طار له صيت في الناس
To exchange questions with s.o.	طارحه الاسئلة
To chat with s.o.	طارحه الحديث
To converse with s.o., have a conversation with s.o.	طارحه الكلام
To be on the wrong track, bark up the wrong tree, fail, be unsuccessful	طاش سهمُهُ
To lose one's head	طاش صوابُه
To miss the mark, target	طاش عن الغرض

Aged, old, advanced in years	طاعن في السن
The bubonic plague	الطاعون الدُّمَّلي
He had a sudden impulse or urge	طاف به طائف
Tragedy befell him, he met with a harsh fate	طاف عليه طائف من القدر القاسي
Sooner or later, before long	طال الزمان أو قصُر
It took him a long time before he …	طال به الزمن حتى …
To last, or have lasted, a long time	طال به العهد
To ask the Chair for permission to speak, ask for the floor	طالبَ الإذنَ بالكلام
Pupil, student	طالب العلم
Of flawless character, irreproachable	طاهر الثياب
Upright, righteous	طاهر الذمة
Innocent, blameless	طاهر الذيل
Reconnaissance plane	طائرة الاستكشاف
Willingly or unwillingly, whether I (you, etc.) will it or not	طائعاً أو كارهاً
Mighty, powerful, forceful	طائل الصولة
The nature of things, state of affairs	طبائع الأشياء
To be innate, inherent in s.o., be native, natural to s.o.	طُبع عليه
By nature, by natural disposition, naturally! Of course! Certainly!	طبعاً
To place, set, or leave one's stamp, mark, or impress on s.o., impart one's own character on s.o. or s.th.	طبعه بطابعه
His (its) fame spread throughout the world	طبّق صيتُه الآفاق
According to, corresponding to	طِبقاً لـِ
According to schedule, as planned	طِبقاً لخطّة مرسومة

الطبقات النجسة	The impure castes, the pariahs
الطبقة الوضعية	The lowest class
طبّقت شهرتُهُ الآفاق	He (it) enjoyed, or achieved, worldwide fame
طَبيقُ ...	S.th. in agreement, in conformity with, analogous to s.th., compatible with ...
طرأت عليه فكرة	An idea occurred to him, he had an idea
طراوة الخلق	Gentleness, softness of character
طرّح (ه) إطراحاً	To throw s.th. far away
طرح عليه سؤالاً	To put a question to s.o.
طرح مسألة على بساط البحث	To broach or raise a question, present a problem for consideration
طرّحت به الطوائح	Fate dealt him severe blows
طرحه في المناقصة العامة	To invite tenders, or bids, publicly for s.th.
طرده إلى حيث التسكّعُ	To drive s.o. out into the dark, leave s.o. to an uncertain fate
طرده من منصبه	To relieve s.o. of his office, dismiss s.o.
طَرَف ...	On the part or side of ...
طَرَفٌ مِنْ	A part of, a bit of, some, party (as to a dispute, of a contract)
طرفَي النهار	In the morning and in the evening, mornings and evenings
طرق أذنَه	To strike s.o.'s ear, reach s.o.'s ear
طرق بباله	To occur to s.o., come to s.o.'s mind
طرق سمعَه (مسامعه)	To reach s.o.'s ear, come to s.o.'s knowledge or attention
طرق طريقاً	To tread, travel, follow, take or use a road

To occur to s.o., come to s.o.'s mind	طرق في ذهنه
To treat of a subject, discuss a topic, to broach a theme	طرق موضوعاً
One (two) knock(s) (e.g. at a door)	طرْقةٌ (طرْقتين)
Delicate to the touch, fresh	طَرِي الجَسّ
Sea route	طريق البحر
Air route	طريق الجو
Main road	طريق رئيسي
A public, much-frequented road	طريق سابلة
Path of errors	طريق شاردة
Public road, highway, thoroughfare	طريق عام
Self-service	طريقة اخْدِمْ نفسَك بنفسك
Directions for use	طريقة الاستعمال
Manner of speaking, diction	طريقة الكلام
Cannon fodder	طعمةٌ لمدافع الحرب
To speak evil of	طعن في
To be advanced in years, be old	طعن في السن
To contest, challenge, impeach	طعن في حكم
To refute a theological doctrine	طعن في قول
To bring s.th. to the surface	طفا به إلى السطح
Her bosom heaved violently (with joyous agitation)	طَفَرَتْ جوانحها
She became happily excited, she trembled with joy	طَفَرَتْ جوانحها
To sponge on s.o., at s.o.'s table	طفّل على مائدته
Petitioners	طلاب الحاجات
One with high-flung aspirations	طلّاع الثنايا
Efficient, energetic, vigorous	طلاع الثنايا والأنجُد
Curious, eager for news	طلاع إلى التعرف
Definite divorce	طلاق بالثلاثة
Revocable (not definite) divorce	طلاق رجعي

طلاقة اللسان	Fluency, eloquence
طلاقة الوجه	Cheerfulness of the face, gaiety
طلاه بالذهب	To gild s.th.
طلاه بالكهرباء	To galvanise, electroplate s.th.
طلاه بالميناء	To enamel s.th.
طلب عدم الثقة	Motion of no confidence
طلب يدَ المرأة	To propose to a woman, ask her hand in marriage
طلع على باب الله	To pursue one's livelihood, earn one's bread
طلع عليه بِـ	To take or bring to s.o. s.th.
طلْقُ اللسان	Eloquent
طلْقُ المُحَيَّا	With a happy, cheerful face, bright-faced
طلْقُ الوجه	Cheerful face, bright-faced
طلْقُ اليدين	Open-handed, liberal, generous
طلّق زوجتَه	To divorce one's wife
طلْقٌ من	Free from, rid of
طلق ناري	Gunshot
طلقة بالثلاثة	Definite divorce
طلقة نارية	Shot
طُلّقَت عليه	She was granted a divorce from him (by judicial decree)
طلّقت نفسَها	She dissolved her marriage, got a divorce
الطَّمُّ والرِّمُّ	Tremendous riches
طمع أشعبي	Insatiable greed
طمّن الخواطرَ	To calm the excitement
طهارة الذيل	Innocence, probity, integrity
طِوالَ بِضعَةَ عشر قرناً	During more than ten centuries
طور الانتقال	Transition period

Tractable, docile, amenable	طوع العنان
At your disposal	طوعَ أمرك
To be at one's beck and call, to be in one's power	طوعَ أيدينا
Under s.o.'s thumb, at s.o.'s beck and call	طوعَ يده
Voluntarily, of one's own free will, of one's own accord	طوعاً
Willingly or unwillingly, willy-nilly, whether I (you, etc.) will it or not	طوعاً أو كرهاً
He allowed himself to do s.th., he had no qualms about doing s.th. (lit. his soul permitted him, made it easy or feasible for him)	طوّعت له نفسُه
To embrace s.o.	طوّق شخصاً بذراعيه
To present s.o. with, bestow upon s.o. s.th.	طوّق عنقه بِـ
To take s.o. in one's arms, embrace, hug, clasp s.o.	طوّقه بذراعيه
During, throughout ...	طول ...
Long-suffering, longanimity, forbearance, patience	طُول الأناة
Far-sightedness, hyperopia	طول النظر
All day long	طول النهار
To be patient with	طوّل بألَه عليه
As long as	طول ما
During this period, during all this time	طول هذه المدة
Lengthwise, longitudinally	طولا (بالطول)
To rush through a country	طوى الأرض طيا
To bring the matter to an end, settle it once and for all, wind up an affair	طوى البساطَ بما فيه

طوى الطريق إلى	To hurry or rush to
طوى الماضي طي السجل	To break with the past, let bygones be bygones
طَوَى بساطهُ	To be finished, be done, come to an end, finish
طوى جوانحَهُ على	To harbour s.th., conceal s.th. in one's heart
طوى صدرَه على	To harbour or lock (a secret) in one's bosom, conceal, hide
طوى صفحتَه	To have done with s.th., be through with s.th., give up, abandon s.th.
طوى كشْحَهُ (كشحاً) على	To harbour or lock (a secret) in one's bosom, conceal, hide, to turn away from s.o., break with s.o., to keep s.th. to o.s., keep s.th. secret
طُوِيَ على	To be folded around or over, i.e. to bear within itself, harbour, contain, involve s.th.
طويل الأجل	Long-term, long-dated
طويل الأناة	Long-suffering, forbearing, patient
طويل الباع	Capable, knowledgeable, powerful, generous, efficient
طويل الروح	Long-suffering, forbearing, patient
طويل القامة	Tall
طويل اللسان	Insolent, impertinent, pert, saucy
طويلا	Long
طيَّ هذا	Herein enclosed, herewith
طِيْبُ (طيّب) العرق	Noble birth, noble descent
طيّب الخلق	Good-natured, genial
طيّب الرائحة	Sweet-smelling, fragrant, sweet-scented
طيّب السريرة	Guileless, simple-hearted

طيّب العرق	Noble descent
طِيبُ العرق	Noble descent
طيّب الله ثراه	God give him peace! May God make his earth light (a eulogy added after mentioning the name of a pious deceased)
طيب المكسر	Standing the test, proving its value, of excellent quality
طيب النحيزة	Good-natured, good-humoured
طيّب النفس	Gay, cheerful, in high spirits
طيّب خاطرَه	To mollify, soothe, placate, conciliate s.o., set s.o's mind at rest
طيّر رأسَه	To chop off s.o.'s head, behead s.o.
طير كاسر (كواسر الطير)	Bird(s) of prey
طيَّةُ	Herein enclosed, herewith (in a letter)

ظ

Oppressors of all kinds	ظالمون على أنواعهم
The literal meaning of an expression	ظاهر اللفظ
It seems, it appears that ...	الظاهر أن ...
Externally, seemingly, outwardly, presumably, ostensibly	ظاهراً
Adverb of place (gram.)	ظرف المكان
Extenuating circumstances	ظروف التخفيف
Extenuating circumstances	ظروف مخففة
Aggravating circumstances	ظروف مشددة
He remained silent, persisted in his silence	ظل صامتاً
To persist in a standpoint or attitude	ظل على موقف
He remained as he had always been, as everybody used to know him	ظلّ كعهده
He continued to live in the house	ظل يسكن البيت
Unjustly, wrongfully	ظلماً
To think ill of s.o., have a low opinion of s.o.	ظن به الظنون
To suspect s.o. of stupidity	ظن به الغَبَاءَ
He considered him capable of ...	ظن فيه القدرةَ على ...
Since he believed that ...	ظنّاً منه أن ...
To think s.o. capable of doing s.th., believe of s.o. that he would do s.th.	ظنه يفعل
To turn up, appear on the scene	ظهر في الميدان
From the ground up, radically, entirely, completely	ظهراً على عقب
Upside down, topsy-turvy	ظهراً لبطنٍ
Biological phenomena	ظواهر الحياة

ع

Wanderer, wayfarer	عابر الطريق
To create disaster, cause havoc, rage, rave	عاث فساداً في الأرض
To squander, or dissipate, one's fortune	عاث في ماله
Soon, presently, before long	عاجلاً
Sooner or later, now or later on	عاجلاً أو آجلاً
To lose the game, return empty-handed	عاد (رجع) بصفقة المغبون
To retrace one's steps, to turn back, go back	عاد أدراجَه
To fall back, retreat, withdraw	عاد القهقري
Peace has been restored	عاد الهدوء إلى نصابه
To start s.th. all over again	عاد إلى رأس أمره
To regain consciousness, come to, examine o.s. introspectively, search one's soul	عاد إلى نفسه
He returned safe and sound	عاد سالماً غانماً
To retrace one's steps, turn back	عاد على عقبيه
To bring about, entail s.th. for s.o., yield	عاد عليه بِـ
He continued (after a pause in his speech)	عاد يقول
The war broke out again, started all over again	عادت الحرب جَذْعَة
The situation returned to normal	عادت المياه إلى مجاريها
To retrace one's steps, turn back	عادوا على أعقابهم
The cheeks	العارضان
Mannequin	عارضة الأزياء

عاش الملك!	Long live the king!
عاش حياتَه	To enjoy one's life, make much of one's life
عاصفة من الهتاف	Storm of applause, thundering applause
عاظل الكلامَ	To be repetitious in one's speech, use tautologisms, repeat o.s. in speaking
عال صبرُه	To lose patience
عالة على	Living at the expense of, entirely dependent on, being a burden on (s.o.)
عالج الرَّمَقَ الأخير	To be on the verge of death, be dying
عالجه بطعنة	To land a stab on s.o., stab s.o.
العالم الإسلامي أجمعَ	The entire Islamic world
العالم من حيث هو	The world in itself, the world as such
عالَمون	Inhabitants of the world
عامة الناس	The common people, the masses, the populace
عامر الجيب	With a full pocket
عامر الذمة بِ	Obliged to s.o., committed to s.o.
عامر النفس بِ	Obsessed by, possessed by
عامر بالأمل	Full of hope
عامله بالمثل	To repay s.o. like for like, treat s.o. in like
عائد الأرباح	Net profit, net gain
عبء الإثبات	Burden of proof
عبّأ جيشاً	To mobilise, call up an army
عبارة عن	Consisting in, tantamount to, equivalent to, meaning
عبارة فعبارة	Sentence by sentence, word by word

In vain, futilely, to no avail, uselessly, fruitlessly	عَبَثاً
The crucial factor(s) is (are), decisive is (are) ...	العبرة في ...
To give s.o. an angry look, scowl at s.o.	عبس في وجهه
To cross the threshold of s.o.	عَتَبَ بَابَهُ
Old-fashioned, outmoded	عتيق النمط
To raise, swirl up (the dust)	عجّ الغبارَ
Most prodigious happening, wonder of wonders	عَجَبٌ عجاب
How strange! How odd! How astonishing! How remarkable!	عجباً
His obvious and hidden shortcomings, all his (its) faults	عُجَرُهُ وبُجَرُهُ
Steering wheel (of an automobile)	عجلة القيادة
To try, test s.o., put s.o. to the test	عَجَمَ عُودَه
To watch closely over s.o., keep a sharp eye on s.o., watch s.o.'s every move (lit. to count s.o.'s breaths)	عدّ الأنفاسَ عليه
To put down, or charge, s.th. to s.o.'s disadvantage	عده على
To transcend one's bounds or limits	عدا طورَه
Professional jealousy, trade rivalry	عداوة الكار
Clockwork, watchwork	عدة الساعة
Several times	عدة مرات
Fate dealt them heavy blows, they fell on evil days	عَدَت عليهم عواد
To enumerate the merits of the deceased, to eulogise	عدّد الميتَ
Special number, special issue (e.g. a periodical)	عدد خاص

عدد صحيح	Whole number, integer (maths)
عدد عديد	Enormous quantity, great multitude
عدد مشؤوم	Unlucky number
عدل ببصره إلى	To let one's eyes stray towards
عدل به عن	To make s.o. desist, abstain or turn away from
عدل بينَهم	To treat everyone with indiscriminate justice, not to discriminate between them
عدلاً	Equitably, fairly, justly
عدم الاتساع لـ	Inadequacy for
عدم الاختصاص	Non-competency
عدم الاشتباك في القتال	Non-intervention in battle
عدم الالتفات	Inattention
عدم الإمكان	Impossibility
عدم الانحياز	Non-alignment (political)
عدم الاهتمام	Inattention, indifference
عدم التنازل	Relentlessness
عدم الكفاية الجنسية	Sexual impotence
عدم الوجود	Non-being, non-existence
عدم قبول التفرقة	Indivisibility
عدو ألَد (لَدود)	Mortal enemy, archenemy
عدو لدود	Foe, arch-enemy
عديم الحياة	Lifeless, inanimate
عديم الذِّمة	Without conscience
عديم الشعور	Unfeeling, insensitive
عديم النظَر	Unparalleled, matchless, unique of his kind
عديم النظير	Unequalled, incomparable, unique
عَذْب الحديث	Entertaining, amusing, companionable, personable

Noble descent	عِراقة النسب
Baby carriage	عربة الأطفال
Hackney	عربة الركوب
Wagon, lorry, freight car	عربة الشحن
Pushcart, wheelbarrow	عربة يد
Fashion show	عرض الأزياء
A thought occurred to him, he had an idea	عرض له خاطر
An obstacle arose in his path	عرض له عارض
Supply and demand	العرض والطلب
Incidentally, by chance	عَرَضاً
To hold s.th. against the light	عرّضه للنور
To know for sure, be sure (of), be positive (about), know very well	عرف حقَّ المعرفة
Gratitude, thankfulness	عرفان الجميل
Gratitude, thankfulness	عرفان الفضل
In recognition of what he owed her	عرفاناً لحقها عليه
She was grateful to him, she appreciated his service, she gratefully acknowledged his service	عَرَفَتْ له الجميل
Blood will tell, what is bred in the bone will come out in the flesh	العِرقُ دسّاس
The firm, reliable grip or hold, the firm tie	العروة الوثقى
Bonds of friendship	عُرَى الصداقة
To take off one's clothes, strip (naked)	عَرِيَ عن ثيابه
To be completely unfounded, be without any foundation	عَرِيَ عن كل أساسٍ
Ancient, centuries old	عريق في القِدَم
He is sorry that ...	عَزَّ عليه أن ...
To be forgotten, sink into oblivion	عَزَبَ عن الأذهان

عزة الجانب	Power, might
عزة النفس	Sense of honour, self-esteem
عزّز جانبَه	To strengthen, reinforce, make s.th. strong
عزله عن منصبه	To depose s.o. of his office
عزها	Her Highness (title)
عزيز الجانب	Powerful
عزيزي	Dear!
عسى أن	It might be, it could be that, maybe, perhaps
عسى أن يكون	What might be ...?!
عَسِيٌّ بِـ (أن) ...	It befits him (them) to or that he (they), it is proper from him (them) to or that he (they) ...
عشاء رسميّ	A formal dinner
عشرات الألوف	Tens of thousands
مئات الألوف	Hundreds of thousands
عَشِية أمس	Last night
عصابات الخطف	Bands of robbers
عصب الريقُ فاه	The saliva dried in his mouth, clogged his mouth
العصر الحاضر	The present (time), our time
عصفور في اليد خير من ألف على الشجرة	A bird in the hand is worth two in the bush (proverb)
عِصمة النكاح	The bond of marriage
عَصِي النطق	Unable to speak, incapable of speech
عض بالنواجذ	To grit one's teeth
عض بالنواجذ على	To cling stubbornly to
عض على ناجذيه	To have reached the age of manhood
عضده المتين	He is an indispensable aid to him
عضّه الزمان	Time, or fate, gave him a raw deal, heaped trials and tribulations upon him, he suffered reverses
عضه الدهر بِنَابِهِ	

Regular member	عضو أصلي
A transplanted organ	عضو مزروع
To incline, dispose s.o. towards, make s.o. appreciate s.th., bring s.th. close to s.o.'s heart	عَطَفَ به على
To dissuade, alienate s.o. from	عطف به عن
Worthless people	عُفاشة من الناس
Spontaneously, unhesitatingly, casually	عفو الخاطر
Amnesty	عفو عام (شامل) عن
Unselfish, selfless, altruistic	عفيف النفس
To tread in s.o.'s footsteps	عقب آثاره
Insurmountable obstacle	عَقَبَة كأداء
To give s.th. a top rating because of its excellence, put s.th. above everything else	عقد الخنصر (الخناصر) على
Marriage contract	عقد الزواج
To make up one's mind to do s.th., be (firmly) determined to do s.th.	عقد العزمَ (العزيمة) على
To determine on s.th., resolve to do s.th., direct one's intention to, decide on s.th.	عقد النية على
To pin, or set, one's hope(s) on	عقد أملاً على
To knit, or wrinkle, one's brows, frown	عقد جبهتَه
To convene a session	عقد جلسةً
She became engaged to	عقد خطبتها على
To contract a marriage	عقد زواجاً
To conclude a bargain, effect a transaction	عقد صفقةً
To marry a woman	عقد على المرأة
To silence s.o.	عقد لسانَه

عقد له لواء المجد (النصر)	He was awarded the laurel of fame (of victory)
عقد لواء الشيء	To found, start, originate, launch, produce, kindle, provoke s.th.
عقد محادثةً	To strike up a conversation
عقد ناصيته	To form a cordon
عقد نطاقاً حوله	To form a cordon around s.o.
عقل لسانه	To tongue-tie s.o. speechless
عقل مَسْبُوه	Impaired mind (esp. due to old age)
عكر الصفو	To destroy the untroubled state, disturb
عكر عليه الصفوَ	To kill s.o.'s good spirits, spoil s.o.'s good humour
عكس ذلك	In contrast with that, contrary to that
عل لسانه	From his mouth, through him
علا الاداة الصدأ	Rust has covered his tool
علا السطحَ	To climb the roof
علا به	To raise s.th., or s.o, to exalt, extol s.o.
علا صوتُه ...	His voice rang out with, he exclaimed, aloud ...
علاج نهائي	Extreme remedy
علامَ؟	Wherefore? What for?
علامات التنصيص	Quotation marks
علاوة على	In addition to
علة العلل في	The principal cause of, the deeper reason underlying
علة متنقلة	Contagious disease
العلة والمعلول	Cause and effect
علت السآمة	He was overcome by fatigue
علت به السنُّ	He had attained great age, he was an old man

Foam appeared on his lips	علت شفتيه رغوة
Deathly pallor suffused his face	علت وجهه صفرة الأموات
To set one's hopes on	علّق الآمال على
To attach importance to s.th.	علّق أهمية (خطورة) على
To cherish the hope of	علّل الآمال بـ
To indulge in the hope that, entertain or cherish the hope of or that	علّل نفسَه
To indulge in hopes, to entertain vain hopes	علّل نفسه بآمال
To put s.o. off with promises	علّله بالوعود
Elocution	علم الإلقاء
Scholastic theology	علم الكلام
Theology	علم اللاهوت
Mystic knowledge	العلم اللدني
Lexicography, philology, linguistics	علم اللغة
Geography	علم تقويم البلدان
To know exactly, know very well	علم حقَّ العلم
Theoretically and practically	علماً وعملاً
Sound volume, sound intensity	علو الصوت
High rank, outstanding position	علو الكعب
Supremacy, hegemony	علو الكلمة
Tremendous height	علو شاهق
Alongside, parallel to	على (في) مُحَاذاة
Like, similar to	على (من) غرار
In the long run	على (مع) طول التمادي
In touch with	على اتصال بـ
Fully prepared, totally ready	على أتم استعداد
In the most perfect manner conceivable, as perfect(ly) as possible	على أتم ما يكون

على أحر من الجمر	On pins and needles, on tenterhooks, in greatest suspense or excitement
على أحسن ما يرام	To be as well as one can possibly wish
على اختلاف أحزابهم	Whichever faction they may belong to
على ارتفاع ألف قدم عن سطح البحر	A thousand feet above sea level
على إزاء	In the face of (e.g. a situation)
على أساس	On the basis of, on account of
على أطراف قدميه	On tiptoe
على اعتبار أن …	Considering (the fact) that, with regard to the fact that, in view of the fact that, on the assumption that …
على أعظم جانبي من الخطورة	Of utmost significance
على أقساط	By instalments, gradually
على أقل تقدير	At the lowest estimate, at least
على أكثر تقدير	At most
على الأبد، إلى الأبد، أبد الدهر	Forever
على الأبواب	Near, imminent
على الإجمال	On the whole, in general
على الأخص	Especially
على الأرجح	Probably, in all probability
على الإطلاق	Absolutely, unrestrictedly, without exception, in any respect, under any circumstances, unfriendly
على الأقدام	On foot
على الأقل	At the very least
على الأكثر	At most, latest
على الانفراد	Alone, apart, in solitude, singly, by o.s.

Offhand	على البديهة
To be exact, strictly speaking	على التحديد
Strictly speaking, properly speaking	على التحقيق
Approximately, almost, nearly, about	على التقريب
Side by side, parallel	على التوازي
Continuously, incessantly	على التوالي
In short, in a word	على الجملة
On the spot, right away	على الحافر
Neutral	على الحِياد
Especially, in particular, specifically, particularly	على الخصوص
Very gladly, with pleasure, just as you wish	على الرأس والعين
Welcome	على الرُّحب والسَّعة
In spite of himself	على الرغم من أنفه
Silently, in silence	على السكْت
To be the talk of the town, be on everyone's lips	على ألسنة الخاص والعام
On tenterhooks, on pins and needles	على الشوك
In common, jointly, in joint possession	على الشيوع
Happy journey, Godspeed	على الطائر الميمون
On an empty stomach, without having eaten	على الطَّوَى
Very gladly, with pleasure	على العين والرأس
Immediately	على الفور
By analogy	على القياس
According to general belief, as it was generally understood	على المشهور
Openly, publicly, overtly, for everyone to see	على المكشوف (بالمكشوف)

على الملأ	Publicly, in public
على المودة	Of the latest fashion, fashionable, stylish
على النقيض	On the contrary
على الواقف	Instantly, on the spot
على الوجه التالي	In the following manner, as follows
على امتداد	Along, alongside of
على أملٍ أن	In the hope that
على أن ...	On the condition that, provided that ...
على أنَّ ...	However, but, on the other hand, nevertheless, yet, still ...
على أهبَة الاستعداد	Fully prepared, on the alert
على أهبَة الرحيل	Ready to set out
على أي حال	In any case, at any rate, anyhow, by all means
على أيدي الناس	With the help of other people
على بصيرة من الأمر	In cognisance of the matter, knowing the matter
على بُعْد	In the distant, far off
على بعد مائة متر	At a distance of 100 meters
على بَكْرَة أبيهم	All without exception, all of them
على تخصيص	Specifically
على تخمين	Approximately, roughly
على تعاقب العصور	In the course of centuries
على تواتر	Successively, one after another
على توالي الأيام	In the course of time
على تؤدة	Slowly, deliberately
على ثقةٍ (من)	Trusting in, relying on, certain, sure
على ثقة من أنه ...	He is certain that he ...
على جانب عظيم من الأهمية	Of great importance

He is very …	… على جانب كبير من
In the sky	على جبين السماء
Aside, apart	على جنب
On the brink of ruin, on the verge of destruction	على حافة الخراب
On the verge of an abyss, on the rime of a precipice	على حافة الهاوية
According to, commensurate with	على حد
In the same manner, likewise	على حدّ سَواء
In the same manner, likewise	على حد سوى
Within narrow confines, on a limited scope	على حد ضيّق
According to his statement, in his own words	على حد قوله
Alone, by o.s., apart from others, detached, isolated	على حِدَةٍ
Cautiously, warily	على حذر
Irresolute, wavering, on the fence	على حرف
At s.o.'s expense	على حساب فلان
At his expense	على حسابه
According to, in accordance with, commensurate with, depending on	على حَسَبٍ
To be in the right	على حق
Aside, apart, to one side	على حَيْدَةٍ
Upright, erect	على حَيْلِه
At the same time when, whereas	على حين أن
Unexpectedly, inadvertently, surprisingly	على حين غِرَّة
Suddenly, all of a sudden, unexpectedly, surprisingly	على حين غفلة

على حين هم يزعمون	Whereas they, on the other hand, claim
على خاطرك	As you like
على خط مستقيم	Straightaway, in a straight line, outright, out and out
على خلاف ذلك	Unlike that, contrary to that, on the contrary
على خلوةٍ	Alone, in seclusion
على دراية	In full cognisance of the situation
على ذلك	In this manner, thus
على ذمّتي	On my honour
على رأي المثل	As the proverb says
على رؤوس الأشهاد	In public, for all the world to see
على سبيل	As, by way of, for
على سبيل الاحتياط	As a precaution, to be on the safe side
على سبيل الاختبار	Experimentally
على سبيل التجربة	For a try, tentatively
على سبيل الحصر	Exhaustively
على سبيل الفكاهة	For fun
على سبيل المجاز	Figuratively, metaphorically
على سنه قوي	He bears his years well
على شاكلة	In the manner of, of the kind of, like
على شاكلتهم	Of their kind, like them
على شرط أن ...	On the condition that ...
على شريطة أن ...	On the condition that ...
على شفا مجاعة	On the verge of a famine
على شَفْرَة الهاوية	On the brink of the abyss
على شيء كثير من	Very, extremely
على شيء كثير من البساطة	Very simple

To have certain …	على شيء من …
To have a good deal of intelligence	على شيء من الذكاء
On the (surface of the) cheek	على صحن الخد
Congenial, like-minded, kindred in spirit, agreed	على صعيد واحد
He is right	على صواب
Within shouting distance	على صيحة
In light of, under the circumstances of, as seen from, according to	على ضوء
Within easy reach, handy	على طرف الثُّمَام
Her obeying, without opposition on her part	على طوع منها
Along, alongside of	على طول
All along the line	على طول الخط
On the ground, on the water, etc.	على ظهر (الأرض، الماء)
Aboard the steamer	على ظهر الباخرة
On horseback	على ظهر الخيل
According to his habit, as was his wont, as he used to do	على عادته
In a hurry, hurriedly, speedily	على عجل
Immediately after …	على عقب …
In contrast with that, contrary to that	على عكس ذلك
In spite of his weaknesses, such as he is	على علاته
Against me	على عندي
At the time of	على عهد
At or in his time	على عهده
In a hurry, hastily	على غرار
After one pattern, alike, likewise	على غرار واحد
In the like manner	على غَرارة
Unexpectedly, inadvertently, surprisingly	على غرة

على غفلة	Suddenly, all of a sudden, unexpectedly, surprisingly
على غير انتظار	Unexpectedly
على غير جدوى	Of no avail, useless, futile, in vain
على غير شعور منه	Without his being aware of it
على غير معرفة منه	Without his knowing about it, without his knowledge, unwittingly
على غير ميعاد	Untimely
على غير هداية	Without divine guidance, aimlessly, at random
على غير هدي	Aimlessly, at random
على غير وجهه	Improperly, incorrectly
على فرض أن …	On the assumption that, supposing that, on the premise of …
على قاب قوسين	Quite near, very close, imminent
على قارعة الطرق	On the open road
على قدر الإمكان	As far as possible, as much as possible, in the best way possible, to the best of one's abilities
على قدر المستطاع	As far as possible, as much as possible, in the best way possible, to the best of one's abilities
على قدر سَعتي	To the best of my abilities
على قدر طاقته	According to his capability
على قدر ما	To a certain extent, relatively
على قدم الأهبة والاستعداد	In a state of extreme alertness
على قدم الحَذَر	Anxious, timid, fearful
على قدميه	On foot
على قده	Of the same size, of equal size, just as (large)
على قرب لمحة	In a moment

Within a few hours	على قيد ساعات معدودة
At a distance of 10 km	على قيد عشر كيلمترات
In the vicinity (of a neighbourhood), near	على كَثَبٍ من (عن كثب من)
In the course of time	على كر الدهور (الزمن)
Unwillingly, grudgingly, forcedly	على كراهية
Unwillingly, reluctantly, under compulsion	على كُرهٍ منه
In any case, at any rate	على كل
In any case, at any rate, anyhow	على كل حال
At his expense	على كيسه
At your discretion, as you please, as you wish	على كَيفِك
Through the organ of the press	على لسان الصحف
As the heart dictates, i.e. as chance will have it	على ما خيّت النفسُ
As they say, as it is said	على ما يقال
As it seems, apparently	على ما يلوح
As far as I can judge for myself	على مبلغ تقديري
Aboard (a ship or airplane)	على متن (سفينة – طائرة)
By sea, sea-borne	على متن البحر
Aboard the plane	على متن الطائرة
Through the air, air-borne	على متن الهواء
In the manner of, after the pattern or model of	على مثال
After the same pattern	على مداد واحد
Within sight	على مدى البصر
At a distance of 10 metres	على مدى عشر أمتار
In the course of time	على مر الزمان
Before s.o.'s eyes	على مرأى من
In full view of	على مرأى من

على مرأى ومسمع من	Before the eyes and ears of, with full knowledge of
على مشارف	Within view, in the visual range of, in front of
على مضض	Unwillingly, reluctantly, begrudgingly
على مضى الزمان	Lastingly, for long, permanently
على مقربة (مِن)	Nearby, close at hand, in the vicinity of
على ملأ العالم	For everyone to see, before all the world
على ممر العصور	In the course of centuries
على مهل	Slowly, leisurely, in no hurry
على مهلك	Take it easy! Take your time!
على نحو ما	In the manner of, as
على نحوٍ ما	Pretty much, rather
على نسبة	In proportion to, corresponding to
على نَسَق	In the manner of
على نَسَق واحد	In the same manner, uniformly
على نصيب وافر من ...	To have an ample share in ...
على نفقته	At s.o.'s expense
على نقيض	Contrary to, in opposition to, unlike
على نَمَط	In the manner of
على نور	In the light of
على نية ...	With the intention to ...
على هامش ...	On the periphery of, aside from ...
على هذا الاعتبار	From this standpoint, from this viewpoint
على هذا الغرار	In this manner
على هذا المِنوال	In this manner, this way
على هذا النحو	In this manner
على هذا النظام	Along this line, in this manner

In this manner, this way, after this fashion	على هذا النمط
In this manner, thus	على هذا الوجه
In this manner, this way	على هذه الوتيرة
To be convenient to s.o., please s.o.	على هواه
Gently, imperceptibly	على هون
At your convenience	على هونك
In the same manner	على وتيرة واحدة
In the manner of, in the shape of, with regard to, concerning	على وجه
On the whole, altogether	على وجه الإجمال
Expeditiously, speedily	على وجه الاستعجال
To be exact, strictly speaking	على وجه التحديد
Specifically	على وجه التخصيص
At great length, in detail, elaborately	على وجه التفصيل
In a condensed form, in a nutshell	على وجه الحصر
Especially, in particular, specifically, particularly	على وجه الخصوص
Generally	على وجه العموم
With certainty	على وجه اليقين
In his own way, in the right manner	على وجهه
At the hands of	على يد (على أيدي)
Through him, by him, at his hand	على يده
To (or at) his right	على يمينه
Bring, give him (or it) to me!	علي به
Upper class, people of distinction, prominent	علية القوم
Upper class, people of distinction, prominent	علية الناس
Take . . . ! Help yourself . . . !	عليك بـ
You must have patience!	عليك بالصبر

عليك نور	Well done! Bravo!
علينا به	He is the one we must have!
عليه العفاء	It's all over with him, he is done for
عليه أن ...	It is incumbent on him to, it's his duty to, he must, he will have to ...
عليه دَين	He is in debt
عما قريب	Shortly, after a little while, soon
عما قليل	Shortly, soon
عمّت البلوى به	It has become a general
عمر مديد	Great age
عمّر وقتَه	To take up, or claim, s.o.'s time
عمره الآن قد أوفى على التاسعة	He is already past nine years of age
عمره عشرين سنة	He is twenty years old
عمره كذا سنوات	His age is such-and-such many years
عمل أعماله	To behave, or act, like s.o.
العمل بِ	Validity, effectiveness of s.th.
العمل بالقطع	Piecework, job work, taskwork
عَمِلَ حساباً له	To reckon s.o. with s.th.
عمل يستَوجِب الشكرَ	An act deserving of thanks, a meritorious undertaking
عملاً بِ	In execution of, in pursuance of, according to
عملياً	Practically, in practice
العموم	The (general) public, the public at large
عموماً	In general, generally
عموماً – خصوصاً	In general, in particular
عن استحقاق	Deservedly, by rights
عن أمره	By s.o.'s order(s), on s.o.'s initiative
عن بصيرة	Consciously, fully aware of the situation, knowingly

From a distance, from afar	عن بعد
All without exception, all of them	عن بكرتهم
Out of ignorance	عن جَهْلٍ
In good faith, bona fide	عن حسن نية
Justly, rightly, by rights	عن حق
For fear	عن خوف
Of one's own accord, spontaneously	عن سجية
Gladly, happily, joyfully	عن سرور
By way of, via, by means of, through	عن طريق
Voluntarily, of one's own free will, of one's own accord	عن طواعية
Gladly, most willingly, with pleasure, voluntarily	عن طيبة خاطر
By heart, from memory	عن ظهر الغيب
By heart	عن ظهر القلب
On the basis of sound knowledge, in full cognisance of the situation	عن علم
Unintentionally, inadvertently	عن غير قصد
Shortly, presently, after a (little) while, soon	عن قريب
Intentionally	عن قصدٍ
Soon, shortly, before	عن قليل
Out of absolute inner conviction	عن قناعة وجدانية
Within sight	عن قيد البصر
It occurred to him that ...	عن له أن ...
Through the good offices of s.o.	عن وساطة فلان
To (or at) his or its right side, at (or on) his or its right side, to the right of him or it	عن يمينه
In case of emergency	عند الاضطرار

عند الاقتضاء	In case of need, if need be, when necessary
عند الإمكان	When (or if) possible, possibly
عند البيت	Near the house, at the house
عند التحقيق	Properly speaking, strictly speaking
عند الحاجة	If or when necessary, if need be, in case of need
عند الحافرة	On the spot, right away
عند الضرورة	In case of need, if need be, when necessary
عند الضرورة القصوى	In case of dire necessity, when worst comes to worst
عند الطلب	On demand, by request, if desired, on application
عند اللزوم	In case of need, when (or if) necessary, if need be
عند أنفسهم	In their own opinion
عند تقليب النظر	On closer inspection or examination, when examined more closely
عند توفر الشروط	As soon as the conditions are fulfilled
عند ذلك	Thereupon, then, at that moment
عند طلوع الشمس	At sunrise
عند مسيس الحاجة	Should the necessity arise, if (or when) necessary
عند مقتضيات الأحوال	Should the circumstances require it
عندي	In my opinion, as I think
عندي دينار واحد	I have only one dinar (with me)
عنوانًا على (لِـ)	In token of s.th.
عَهِدَ وعدَه	To fulfil, or keep, one's promise
عهدته عليه	He is responsible for it

عهدُنا بهذه المسألة	Our long-standing knowledge of this question
عهده	His familiar nature or manner
عهدهم به	The nature of manner that they know (knew) of him (or of it), that they are (were) used to
عوادي الوحوش	Beasts of prey, predatory animals
عود كبريت	Matches, matchstick
عِوَضاً عن	As a substitute for, in replacement of, in lieu of
عياذ الله	God forbid! God save me (us) from that
العياذ بالله	God forbid! God save me (us) from that
عيال على	Living at the expense of, entirely dependent on, being a burden on (s.o.)
عيب عليك	Shame on you! You ought to be ashamed!
عيد القيامة	Easter
عيد صوم الغفران	Day of Atonement
عيد مؤوي	One hundredth anniversary
عِيلَ صبرُه	To lose patience
العين بالعين	An eye for an eye
عيّن سبباً	To give a reason
عينُه فرارُه	His outward appearance bespeaks his inner worth, you need only look at him to know what to think of him
عيون الشِّعر	Gems of poetry, choicest works of poetry

غ

The matter has slipped from his memory, he has forgotten the matter	غاب الشيء عن باله
To lose consciousness	غاب عن الشعور
To lose consciousness	غاب عن الوجود
To lose consciousness, to faint, become unconscious	غاب عن صوابه
Completely taken aback, deeply shocked, utterly dismayed	غارق في الدهشة
His face lost all colour, he turned pale	غاض لونُه
To struggle, wrestle with difficulties	غالب المصاعب
Mostly, in most cases, in general, generally	غالباً
To befall, overcome s.o. (sleep)	غالبه النوم
To engage in daring adventures, risk one's life	غامر بنفسه
Unconscious, senseless	غائب عن صوابه
The utmost degree of, the maximum of	الغاية القصوى من
The ends justify the means	الغاية تبرر الوسيلة
To surpass, outstrip, outdo s.o., be superior to s.o.	غبّر في وجهه
The earth	الغبراء
To suppress one's laughter, bite one's lip	غت الضحك
To feel like vomiting, feel sick, be indisposed	غثّت نفسُه
Be indisposed	غثيت نفسه
Tomorrow, the following day	غداً
To come and go	غدا وبرح

To go back and forth	غدا وراح
In a hurry, hastily	غراراً
To get around in the world, see the world	غرّب وشرّق
Westwards, towards the west	غرباً
South-westwards, towards the south-west	غرباً بجنوب
The first day of the month	غُرَّة الشهر
To expose o.s. to danger, risk one's life	غرّر بنفسه
A goal much sought after or worth striving for	غَرَضٌ تُحْدَى إليه الركائبُ
Dining room	غرفة الأكل
Chamber of commerce	غرفة التجارة
Bedroom	غرفة النوم
A chamber under the roof	غرفة تلي السقف
To flood the market with	غرّق السوقَ بِـ
Self-deception, self-delusion	الغرور بنفسه
Of odd behaviour, whimsical, capricious, eccentric	غريب الأطوار
To flood the market	غزا السوق
Well-informed, learned, well-read	غزير المادة
Offering a wealth of information	غزير المواد
To lose consciousness, faint	غُشِيَ عليه
The place was overcrowded	غص بهم المكانُ
Forcibly, by force	غصباً
Against his will, in defiance of him	غصباً عنه
Agony of death	غصة الموت
To overlook, let pass, disregard s.th., pay no attention to s.th.	غض النظرَ (الطرف) عنه
To lower one's eyes	غض طرفَه
For the protection of	غضباً لِـ

غفر الله له ما تقدم وما تأخر	God has forgiven all his sins
غفراً	Pardon me! I beg your pardon!
غُفْلٌ من الإمضاء (التوقيع)	Unsigned, anonymous
غُفْلٌ من التأريخ	Undated, bearing no date
غلّ يدَه إلى عُنُقهِ	Not to spend or give away anything (lit. to fetter one's hand to one's neck)
غلب على الظن	To be probable, be likely
غُلِب على أمره	He suffered a complete defeat
غلط الحس	Illusion, deception of the senses
غلطة كتابية	Slip of the pen, clerical error
غلّظ اليمين	To swear a sacred oath
غمرات الموت	Mortal throes
غمز الجرسَ	To press the bell button, ring the bell
غمز قناته	To sound s.o. out, probe into s.o.
غمض جفونه على القذى	To bear annoyance patiently, to grin and bear it, swallow the bitter pill
غمّض عينيه عن	To shut one's eyes to, over, towards, or in the face of
غمطه حقَّه	To encroach upon s.o.'s rights, refuse to recognise s.o.'s rights
غَنِيٌّ عن البيان	Self-evident, self-explanatory
غنيمة باردة	Easy prey
غوامض أفكاره	S.o.'s innermost thoughts
غيباً	By heart, from memory
غيّبه الثرى	The earth covered, or buried him
غيّبه عن الوجود	It drove him out of his mind
الغير	The others, fellow men
غير أن ...	Except that, however, but, yet ...

Not topical	غير ذي موضوع
Indifferent, unconcerned	غير عابئ
Irremovable, appointed for life tenure (judge)	غير قابل للعزل
Illegal	غير قانوني
Reckless of, without regard for	غير لاوٍ على
Heedless of	غير مبالٍ بـ
Indeclinable (gram.)	غير متمكن
Unlimited, unending	غير متناه
Useless	غير مُجْدٍ
More than once, quite often, repeatedly, several times	غير مرة
Unsatisfactory	غير مرضي
Incredible	غير مُصَدَّق
Unintelligible, incomprehensible	غير معقول
Unlimited, unrestricted	غير مقيد
Impossible	غير ممكن
Irregular	غير منظّم
Invisible	غير منظور
Incessant, unceasing, uninterrupted, continual	غير منقطع
More than one, several	غير واحد
Untrue	غير واقع

ف

It is too late	فات الأوان
It is (too) late	فات الوقت
He missed the opportunity	فاتته الفرصة
Stimulating the appetite, appetising	فاتح الشهية
He missed the train	فاته القطار
It escaped him that, he omitted, failed or forgot to, he failed to see that, he overlooked the fact that …	فاته أن …
He was reputed to be a holy man	فاح منه شذا القداسة
Pitch black, jet-black	فاحم السواد
There he beheld before him, there stood before him …	فإذا به …
A master of, excelling or outstanding in	فارس حلبةٍ بِـ
Tall and slender	فارع القامة
Interval (time)	فاصل زمني
To give up the ghost	فاضت أنفاسه
To give up the ghost, die	فاضت روحُه
To die	فاضت نفسُه
To compare two things in order to determine which deserves preference	فاضل بين شيئين
To expire, die, give up the ghost	فاق بنفسه
This amount was many times as much as his salary	فاق هذا المبلغ مُرَتَّبَه أضعاف أضعافه
Unmannered, uneducated	فاقد التهذيب
Unconscious, insensible, senseless	فاقد الشعور

Unscrupulous	فاقد الضمير
Dumbfounded speech	فاقد النطق
In that case it's all right	فَبِهَا ونِعمَتْ
To weaken s.o.	فتّ في ساعده
To weaken s.o., sap s.o.'s strength, discourage, enervate s.o.	فت في عضده (ساعده)
Maiden, virgin	فتاة عذراء
Opening of a credit	فَتْحُ الاعتماد
To tell fortunes	فتح البختَ
To stimulate the appetite	فتح الشهيةَ
(S.th.) got under way, was begun	فُتِحَ بابُ
To open negotiations	فتح بابَ المفاوضات
To open up a new way, a new possibility	فتح باباً جديداً
To open one's eyes wide, stare wide-eyed	فتح عينيه على آخرهما
To open one's mouth in order to say s.th., prepare to say s.th.	فتح فمَه بالكلام
Interim period, interim stage, stage of transition	فترة الانتقال
Morning rush hour	فترة الذروة الصباحيّة
To make s.o. see his way clear, cause s.o. to see things in their true light	فتق الذهنَ
A ruse came to his mind	فُتِقَتْ له حيلةٌ
To cut off, destroy, wipe out, eradicate, to decimate, thin the ranks of (esp. said of a disease)	فتك به فتكاً ذريعاً
To straddle	فج رجليه
He was stricken by the death of his son	فُجِعَ بولده
And that's all, and no more, only	فحسب

فرداً فرداً	Singly, one by one, one after the other
فرصة من الزمن	For a short time, briefly
فرض ارادتَه عليه	To force one's will on s.o.
فرض الحصارَ	To impose a blockade
فَرَضَ جَدَلاً	To assume for the sake of argument, propose as a basis for discussion, assume hypothetically
فَرَطَ منه الشيءُ	He missed the thing, lost it
فرغ إلى نفسه	To collect one's thoughts
فرّق تَسُدْ	Divide and conquer!
فرى كذباً	To fabricate, or invent, a lie
فريد في بابه	Unique of its kind
فسّح له الطريق	To open or pave the way for s.o. or s.th.
فسّح مجالا له	To make room for s.o. or s.th., give s.o. or s.th. free play or free scope, to open up an opportunity for s.o.
فسخ عقد زواج	To dissolve a marriage
فشل ذريع	A catastrophic failure
فصاعداً	And beyond that, and more
فصل (مقال) افتتاحي	Opening speech
فصلته عن الرضاع	To wean the infant from sucking
فض بكارتَها	To deflower a girl
الفضل في ذلك عائد عليه	The merit thereby is his due, he deserves all credit for it
فضلا عن	Beside, aside from, let alone
فضلا عن ذلك	Besides, moreover, furthermore
فضول الأحاديث	Futile talk, idle words
فُطِرَ على	(S.th.) is native of him, is in his nature
فعل عوداً إلى بدء	He did it all over again, he began anew

He did it all over again, he began anew	فعل عودَه على بدئه
To have unpleasant effect on s.o.	فعل فيه فعلاً كريهاً
He did it all over again, he began anew	فعله عوداً وبدءاً
To deal s.o. (an opponent, an enemy) a heavy blow, ruin s.o.	فقأ عينَه
To lose one's mind	فقد صوابَه
To lose consciousness, faint, pass out	فقد وعيه
Loss of memory, amnesia	فقدان الذاكرة
The deceased	الفقيد الراحل
Disengagement of forces	فك الاشتباك
To raise, lift (the confiscation of s.th.)	فك الحجزَ عن
To revoke the husband's matrimonial authority over his wife (jur.)	فكّ عصمتَها من زوجها
Just imagine how much more (or less) . . .!	فكيف بِـ
To weaken s.o., to dampen, subdue s.o.	فل حديده
To weaken s.o., to dampen, subdue s.o.	فلّ غربَه
To weaken s.o.	فلّ من حدّته
To weaken s.o.	فلّ من شَبَاه
So-and-so in his private life	فلان في مَبَاذِلِه
His own blood, his own child	فِلذة كبده
And upwards, and more (than that)	فما فوقه
He had no sooner made his plan than he carried it out	فما هي إلا أن همّ حتى فعل
To fully understand, be fully aware	فهم حق الفهم
To understand s.o., understand what s.o. says or means	فَهِمَ عنه

فوات الأجل	Expiration of the deadline
الفواكه على اختلافها	Fruits of every kind
فوائد جمة	Numerous advantageous, ample benefits
فوراً	At once, right away, instantly, immediately
فوز نهائي	Ultimate triumph
فوق الحد	Boundless, infinite, excessive
فوق الطبيعة	Supernatural
فوق العادة	Extraordinary, unusual, uncommon, exceptional
فوق أنه ...	In addition to the fact that it, beyond its being ...
فوق ذلك	Moreover, besides, in addition to that, furthermore
فوق شهور لا تُقَدِّم ولا تُؤَخِّر	A difference of a few months which is of no consequence
في الغد	Tomorrow, the following day
في أثره، على أثره	On his (its) track, immediately afterwards
في أثناء	During, in the course of, meanwhile, in the meantime
في إجماله	As a whole, in its entirety
في أجواز	Amid, in the middle of
في أجواز الفضاء	In space
في أحشاء	In the interior of, within, in
في أحضان	Amid, among, in the presence of s.o.
في أحضان الصحراء	In the heart (or folds) of the desert
في أحيان كثيرة	Frequently, often
في آخر المطاف	In the long run, finally
في أصل الأمر	Originally, at first, actually
في إطار	Within the scope of

In	في أطواء
Reluctantly	في إعراض
At the end of the month	في أعقاب الشهر
At daybreak, immediately after night was over	في أعقاب الليلة
Mostly, most of the time, in most cases	في أغلب الأحيان
Most likely, most probably, in all probability	في أغلب الظن
In the best case, at best	في أفضل الحالات
In the quickest time possible, in the earliest opportunity	في أقرب وقت ممكن
In the twinkling (blink) of an eye, in a moment, in a flash, instantly	في أقلَّ من لمح البصر
Most probably, most likely	في أكثر الظن
Under his protection, under his sponsorship	في أكنافه
At times, once in a while	في الأحايين
Originally, at first, actually	في الأصل
In most cases, in general	في الأغلب
In most cases, in general	في الأغلب والأعم
There is s.th. wrong, there is a fly in the ointment	في الأمر شيء
There is a but in the case, there is a hitch somewhere	في الأمر غلط
In the realm of possibility	في الإمكان
Recently	في الآونة الأخيرة
Straight, directly	في التو
On the spot, immediately	في الحال
In the sixth decade of his life, in his fifties	في الحَلْقَة السادسة من عمره

Abroad, in foreign countries, outside	في الخارج
Secretly	في الخَفَاء
Under the open sky, outdoors, in the open air	في الخلاء
To the back, at the back	في الخلف
On the fourth of the current month	في الرابع من الحالي
Formerly, at one time, once	في السابق
In good and bad days, for better or for worse	في السراء والضراء
Early in the morning	في الصباح الباكر
In the foreground	في الصدر
It is possible to …	في الطاقة …
In front, at the head, in the lead	في الطليعة
Apparently, obviously, evidently	في الظاهر
Now and in the future	في العاجل والآجل
In the open air, outside, outdoors	في العَرَاء
Mostly, in most cases, in general, generally	في الغالب
He had a thousand other things to think of than …	في ألف شاغل عن …
At certain intervals, now and then, off and on, once in a while	في الفترة بعد الفترة
From time to time, now and then, once in a while, sometimes	في الفينة بعد الفينة
Near and far	في القاصية والدانية
In ancient times	في القديم
In the near future, in the immediate future	في القريب العاجل
After all, when all's said and done, in the last analysis	في المدى الأخير

All over the world, throughout the world	في المشرقين وفي المغربين
In good and bad times, for better or for worse	في المصلحة والمفسدة
Externally, in outward appearance, outwardly	في المظهر
All over the world	في المغربين وفي المشرقين
On the twentieth day of the month	في المُوَفَّى عشرين من الشهر
Per cent	في المئة
Rarely	في النادر
In good and bad days	في النعماء والبأساء
In the end, at last, finally, ultimately	في النهاية
It is intended to …	في النية أن …
Outdoors, in the open, under the open sky	في الهواء الطلق
In love	في الهوى
In the very centre, midway, of medium quality	في الوسط
At present, now	في الوقت الحاضر
At the same time, simultaneously	في الوقت نفسه (في نفس الوقت)
At first, first off	في الوهلة الأولى
In hand, on hand, available	في اليد
It is in his power, he is in a position to …	في إمكانه أن …
Methodical, systematic	في انتظام
All over the world	في أنحاء الأرض
He is stuck up	في أنفه وَرَمٌ
Towards the end, at the end of	في أواخر
The end of the month	في أواخر الشهر
At the end of the twenties	في أواخر العشرينات
In the middle of this week	في أواسط هذا الأسبوع
At the right time	في أوانه

في أوائل الخمسينات	In the beginning of the fifties
في أوائل الشهر	In the beginning of the month
في أول الأمر	In the beginning, at first
في أول وقت	One these days, at the first opportunity
في بادئ الأمر	At first, in the beginning
في بادئ الرأي	Beginning with the first impression, right away
في باطن الأمر	At bottom, after all, really
في حبوبة من	Amidst
في بحر	In the course of, during
في بحر سنتين	In the course of two years
في بداية الأمر	In the beginning, at first
في بطانة	Among, amidst, within
في بطن	In, within, in the midst of
في بطون	Inside, within, in
في بعض الأحيان	Sometimes, occasionally
في بعض الأوقات	At times, sometimes
في بعض الطريق	On the way, after passing a certain stretch of the way
في بعض النهار	Sometime during the day, at a certain time of day
في بعض الوقت	Sometimes
في بُهْرَةِ	Middle, centre, amidst
في بيضة الصيف	In the heat of summer
في بيضة النهار	In broad daylight
في تلافيف الظلام	In the dark
في تلافيف سويدائها	In the depth of her heart
في تلك الأثناء	Meanwhile, in the course of
في تمام الساعة السادسة	At six o'clock sharp

في ثنايا	In, inside, among, between
في ثنايا الكتب	In the books
في ثنايا نفسه	In his heart, inwardly
في ثوب بسيط	In plain, homely form
في جانب	With regard to, as compared with
في جَفَاف	In a cold, unemotional tone
في جنبات البيت	All over the house
في جنبات المدينة	Throughout the whole town
في جَنَبَاتِه	In it, inside
في جُنْح الليل	In the dark of night, under the cover of night
في جوانب الدار	All over the house
في جوف	Inside, in the middle of
في جوف الليل	In the middle of the night
في حال من الأحوال	If occasion should arise, anyway
في حالة	In case of, in the event of
في حالة الوفاة	In case of death
في حالة حرب	In a state of war
في حالة غيابه	In case of his absence
في حالة ما إذا	If
في حد ذاته	In itself, as such
في حِدَّةٍ	Sharply, keenly
في حدود	Within, within the framework
في حركاته وسكناته	In all his doings, in every situation
في حِصَّةٍ وجيزة	In a short time
في حضرة	In the presence of
في حظيرة	Inside of, within
في حقيقة الأمر	In reality, actually
في حكم العدم	It is as good as nothing, it is practically non-existent

في حكم	As good as, all but
في حنايا صدره	In his bosom
في حنايا نفسه	Deep inside him
في حوزة يده	In his possession
في حوزته	In his possession
في حَيْرَةٍ	Embarrassed, at a loss, helpless
في حيز الإمكان	Within the realm of possibility, quite possible
في حين (يفعل)	Whereas he does
في حين أن	At the same time when, whereas
في حينِهِ	Then, at the time
في خاصة أنفسهم	At the bottom of their hearts
في خدمة شيء	In the service of s.th.
في خدمتكم	At your service
في خصوص	As to, with respect to, as regards, concerning
في خَطْفَةِ البَرْقِ	Instantly, like a bolt of lightning
في خَفْضٍ من العيش	To live in ease and comfort
في خُفيةٍ	Covertly, secretly
في خلال	During, in the course of, within
في خلال ذلك	Meanwhile, in the meantime
في خُلْسَةٍ	Unobtrusively, unnoticeably
في خَلَلِ	During, in the course of, within
في ذلك مَقْنَعٌ له	That is enough for him, he may content himself with that
في رأيي	In my opinion
في ريعان النهار	In broad daylight
في ساعة مبكرة	At an early hour
في سبيل	For the sake of, for, in behalf of, in the interest of

For the cause of God, in behalf of God and His religion	في سبيل الله
To your health! Cheerio! Skoal!	في سركم
Secretly, inwardly, in his heart	في سره
To be concerned with a matter	في شأن
All but completely isolated, as good as completely isolated	في شبه عزلة تامة
Preoccupied with, concerned about	في شغل (من)
Busy, occupied with	في شغل بِ
Not in any way, in no way, by no means, not at all, not in the least (in negative sentences)	في شيء، بشيء
Concerning, regarding, with respect to	في صدد
On a common basis, on common ground, on equal footing, without distinction, indiscriminately	في صعيد واحد
At heart, in his innermost	في صُلْبِهِ
Silently, quietly	في صَمْتٍ
Amid, in	في صميم
In a tremulous voice	في صوت واجف
In human shape	في صورة آدميين
In case that …	في صورة ما إذا …
On a reduced or small scale, in miniature	في صورة مصغرة
In the twinkling of an eye, instantly	في طرْفةِ عين
Inside, within, in, amid	في طوايا
Throughout the country, all over the country	في طول البلاد وعرضها
Secretly, covertly	في طي الغيب
Seen outwardly, externally	في ظاهر الأمر

في ظل	Under the protection or patronage of, under the auspices of, under the sovereignty of
في عاجله أو آجله	Sooner or later
في عارض الطريق	In the middle of the road
في عداد	Among
في عدادهم	To be counted among them, he is one of them
في عُرْضِ البحر	At sea, on the high seas
في عرض الناس	Amid the people
في عُرْفِهِ	As was his habit, according to this habit
في عز شبابه	In the prime of his youth
في عُزْلَة عن	Secluded, segregated, detached, cut off, isolated from
في عصمة فلان	Under s.o.'s custody, protection or power, married to s.o.
في عُقْر الدار	Within the house itself
في عُقْر داره	In his own house
في عقر ديارهم	Within the country, in their own country, on their own ground
في عموم القطر	Throughout the country
في عُنفُوَان شبابه	In the prime of his youth
في عهد فلان	During s.o.'s lifetime
في عُهدته	In his care, custody, entrusted to him
في غاية الإتقان	To greatest perfection, of excellent workmanship
في غرة العام	At the beginning of the year
في غضون ذلك	Meanwhile, in the meantime
في غضون	In the course of, during, within
في غنى عنه	To do without him, he can dispense with it
في غير أوانه	The wrong time, untimely

Unnecessarily	في غير حاجة
Without	في غير ما
Without fear	في غير ما تهيُّب
Improper, out of place	في غير محله
In places where he couldn't possibly be	في غير مظانه
Unequivocally, in no uncertain terms	في غير مواربة (بدون مواربة)
In the wrong place	في غير موضعه
Unnoticed, without being noticed	في غير وعي
At the wrong time, untimely	في غير وقته
At infrequent intervals, from time to time	في فترات متباعدة من الزمن
During his lifetime	في قائم حياته
In s.o.'s possession, in s.o.'s hands, in s.o.'s power	في قبضة يده
In s.o.'s possession, in s.o.'s hands, in s.o.'s power	في قبضته
In the depth of the heart	في قرارة النفس
Frequently, often	في كثير من الأوقات
Under the protection or tutelage of s.o., in s.o.'s custody	في كفالة فلان
In every respect	في كل اعتبار
All over the world	في كل المعمور (العالم)
All over the world, throughout the world	في كل أنحاء المعمور (المعمورة)
Everywhere, on all sides	في كل جانب
Every place, everywhere, all over, in all quarters	في كل صوب وحدب
Always and everywhere, at any time any place	في كل عصر ومصر

في كل متجه	In all directions, all fields, in every respect.
في كل مكان	Everywhere
في كل مناسبة	Whenever an opportunity arises
في كل وادٍ	On all sides, everywhere
في كَنَف	Under cover of, in an atmosphere of
في لحظة	In a moment, instantly
في لمح البصر	In the twinkling (blink) of an eye, in a moment, in a flash, instantly
في لمح البصر	Like lightning, in a trice, instantly, in no time
في ليلة ليلاء	In the dark of night, under the cover of night
في مَبْرَقِ الصبح	The first rays of the morning sun
في متناول الجميع	Within everybody's means
في متنوال كل الأفهام	Comprehensible to all, understood by all
في متنواله	Attainable to s.o., within s.o.'s reach
في مجلسه	In s.o.'s presence, in s.o.'s company
في محلّه	In his place, in his stead
في مختلف المجالات	In various fields
في مدة	Within the course of, during
في مسيس الحاجة إلى	To be in urgent need of
في مصلحة فلان	In s.o.'s interest
في مطاوي	Inside, within, in, amid
في مطاويه	Inwardly, at heart, in his bosom
في مَعرِض	In the form of, in ... manner, on the occasion of, at the occurrence or appearance of
في مُعظمِهِ	Mostly, for the most part, largely
في مقتبَل العمر	In the prime of life

To be able to, be capable of, be in a position to, have the possibility to …	في مقدوره أن …
On the occasion of	في مناسبة (لمناسبة، بمناسبة)
Halfway, midway	في منتصف الطريق
At the parting of day, at day's end	في منصَرَف النهار
Storm-swept, exposed to storms, threatened by storms	في مهب الرياح
At (the time of) sunset	في مهبط الغروب
In one and the same place	في موضع واحد
In the right place, time, convenient	في موضعه
On time, punctually	في ميعاده (في الميعاد)
Free from, far from, a long way from	في نجوة من
Around seven o'clock	في نحو الساعة السابعة
In its proper place, in good order, perfectly all right	في نصابه
In my eyes, in my opinion	في نظري
In reality, actually, in fact	في نفس الأمر
He acts according to his own desires	في نَفَس من أموره
This matter calls for careful study, will have to be considered	في هذا الأمر نظر
About this, about this matter	في هذا الباب
In this respect, with regard to this, with relation to this, on this occasion, in this connection	في هذا الصدد
In this connection	في هذا المجال
On this occasion	في هذا المقام
Enough of that, that's enough	في هذا كفاية
In the meantime, meanwhile	في هذه الأثناء
In this case	في هذه الحالة
At that moment	في هذه اللحظة

في واقع الأمر	In effect, indeed, as a matter of fact, actually
في وَسَطٍ مِن	In the middle or midst of, within
في وسطنا	In our midst, among us
في وُسعِهِ أن ...	It is in his power to, he can ...
في وُسعِي أن أقولَ	I can say
في وضح النهار	In broad daylight
فياض الخاطر	Brilliant, overflowing with ideas
فيما	While, in that, as
فيما إذا	In case that, if
فيما اعتقد	As I believe
فيما أعهَدُ	To my knowledge, as far as I know
فيما بعد	Afterwards, later
فيما بين ذلك	Meanwhile, in the meantime
فيما بينهم	Among themselves, among them
فيما بيني وبين نفسي	In my heart, at heart, inwardly
فيما عدا	Except, save, with the exception of, excepting
فيما عدا ذلك	Besides
فيما له مساس بِـ	Concerning, regarding
فيما لو	In case that
فيما مضى	In the past, formerly, before
فيما مضى من الزمان	Formerly, previously, in the past
فيما يتعلق بِـ	With regard to, as to, regarding, concerning
فيما يلي	In the following, in what follows, below
الفَينة بعد الأخرى	From time to time, now and then, once in a while, sometimes

From time to time, now and then, once in a while, sometimes	الفَينة بعد الفَينة
He is a little crazy, he has a bee in his bonnet	فيه (به) لُوثة
He looks like his father	فيه لمحة من أبيه
He has his father's features	فيه ملامح من أبيه

ق

Ruler, potentate, monarch	قابض على الأمر
Subject to, liable, susceptible to	قابل لـ
Irrevocable	قابل للرجوع
Curable	قابل للشفاء
Mortal	قابل للموت
To return like for like	قابله بالمِثل
To welcome s.o. or s.th.	قابله على الرحب والسَّعَة
Divisibility	قابلية القسمة
Damned bastard! (lit. may God fight him!)	قاتله الله
Leading thinkers	قادة الفكر
Flamethrower	قاذفة النار
Minesweeper	قارب التنقيب عن الألغام
Gunboat	قارب مسلح
Motorboat	قارب ناري
Lifeboat	قارب نجاة
Middle of the road	قارعة الطريق
To compare two things, draw a parallel	قارن بين شيئين
The gentle reader	القارئ الكريم
To die a thousand deaths	قاسى الألواء واللَّأْواء
To go through the worst, be exposed to the greatest hardships	قاسى الأمرين
To compare two things	قاسى بين شيئين
Hard-hearted, callous, pitiless, cruel	قاسي القلب
Helpless, impotent, parsimonious, niggardly	قاصر اليد
Chaste, demure, modest (of a woman)	قاصرة الطرف

Mortal blow, catastrophe	قاصمة الظهر
Everybody, all people (lit. the distant one and the near one)	القاصي والداني
Brigand, waylayer, highway robber	قاطع الطريق
To interrupt s.o., cut s.o. short, cut in on s.o.'s talk	قاطعه الحديث
Riverbed	قاع النهر
Slacker, inactive, idle	قاعد عن العمل
Capital of the country	قاعدة البلاد
General rule	قاعدة مطردة
To motion with the head, signal, beckon	قال برأسه
He said in a voice full of mercy ...	قال بصوت ملؤه الشفقة ...
Among other things, he said ...	قال في جملةِ ما قاله ...
To mention casually, say among other things	قال في مِعْرَاض كلامه
He said what he had to say, he had his say	قال كلمته
He said with a smile	قال وهو يبتسم
Chunk of cheese	قالب جُبن
Sugar loaf	قالب سكر
Bar of soap	قالب صابون
Proof had been furnished for	قام البرهان على
Truth became or was manifest	قام الحق
To go to	قام إلى
To consist in, be founded on, be based, to carry out, execute, perform	قام بـ
To assume the burdens of government	قام بأعباء الحكم
To meet one's obligations	قام بالتزاماته
To defray the costs, pay the expenses	قام بالمصاريف

قام بالواجب عليه	To do one's duty
قام بأوَدِهِ	To provide for s.o.'s needs, stand by s.o. in time of need
قام بدورٍ	To play a part
قام بشأنه	To take care of s.o., look after s.o., take s.o. under one's wing
قام بوعده	To keep one's word
قام على	To be built on, to manage, tend, guard
قام على قدم وساق	To become fully effective, be in full progress, be in full swing
قام عليه	To rise or turn against s.o.
قام في وجه فلان	To stand up to s.o., take a stand against s.o.
قام في وجهه	To resist, oppose, defy s.o.
قام له	To rise in honour of s.o.
قام مقامَه	To replace s.o., substitute for s.o., take s.o.'s place, replace s.th.
قام منه مقامَه	To take the place of s.th. with s.o.
قام وقعد	To be in a state of great anxiety, be seriously upset, be very agitated
قام يفعل	To begin to do s.th.
قامت الحرب على ساقٍ	The war was or became violent, war broke out
قامت الصلاة	Time of prayer has come
قامت قيامته	To get excited, get angry, become furious, all hell broke loose in it
قامت قيامته لِـ (عن)	To be upset, be shocked, be violently agitated by s.th.
قامت قيامته لِـ (مِن)	To be upset, be shocked, be violently agitated by s.th.
قامر على	To bet, speculate on
قامر على الجواد الخاسر	To bet on the wrong horse

They rose to a man	قاموا قومة رجل واحد
They set out in our support	قاموا لمعاونتِنَا
Constitutional law	قانون الأساسي
Rectangular, right-angled	قائم الزاوية
Self-existent	قائم بالذات
Self-existent	قائم بذاته
Self-existent	قائم برأسه
Self-existent	قائم بنفسه
Revolting, rebelling against, vertical to, perpendicular to	قائم على
Everything without exception	قائم وحصيد
Menu	قائمة الطعام
To denounce s.o.'s action as ugly, ignominious, shameful	قبّح عليه فعلَه
To constipate the bowels	قبض البطنَ
To oppress, deject, dishearten, dispirit, depress	قبض الصدرَ (النفس)
God made him die	قبض الله روحه (قبضه الله)
To hold the reins of power	قبض على أزمة الأمر
Revenues and expenditures	القبض والدفع
To keep o.s. from seizing s.o. or s.th., to be stingy towards	قبض يدَه عن
Fist	قبضة اليد
To die	قُبِضَت روحُه
Skates	قبقاب الانزلاق
Before, prior to	قَبلَ
Fore part, front	قُبْل
Power, ability	قِبَل
In the presence of, near, in the direction of (prep.)	قِبَل
Before, previously, formerly	قبل الآن

قَبِلَ الذهابَ معي	He was willing to go with me
قبل الظهر	In the forenoon, a.m.
قبل أن	Before
قبل أوانه	Prematurely
قَبِلَ شكًّا	To admit doubt
قبل فوات الوقت	Before it is too late
قبل كل شيء	First of all, above all
قبل مجيئه بساعة	An hour before his arrival
قِبلة الأنظار	Focus of attention, target of all eyes, ideal, goal sought after and aspired to
قِبلة الاهتمام	Object of widespread interest, focus of attention
قَبِلَهُ بالحِضْنِ	He received him with open arms
قبلئذٍ	Previously, in former times
قُبَيلَ (أن)	Shortly before, prior to
قتل البردَ	To alleviate the cold
قتل الجوعَ	To alleviate hunger
قتل الدهرَ خِبرةً	To have long experience with life, be worldly-wise
القتل العمد مع سَبق الإصرار	Premeditated murder
قتل الموضوعَ بحثاً	To study a topic most thoroughly, treat a subject exhaustively
قتله خُبراً (علماً)	To know or master s.th. (e.g. a skill, a field of study) thoroughly
قتله درساً وبحثاً	To know or master s.th. (e.g. a skill, a field of study) thoroughly
قتله صبراً	To kill s.o. in captivity
قتله غيلةً	To assassinate s.o.
قتله في مهده	To nip s.th. in the bud
قتلوا عن آخرهم	They were killed to the last man

It has come to our knowledge that ...	قد اتصل بنا أن ...
It's all over between him and them, they are through with each other	قد انبتَّ الأمر بينه وبينهم
To have a heart of stone	قُدَّ قلبُه من حجر
To strike fire (with a flint)	قدح النارَ
To ponder, think hard, rack one's brain	قدح زنادَ الفكر
To strike or emit sparks	قدح شرراً
To think hard	قدح فكرَه
To reprove, censure, belittle	قدح في
As far as possible, as much as possible, in the best way possible, to the best of one's abilities	قدرَ الإمكان
As far as possible, as much as possible, in the best way possible, to the best of one's abilities	قدرَ الطاقة
As far as possible, as far as it is feasible	قدر المستطاع
The inevitable happened	قُدِّر فكَانَ
A certain extent of, a certain degree of	قدر من
Deterring power	قدرة ردعيّة
Inflammability, flammability	القدرة على الاشتعال
May God sanctify his secret (eulogy used when mentioning the name of a deceased Muslim saint)	قدّس الله سرّه
To offer condolences	قدّم التعازي
To extend one's thanks to s.o.	قدّم الشكر له
To send s.th. ahead of s.th. else, let s.th. precede s.th. else	قدّم بيد يديه
To render a service	قدّم خدمةً

قدّم خطوةً	To make a step forwards
قدّم عطاء	To make an offer or tender
قدِمُ عهدهِ بِـ	His long-standing familiarity with
قدّم له الثمنَ	To pay the price to s.o. in advance
قدم مكعب	Cubic foot
قدّم نفسه إلى الشرطة	To give o.s. up to the police
قدّم وساطتَه لِـ	To offer one's good offices for
قدِماً	In old(en) times, of yore
قدّمه باليد	To hand s.th. over personally, deliver s.th. in person
قدير على	Having mastery over
قديم الطراز	Old fashion
قديم العهد	Of an early date, long past, long-standing
قديم العهد بِـ	Of long experience in, long acquainted with
القديم الغابر	Old times, ancient times
قديماً	In ancient times
القذف بالقنابل	Bombardment
قذف عليه الشتائم	To hurl abusive language at s.o.
قذفه بالقنابل	To bomb s.th. strafe s.th. with bombs
قذىً في عينه	An odious thing, an eyesore, a thorn in the flesh
قر الرأي على ...	It was decided to, a resolution was passed on s.th., the decision was reached to ...
قر رأيه على	To resolve, determine on s.th., decide
قَرَّ عيناً	To be of good character
قرأ الفأل	To tell fortunes, predict the future
قرأ حسابَه لـ	To reckon with s.th., take s.th. into account

To study s.th. under s.o.	قرأ عليه
To greet, salute s.o., to extend greetings to s.o.	قرأ عليه السلامَ
To have a thousand apprehensions about s.th.	قرأ له ألفَ حساب
Palmistry	قراءة الكف
Almost three years	قرابة ثلاثة أعوام
I read a book by him, I read one of his books	قرأت له كتاباً
Towards noon	قُربَ الظهر
To bring people together, make peace, reconcile	قرّب بينَهم
Joy, pleasure, consolation for the eye, delight for the eye, darling	قرة العين
To be glad, be delighted	قرّت عينُه
Dial (of a telephone)	قُرص الأرقام
To shape (dough) into round, flat loaves	قرّص العجين
Honeycomb	قرص عسل
To hurt s.o. with words	قرصه بلسانه
Disk-like, discoid	قُرصي الشكل
To die	قرض رباطَه
To write poetry, make verses	قرض شعرَه
To ring the bell	قرع الجرسَ
To touch glasses, drink to s.o.'s health	قرع الكأسَ (لِـ)
To reach s.o.'s ear	قرع سمعَه
To repent s.th.	قرع سِنَّ الندم لِـ (على)
To gnash one's teeth	قرع سِنَّه
Enlistment, draft recruitment	قرعة عسكرية
His conscience tormented or smote him, he had a guilty conscience, he felt grave compunctions	قرعه ضميرُه

قرقع بسوطه	To crack the whip
قرقع ضاحكاً (بالضحك)	To burst into loud laughter, guffaw
قرن البحر	Coral
القرون الخالية	The past centuries
القرون الوسطى	The Middle Ages
قريب الشَبَهِ إلى	Very similar to
قريب العهد	New, recent, young
قريب العهد بِـ	Having adopted or acquired (s.th.) recently, inexperienced at (s.th.), new at (s.th.)
قريب المأخذ	Easy to handle or to use
قريب المتناول	Easy to understand
قريب المنال	Easy to understand
قريب عهد بالفطام	Newly weaned
قريب من الحسن	Fairly good
قريباً	Soon, shortly, in the near future
قرير العين	Happy, delighted, glad
قريع الدهر	The greatest hero of his time
قساوة القلب	Callousness, hard-heartedness, cruelty
قسماً	I swear
قسماً بِـ	I swear by
قشر الرأس	Dandruff
قص أثرَه	To follow s.o.'s tracks, track s.o.
قص عليه	To relate, narrate, tell
قص عليه طرفاً (أطرافاً) من حياته	To tell s.o. an episode(s) of one's life
قصاراك أن تفعل هذا	The most you can accomplish is to do this, you must limit yourself to doing this

In short, in brief, to make a long story short	قصارى الأمر
In brief, in short	قصارى القول
The matter is so that, the thing is best described by saying that ...	قصة هذا الشيء أن ...
To move towards s.o., walk up to s.o.	قصد شطرَه
Intentionally, purposely, advisedly, deliberately	قصداً
He is in front of you, before you, opposite you	قصدك
The most you can hope to accomplish is to do this, you must limit yourself to doing this	قصرك أن تفعل هذا
To be a mortal blow to s.o. (lit. to break s.o.'s back)	قصم ظهرَه
Powerlessness, impotence, helplessness	قصور الباع
Short-term, short-lived	قصير الأجل
Short-lived	قصير الأمد
Short-sighted, myopic	قصير البصر
Short-sighted	قصير النظر
Powerless, helpless	قصير اليد
Jurisdiction based on the Sharia, canonical law	القضاء الشرعي
Death	قضاء الله
Condemnation, sentencing, extermination, foiling, thwarting	قضاء على
Inescapable fate	قضاء مُبرَم
Fate and divine decree	القضاء والقدر
Criminal cases in which the perpetrator was caught in the act	قضايا التلبس

قضى أجلَه	To die
قضى الحاجة	To relieve o.s., answer the call of nature
قضى العجبَ من	To be full of amazement at, be very astonished at
قضى حاجتَه	To fulfil s.o.'s wish
قضى نحبَه	To fulfil one's vow, to pass away, die
قضى وطرَه	To attain one's aim or end, see one's wish fulfilled
قُضِيَ الأمرُ	The matter is decided and done with, the die is cast
قُضِيَ القضاء	The divine decree was fulfilled, i.e. death came with God's will
قُضِيَ أمرُه	It's all over with him
قُضِيَ عليه	It's all over with him, he's done for
قُطب الرَّحَى	Pivot (of s.th.)
قَطَبَ حاجبيه	To frown, scowl, knit the brows, glower
القُطْر الشقيق	The brother country
قُطِعَ (الحبل)	To break apart, become interrupted, to snap (rope, string of a musical instrument)
قطع أشواطًا	To make progress
قطع أشواطا شاسعة	To make good progress
قطع الأملَ (الرجاءَ)	To give up hope, to despair
قطع الثمنَ	To fix the price, agree on the price
قطع الحسابات	Settlement of accounts

قطع الرَّحِم	To break with one's relatives, to violate the rules of consanguinity, to sever the bonds of kinship
قطع الطريق	Highway robbery, brigandage
قطَع الطريق	To commit highway robbery
قطع الطريق على	Forcible prevention of s.th., radical stop to s.th.
قطع النظر عن	To take no account of, disregard s.th.
قطع الوعدَ على نفسه بِـ	To vow s.th., pledge o.s. or bind o.s. to do s.th.
قطع الوقتَ	To while away the time, kill time
قطع بأن ...	To affirm confidently, aver, to prove that ...
قطع برأي	To express a firm opinion, to decide in favour of an opinion
قطع برأيه	To be guided in one's decisions by s.o., proceed in accordance with s.o.'s opinion or decision
قطع تذكرة (بطاقة)	To buy a ticket
قطع دوراً	To pass through a phase or period, go through a phase or period, go through a stage
قطع شوطاً كبيراً (بعيداً) (الرُّقِي) في التقدم	To make good progress or headway, advance in great strides
قطع على نفسه عهداً بِـ	To vow s.th., pledge o.s. or bind o.s. to do s.th.
قطع عليه الطريقَ	To cut off s.o.'s way, interrupt s.o., to engage in highway robbery, to rob s.o.
قطع عليه حديثه	To interrupt s.o.'s talk, cut s.o. short, cut in on s.o.'s talk
قطع عهداً	To conclude a treaty, make a contract

قطع عهداً (لِـ)	To make a contract, to make a promise, vow or pledge
قطع في ميدان الرقي أشواطاً	To make good progress or headway, advance in great strides
قطع لسانَه	To silence s.o., seal s.o.'s lips
قطع نفسه عهداً على	To assume an obligation, commit o.s., obligate o.s.
قطع نياط القلوب	To break the heart
قطعاً	Decidedly, definitely, for certain
قطعاً للوقت	As a pastime, just to kill time
قطعي	Decided, definite, definitive, final
قطعياً	Definite, definitive
قعد به	To make s.o. sit, seat s.o.
قعد به عن	To hold back, restrain, discourage, or prevent s.o. from
قعد عن	To desist, refrain from, renounce
قعد عن الذهاب	He decided not to go
قعد لـ	To be very alarmed by
قعدت به ركبتاه	His knees buckled under him
قعر في كلامه	To speak gutturally
قعيد المنزل	Confined to one's house or to one's quarters
قفر أثره	To follow s.o.'s tracks, track s.o.
قَفِر من	Destitute, devoid (of)
قفز طويل	Long jump
قفز عال	High jump
قَفَلَ باب الشيء	To put an end to s.th., close s.th.
قلّ صبرُه	To be impatient, to lose patience
قلّب ظهراً لبطن	To turn s.th. completely upside down, turn s.th. topsy-turvy
قلّب فيه البصرَ (النظر)	To scrutinise, eye, regard s.th.
قلّب كَفَّيه	To repent, to be embarrassed

To give s.o. the cold shoulder, become hostile to s.o. (lit. to show s.o. the back of the shield)	قَلَبَ له ظهرَ المِجَنِّ
With heart and soul, inwardly and outwardly	قلباً وقالباً
To turn s.th. over in one's mind, reflect on s.th., ponder s.th., brood over s.th.	قلّبه بعقله
To turn s.th. in one's hands, fidget with s.th.	قلّبه بين يديه
To turn s.th. upside down	قَلَبَه رأساً
Insensitivity, obtuseness	قلة الإحساس
Indifference, apathy	قلة الاكتراث
Misfortune, bad luck	قلة البركة
Immodesty, impudence, shamelessness, impertinence	قلة الحياء
Want of appetite	قلة الشهية للطعام
Impatience	قلة الصبر
Scarcity, rarity, rareness	قلة الوجود
To pull out s.th. with the roots	قلعه من جذوره
To neutralise, disarm one's opponent	قلّم أظافرَ خصمِهِ
Head office	قلم الإدارة
Editing room	قلم التحرير
Accounting department	قلم الحسابات
Impolite	قليل الأدب
Impatient	قليل الصبر
Inexpensive, cheap	قليل النفقات
A little, somewhat, seldom, rarely	قليلاً
Seldom, rarely	قليلاً ما
Crown of the head	قِمّة الرأس
The sun and the moon	القمران

Cigar butt	قمع السيكارة
Nightgown	قميص النوم
Time bomb	قنبلة زمنية
By force, forcibly	قهراً
To have little appetite	قَهِي (أقهى) من الطعام
They lent him their ears, they listened to him	ألقوا إليه أسماعهم
Beginnings	قوابل
Ground, sea and air forces	قوات برية وبحريه وجوية
Biting words	قوارص الكلمات
The provider, or supporter of his family	قِوَام أهله
Reserves (military)	قوة احتياطية
Will power	قوة الإرادة
Inertia	قوة الاستمرار
Volume, intensity (radio)	قوة الصوت
Eloquence	قوة العارضة
Legal force	قوة القانون
Centrifugal force	القوة النابذة
Memory	قوة حافظة
Purchasing power	قوة شراء
Intellectual power, faculty of perception	قوة عاقلة
Working power, output capacity	قوة على العمل
Brute force	قوة غاشمة
Moral strength, morale, spirit	قوة معنوية
Regular army	قوة نظامية
Rainbow	قوس قُزَح
Parentheses (punctuation marks)	قوسان
The last word, the final decision	القول الفصل
By word and deed	قولاً وعملاً

قُوَى البَطْش	Thugs, goon squads
قوي الشكيمة	Energetic, vigorous, active
قَوِيُّ العارضة	Eloquent, quick-witted
قَوِيَ على	To be able to cope with s.th., be able to do s.th.
قياس عالمي	World record
قياس فاسد	Wrong inference, false conclusion, fallacy, sophism, paralogism
قياساً على ذلك	Analogy (with it), analogously (to it), correspondingly
قِيام أهله	The provider, or supporter of his family
القيام بالعمل	Performance, working, functioning
قيد الأسنان	Gums
قيد الأنساب	Genealogical tree, family tree
قيد شعرة	By a hair breadth, within a hair's breadth
قيل على لسانه ما	He was supposed to have said things which, statements were ascribed to him which …
قيل في المثل	The proverb says

ك

كاتب السر	Private secretary
كاتب المحكمة	Court clerk
كاتب قصصي	Writer, novelist
كاتم السر	Secretary
كاد لِـ	To harm by artful machinations, lay snares, conspire against s.o.
كاد يموت	He almost died
كادَه	To deceive s.o.
كارتداد الطرْفِ	In the twinkling of an eye, instantly
كارثة الأمطار	Natural catastrophe, torrential rains
كأس التمويه	Overfull cup
كاسحة الألغام	Minesweeper
كاشَحَهُ بالعداوة	To harbour hatred towards s.o.
كاشفه بالعداوة	To manifest open hostility towards s.o.
كافح أمورَه	To manage one's affairs personally
كافح عن	To defend s.th., fight for s.th.
كافر بالنعمة	Ungrateful
كال – بِـ	To compare by measuring
كال له الشتائمَ	To heap abuse on s.o.
كال له الصاع بصاعين	To pay s.o. back twofold, bring double retaliation on s.o.
كال له اللطمات	To give s.o. a beating, thrash s.o.
كالأول	As before, as at the beginning, as from the outset
كالسابق	As before
كاللازم	As it must be, properly
كالماء الجاري	Fluently, smoothly, like clockwork

As usual	كالمعتاد
To measure s.th., to weigh s.th.	كاله
Latent, hidden, concealed, secret	كامن
Expressing duration in the past = English progressive past (past continuous) 'used to', 'would'	كان (يفعل)
It was his greatest worry	كان أكبر شاغل له
It was hoped that …	كان الأملُ معقوداً أن …
To be the cause of s.th., it was because of	كان السبب فيه
Some of the group were silent and some were talking	كان القوم بين صامت ومتكلم
To be assigned to, be the lot or share of, be left to, be due (s.o.)	كان إلى
The first thing he did was …	كان باكورة أعماله
To keep away from, remain aloof from, not get involved in	كان بمنأى عن
To be safe from, be secure from, be safeguarded against	كان بمنجاة من
We should be please if …	كان بودنا لو …
To be entirely dependent on	كان حُبْساً على
He had not known Europe until recently	كان حديث عهد بأوروبا
To be incumbent on, be the duty of	كان على
To be on tenterhooks, be in great suspense, be dying with curiosity	كان على أحرَّ من الجمر
To be prepared, be set for, to be ready, willing, inclined, in a position to	كان على استعداد لِـ
To be on the wrong way, be wrong, be mistaken	كان على الباطل
To do or think the opposite, take an opposite stand	كان على الضد من ذلك

كان على العكس من	To be in contrast to that, be in opposition to
كان على انتظاره	To wait for s.o. or s.th.
كان على أوفاز	To be on one's toes, be on alert
كان على بصيرة من	To have insight into s.th., be informed about s.th.
كان على بيّنة من	To be fully aware of, to be well-informed, up-to-date about
كان على جانب عظيم من الكرم	To be very generous
كان على حق	To be on the right way, have hit on the right thing, be right
كان على خطأ	To be on the wrong way, be wrong, be mistaken
كأن على رؤوسهم الطيرَ	Motionless or silent with awe
كان على شاكلته	To be of the same kind, of the same strain as s.th.
كان على علم بِـ	To be informed about, be acquainted with
كان على قسط كبير من	To possess s.th. (a quality, a characteristic) to a large extent, have a great deal of
كان على موعد معه (منه)	To have an appointment with s.o.
كان على ميعاد مع	To have an appointment with
كان على نار	To be on pins and needles
كان على هدى	To be on the right way, to embrace the true religion
كان عند حسن الظن به	To have a good opinion of s.o.
كان عند حسن ظنه	To meet, or be up to, s.o.'s high expectations
كان عند نصحه	To follow s.o.'s advice
كان عندي في مقام والدي	He assumed the responsibility of fatherhood for me, he is like a father to me

To be of extraordinary beauty	كان غاية في الجمال
He was present to greet him, he had come to meet him, he received him	كان في استقباله
To be taken into account, be expected, be anticipated	كان في الحُسبان
It was expected that …	كان في الحُسبان أن …
To stand in need, be in want of (s.th.)	كان في حاجة إلى (لِـ)
He reckoned with it, he expected it, he was prepared for it	كان في حسابه
To be subject to s.th.	كان في حكم الشيء
He was free to, he was at liberty to	كان في حلٌّ من (عن)
Be no longer existent	كان في خبر كان
To be wealthy, live in luxury	كان في سَعة من رزقه
To be too busy or preoccupied with to be able to attend to s.th.	كان في شغل عن (بِـ)
To be deaf to s.th.	كان في صمم عن
To have sense, be sensible or normal	كان في طريقه
To forgo, renounce s.th., be in no need of s.th.	كان في غنى عنه
To be uncertain about s.o., to have doubts about s.o.	كان في لَبسٍ من أمره
To be in the right place, to be appropriate, advisable	كان في محله
To be still in its beginnings or infancy, not have progressed beyond the early stages	كان في مهده
To belong to, be one's own	كان لِـ
To be s.o.'s duty to, be necessary for s.o. that he …	كان لزاماً عليه أن …
To make the best impression on everyone	كان له أحسن وقع في النفوس

كان له بيت	He had owned a house
كان لها ضلع في الأمر	She had s.th. to do with the matter, she had a hand in it, she played a role in the affair
كان محطَّ الأنظار	To draw attention to o.s.
كان محلَّ غبطة	To be in an enviable position
كان مضرب المثل (الأمثال)	To be proverbial, be exemplary, be unique, be cited as an example
كان معه	It was with him, he had it with him
كان من	To belong or pertain to, be among, fall under
كان من الأهمية بمكان عظيم	To be of the greatest importance
كان من الضروري	To be necessary
كان من باب	To belong to, to fall under
كان من جملة أصحابه	He was one of his companions
كان من حسن حظه أن ...	He was lucky in that he ...
كان من حقه أن ...	He should have, he ought to have ...
كان من شأنه	It was his wont, he used to
كان من صالحه	It was in his interest
كان من نصيبه	To fall to s.o.'s share or lot
كان من نصيبه أن ...	To be so fortunate as to, have the good fortune to ...
كان من وراء مَقدُرة العقل البشري	To be beyond the power of human comprehension
كان منه وإليه	To depend entirely on s.o., be inseparable from s.o., appertain to s.o.
كان موضعَ حفَاوَةٍ	He was the object of a festive reception
كان نصيبه من ذلك الاخفاق	To have bad luck in s.th., draw a blank
كان نهايةً في الحِذق	To be the ne plus ultra of skill, be extremely skilled

كان هدفاً لـ	To be exposed, be open to
كان وإياه على طرفي نقيض	They held diametrically opposed views or positions
كان وراءه	To be favourably disposed to s.o., stand behind s.o., support, back s.o.
كان وقفاً على	To be entirely dependent on
كانت الحرب بينهم سجالاً	Their battle had its ups and downs, they fought with each other with alternate success
كانت له الصفقة الخاسرة	He had a losing deal
كانت من البراءة بحيث لا ترى	She was so naïve that she couldn't see
كانوا على طرفي نقيض	They were at variance, they carried a feud
كأني بها (تفعل)	I am under the impression that she, it looks to me as if she …
الكائن المطلق	The Absolute Being, God
كائناً ما كان	Whatever it may be, be what it may
كائناً من كان	Whoever it may be
الكائنات	The created beings, the universe, the world
كبّ لوجهه (على وجهه)	To prostrate
كبار الضباط	Senior officers
كبار الموظفين	Senior officials
كبتَ أنفاسَه	To get s.o. out of breath
كبَتَ غيظَه في جوفه	To suppress one's anger
كبَحَ جماحَه	To curb s.o.'s defiance, repress s.o. or s.th.
كبريات	Greater
كبَسَ السنةَ بيومٍ	To intercalate (a day in a leap year)
كبير الأساقفة	Archbishop

Old	كبير السن
Chief justice	كبير القضاة
Proud	كبير النفس
The Quran, the Bible	الكتاب
Credentials (diplomatic)	كتاب الاعتماد
Marriage contract	كتاب الزواج
Bill of divorce	كتاب الطلاق
Textbook	كتاب تعليمي
Bookstore, library	كتاب خانة
Essays, writings	كتابات
In writing	كتابةً
Historical writing	كتابة التاريخ
To be firmly resolved to …	كتب على نفسه أن …
To write from s.o.'s dictation	كتب عنه
To draw up the marriage contract for s.o.	كتب كتابَه
To foreordain, destine (of God)	كتبه الله على (لـ)
Crowds, throngs, masses	كُتَل بشرية
Bulk of the body, frame	كُتلة الجسد
A fearless, husky fellow	كتلة من الأعصاب
To take s.o.'s breath away, drive s.o. out of his senses	كتم أنفاسَه
Density of population	كَثَافة السكان
Sonority, sound intensity	كثافة الصوت
To bare one's teeth, gnash one's teeth	كشّر عن أنيابه
Majority, major portion of	كثرة من
The most part	الكثير
Populous	كثير السكان
Talkative, loquacious, garrulous	كثير الكلام
Too much for	كثير على

Most (of)	الكثير من
The majority of, most of, plenty of, a great many, a lot of	الكثير من (الكثيرون من)
Very, much, to a large extent, often, frequently	كثيراً ما
He doesn't know what he is doing (lit. like one who gathers wood at night)	كحاطب ليل
Heap, pile, stack	كُداسة
I almost went	كِدتُ أذهب
To toil, labour, slave (in or with s.th.)	كدح في
To be angry	كَدِرَ على
To be turbid, muddy, roiled (liquid)	كَدَرَ (الماءُ)
To trouble, spoil s.th. for s.o. (e.g. s.o.'s peace of mind)	كدّره على
So and so, such and such, so-and-so much, so-and-so many	كذا وكذا
Lie after lie, lies upon lies	كذب في كذب
April fool's joke	كِذبَة إبريل
The same goes for, it is also the same with	كذلك الحال في
Attack and retreat (in battle)	الكَرّ والفَرّ
Meatballs	كُرات لحم
The most prized possession(s)	كرائم المال (الأموال)
A second time, once more	كرَّةً أخرى
Terrestrial globe, globe	كُرة الأرض (كُرة أرضية)
Snowball	كُرة الثلج
Basketball	كُرة السَّلّة
Table tennis	كُرة الطاولة
Football	كُرة القدم
Celestial sphere (astrology)	كُرة الكواكب

Water polo	كُرة الماء
Handball	كُرة اليد
Repeatedly, time and again	كرّة بعد كرّة
Workshop, factory (e.g. brothel)	كرخانة
To pose over and over again (a question)	كرّره (السؤال) على
To hide or seek refuge with	كَرَزَ - إلى
To preach, spread the Gospel	كرز بالإنجيل
To consecrate, open ceremonially (Chr.)	كرّس
To devote, dedicate	كرّس في
Royal chair	كرسي المَلِك
Capital, metropolis	كرسي المملكة
Swivelling chair, revolving stool	كرسي دائر
Rocking chair	كرسي هزّاز
To burst out into laughter, roar with laughter	كركر في الضحك
Noble character	كرم الأخلاق
May God honour him!	كرّم الله وجهه
Noble descent	كرم المَحتِد
Most kindly, obligingly, out of kindness	كَرَماً
For your sake, as a favour to you, in your honour	كُرمَاناً لك
For your sake, as a favour to you, in your honour	كُرمَةً لَكَ
To exalt s.o. above another	كرّمه على
Unwillingly, reluctantly, under compulsion, under duress	كَرهاً
The sphericity of the earth	كروية الأرض
Noble-minded, noble	كريم الأخلاق

Noble descent, highbred	كريم الأصل
Noble-minded, of generous disposition	كريم النحيزة
The two noble things, Hajj and Jihad	الكريمان
The two eyes	الكريمتان
Closefisted, miserly, niggardly	كَزُّ اليدين
As was formerly customary, as was usual	كسابق العادة
To encase s.th. in, to cover s.th. with s.th.	كساه بِـ
To give s.th. the appearance of, make s.th. look like	كساه صيغةً كذا
Win acclaim for, be applauded for	كسب هُتَافاً لِـ
Nook of the house	كسر البيت
To break the silence	كسر الصمتَ
To quench the thirst	كسر العطشَ
To humiliate s.o.	كسر أنفَه
To disappoint, offend, affront s.o.	كَسَرَ خاطِرَه
Decimal fractions	كسر عشري
To break s.o.'s power of resistance, crush s.o.'s spirit	كَسَرَ عُودَه
To break s.o.'s heart, to discourage s.o.	كسر قلبَه
To blunt the edge of s.th., tone down s.th., temper s.th or s.o.	كسر من حدته
The wind has calmed down	كُسِرت الريح
To dissuade or hinder s.o. from carrying out his intention	كسره عن مراده
Fractions	كُسُورات
Searchlight	كشاف كهربائي

To harbour enmity towards s.o., hate s.o.	كَشَحَ – له بالعداوة
To disperse, scatter, break up (a crowd)	كَشَحَهُم
To bare or show one's teeth	كشّر عن أسنانه
To bare or show one's teeth	كشّر عن نابه (أنيابه)
To unveil, unmask s.o. or s.th.	كشف القناعَ عن
To uncover, reveal, disclose s.th.	كشف النقابَ عن
Medical examination	كشف طبي
To examine s.o. medically	كشف عليه طبياً
To unveil, reveal, disclose, expose, investigate, examine s.th.	كَشَفَ عن
War flared up, fierce fighting broke out	كشفت الحرب عن (على) ساقها
Discoveries	كشوف
Spine of a book	كعب الكتاب
The Kaaba (in Mecca)	الكعبة
Shrine, object of veneration, focus of interest (fig.)	
Cube(s), cubic structure(s)	كعبة (ـات)
Such as they used to know him	كعهدهم به
To become blind	كفّ بصرُه عن
A strong slap in the face	كف جبّارة
Adequate, appropriate, fit (for), equal to s.o., a match for, qualified, competent	كُفءٌ لِـ
Qualifications, abilities, capabilities	كفاءات
Penance, atonement (for a sin)	كفارة عن
Bail (esp. for due appearance of a person in court, Isl. Law)	كفالة بالنفس
Security, bail	كفالة مالية
To save s.o. the trouble of	كفاه مُؤنَةً كذا
Fighting power	كفاية القتال

To be an infidel, not believe in God, to blaspheme God	كَفَرَ بالله
Godlessness, atheism	كُفر بالله
An unequalled blasphemy	كفر ما بعده كفر
Ingratitude, ungratefulness	كفران بالنعمة
May God give satisfaction in your stead, or may God make up for your shortcoming (said to s.o. making a mistake)	كفى الله عنك
God is the best protector	كفى بالله وكيلاً
Blind	كفيف البصر
Bailsman	كفيل بالنفس
The whole, all, everything	الكل
Every (single) one, each one	كل أحد
Almost everything, nearly all	الكل إلا قليلاً
All hopes are pinned on him	كل الآمال معقودةٌ بناصيته
The whole house	كل البيت
There are all kinds of game in the belly of the wild ass (proverbially of s.o. or s.th. that combines all good qualities and advantages and makes everything else dispensable)	كل الصيد في جوف الفَراء
Everything that concerns him	كل أمرِه
All that	كل ذلك
Every man	كل رجل
In each seven days, every seven days	كل سبعة أيام
Everything, all	كل شيء
Every single detail	كل صغيرة وكبيرة
Everyone by himself	كل على حدةٍ
Everything, all embracing, all-comprehensive, all-powerful	الكل في الكل

كل ما	All that, whatever, whatsoever
كل ما في الأمر أن ...	There is no more to it than, it's nothing but ...
كُل مَنْ	Everyone who, whoever, whosoever
كل من فلان وفلان وفلان	A as well as B as well as C
كل من هب ودب	Every Tom, Dick and Harry (lit. everyone who can stand and crawl)
كل ناعق وناعر	Every Tom, Dick and Harry, all that is alive and astir, everybody and his brother (lit. all the screeches and grunts)
كل واحد	Every (single) one, each one, everyone
كل وقت	At any time, always
كل يبكي (يغني) على ليلاه	Everyone sings his own tune, does as he pleases, follows his own fancy
كل يدعي وصلاً بليلاه	Everybody claims to be the chosen one, everyone brags in his own way (lit. everyone claims a connection with his Leila)
كَلا	Not at all, on the contrary, by no means! Certainly not! Never! No!
كَلَّا ثُمَّ كَلا	No and a hundred times no! Not at all!
الكلام بين أيديكم	You have the floor, you may speak
كلام ذو وجهين	Equivocal statement, ambiguous words
كلام فارغ	Idle talk, prattle, poppycock, bosh, nonsense
كلام في كلام	Just so many words, idle talk
كلب البحر	Shark
كلب الماء	Otter, beaver

Greed (for)	كَلَب على
To covet	كَلِبَ على
Very fond of, very attached to, very much in love with	كَلِفٌ بِـ
To take the trouble, bother s.o.	كلّف خاطرَه
To take the trouble to, go to the trouble of	كلّف نفسَه عَنَاء (مؤونة، مشقة)
To commission, charge, entrust s.o. with s.th.	كلّفه بِـ
To cost s.o. dearly	كلّفه ثمناً باهظاً
To overtask s.o., expect or demand too much of s.o.	كلّفه شططاً
To cost s.o. a certain amount	كلّفه
To perform the marriage ceremony (Chr.)	كلّل
To be crowned by success	كُلِّلَ بالنجاح
To crown (s.o., also fig. s.th.)	كلّله
Whenever, the more, in the same measure as	كلما
The more ... the more	كلما ... كلما
The Ten Commandments	الكلمات العشر
Synonymous words	كلمات مترادفة
Password	كلمة السر
Supremacy, hegemony	الكلمة العليا
The Word of God, the Holy Scriptures	كلمة الله
Password	كلمة المرور
Welcoming speech	كلمة ترحيبيّة
Preface	كلمة تمهيدية
Word for word, literally	كلمةً فكلمة
Proverb	كلمة مأثورة

كلمح البصر	In the twinkling (blink) of an eye, in a moment, in a flash, instantly
كلُّنا أَمَلٌ	We are all full of hope that
كله	He entirely, all of him, it entirely, all of it
كَلُوء العين	Sleepless, awake
كليات	The complete works (of an author)
الكليات	The five logical predicates or general conceptions (philosophy)
كُلِّيَّةً	Wholly, entirely, totally, absolutely
كلية حربية	Military academy
كم بالحَرِي	How much more . . .! How much rather . . .!
كَمَّ فمَه	To silence s.o.
كم مرةً؟	How many times? How often? How often!
كم من مرةٍ؟	How many times? How often? How often!
كم ولداً لك؟	How many sons do you have?
كما اتفق	As chance would have it, at random, haphazardly
كما أن	As, just as, quite as, as also, as on the other hand (introducing a nominal clause)
كما تقدم	As already mentioned
كما لو كان حاضراً	As if he were present
كما مر بنا	As it has passed before us, as we have already mentioned
كما هو	Such as it is, as things are, such being the matter
كما هو الحال في	As is the case with
كما هي الحالة في	As is the case with
كما يأتي	As follows

As it should be, as it must be, *comme il faut*	كما يجب
As follows, like this	كما يلي
As he likes	كما يود
Literary perfection	الكمال الكتابي
Luxuries	كماليات
Similar to, like, just as, the same as, much as	كمثل
Adroit, skilful, active, diligent, industrious	كميش الإزار
To allude with s.th. to	كنا بـ عن
Metonymy, allusion, indirect declaration of (legal) intent (Isl. Law)	كناية
Tantamount to, in lieu of, instead of	كناية عن
It is tantamount to, it means, it stands for, it consists in	كناية عن
To bury a treasure in the ground	كَنَزَ (ه) في الأرض
Such, for example	كهذا
To wind the turban	كوّر العمامة
To clench one's fist	كوّر قبضته
Pyre, stake	كومة الحطب
The existent, reality, the world, the universe, the cosmos	الكون
The Supreme Being, God	الكون الأعلى
You can be sure	كونوا على يقينٍ
In order not to, lest	كي لا
Pillowcase	كيس الوسادة
How are you?	كيف حالك؟
Why shouldn't it be so since …!	كيف لا و …!
To conform, adjust, adapt (s.th. o.s.)	كيّف نفسه

كيفما	However, howsoever
كيفما اتفق	However it may turn out, no matter how, in any case, at any rate
كيفما كان الحال	Whatever the case may be, be that as it may, in any case, at any rate
كيفية الاستعمال	Directions for use
كيفية العمل	Operation (e.g. of a machine)

ل

لَـ / إنَّ – لَـ	Truly, verily, certainly (intensifying particle, frequently after *inna* introducing the predicate)
لِـ	For, on behalf of, in favour of, to (of the dative), because of, due to (preposition)
لِـ (يفعلْ)	That, so that, in order that, in order to (conjunction with the subjunctive)
لا	Not, no! (particle)
لا - بالكلية	Not at all, absolutely not
لا - من قريب أو بعيد	Not – in the least, not by a far cry
لا - ولا	Neither – nor
لا ... غير الشيء اليسير	Only very little
لا ... بتاتًا	Absolutely not, by no means
لا أبالي	I don't care! I don't mind!
لا ابتاعُ منه ولا أبيعُه	I don't trust him
لا أثر له	Ineffective, ineffectual
لا أجد لي نَدحَةً عن	I feel compelled to
لا أرى محلاً لعَجَبٍ	I don't see any reason for amazement, there is nothing to be astonished about
لا أساسَ له من الصحة	Completely unfounded (news, rumour)
لا أصل له ولا فصلَ	Of lowly origin (person), without basis or foundation (speech)
لا أظن أحداً يُنكِر	I don't think that anyone can deny
لا أظن إلا أنه	I am quite sure that he ...

لا أظنك تخالفني	I don't believe that you can contradict me
لا أفعله يد الدهر	I shall never do it!
لا أقل من أن …	The least one can do is to, I (you, etc.) could at least …
لا إله إلا الله	(with indefinite accusative, expressing a general negation) There is not, there is no (e.g. there is no god but Allah)
لا بأس	Never mind! No problem!
لا بأس أن …	It doesn't matter that …
لا بأس به	There is no objection to it, not bad, considerable
لا بأس عليك	Don't worry! It won't do you any harm!
لا بد	Definitely, without fail
لا بد له منه	He simply must do it, he can't get around without it
لا بد من	It is necessary, inescapable, unavoidable
لا بِدْعَ أن …	No wonder that …
لا به يُعمَلُ ولا عليه يُعَوَّل	Null and void
لا تَدمُري	Nobody, not a living soul
لا تدوم له حال	No state is of any permanence with him, he is never the same for a very long time
لا تشوبه شائبة	Blameless, flawless, unblemished, immaculate
لا تغيب عنه الشمس	It is not veiled in darkness (lit. the sun doesn't disappear from him)
لا تفوته شاردة ولا واردة	Nothing escapes him, he doesn't miss a thing

Don't say! (expressing negative imperative)	لا تَقُل
There is no resistance against the enemies, resistance against the enemy is futile.	لا تقوم للأعداء قائمة
You will hardly ever see, you barely see, the moment you see	لا تكاد ترى
Talk of the devil and he will appear!	لا تملأ الدنيا شؤماً
Pardon me! Forgive me!	لا تؤاخذوني
Incontestably, indisputably	لا جدالَ
It won't be held against him if he, it won't do any harm if he …	لا جُنَاحَ عليه أن …
It is not necessary, there is no need of	لا حاجة إلى (لِ)
I don't need it	لا حاجة لي به
Boundless, infinite	لا حدَّ له
There is no objection	لا حرج
Nothing stands in your way, you are at liberty	لا حرج عليك
Immeasurable, innumerable	لا حصر له
He has no knowledge	لا حظ له من علم
Indifferent, of no consequence	لا حفلَ به
He is completely powerless, he can do nothing	لا حول له ولا حيلة
There is no might or power but through God	لا حول ولا قوة إلا بالله
It is not out of place, it is quite appropriate	لا حيفَ به
I have no possibility to, I am in no position to	لا حيلة لي في
It is quite evident, it is quite obvious that …	لا خَفَاءَ في أن …

لا خلاقَ له	Despicable, a worthless fellow
لا خيرَ فيه	There is no good in it, it's no good
لا رجعة فيه	Irrevocable
لا ساحل له	Shoreless
لا سبيل إلى الشك فيه	Doubtless, indubitable, beyond any doubt
لا سلاح بين يديه	He is unarmed
لا سِيَّمَا	Especially, particularly
لا شأن له في ذلك	He hasn't anything to do with this, he has no part in this
لا شأن لي به	I haven't anything to do with it, it's none of my business
لا شكَّ	No doubt
لا شيء	A nothing, nil, non-entity
لا صبرَ لِي	I cannot bear it! This is unbearable!
لا طائل تحته (فيه)	Of no avail, useless, futile
لا عبرة به	It deserves no attention, it is of no consequence
لا عبرة لمن ...	It is of no consequence if s.o ...
لا عجبَ	No wonder!
لا عداد له	Innumerable, countless
لا عليك	Don't worry!
لا عليه	Never mind! It's nothing! No harm done!
لا عهد له بِـ	Not to know s.th., not have experienced s.th., being unacquainted with
لا غبار عليه	Clear, plain, incontestable, impeccable (morally)
لا غَنَاء فيه	Useless, it is inadequate, it is of little use

Indispensable	لا غِنى عنه
And that's all, no more, only	لا غير
Nothing at all, not the least bit	لا فتيل ولا نقير
How well you have spoken!	لا فُضَّ فُوكَ
In no way, in no manner, unimportant, of no consequence	لا في العير ولا في النفير
Not be lasting and durable	لا قام ولا قعد
He has no power over it, it is not in his power, he is incapable of accomplishing it	لا قِبَل له به
(which) God forbid!	لا قدّر الله
Unstable, inconstant, unfathomable	لا قرارَ له
Absolutely not, not at all, by no means, not in the least	لا قطعاً
Completely helpless and paralysed	لا قوة له ولا حَيْلَ
Worthless	لا قيمةَ له
Flawless, irreproachable	لا مأخذ فيه
There is nothing in the way, nothing prevent me (you, etc.) from	لا مانع (عن)
Indifference	لا مبالاة
Unjustifiable	لا مبرر له
Incomparable, matchless, unrivalled, unparalleled	لا مثيل له
There is no possibility of or for	لا مجال لِـ
It is incontestable	لا مجال للطعن فيه
It is inevitable, there is no doubt about it	لا محالة
It is inevitable, there is no doubt about it, absolutely, most certainly	لا محالة منه
There is no room for, it is out of place	لا محلَّ لِـ

لا محيدَ عنه	It is unavoidable
لا مخرجَ منه	Hopeless situation
لا مِراءَ فيه (بلا مِراء)	Incontestable, indisputable
لا مِراءَ فيه أَن ...	It is an incontrovertible fact that, unquestionably ...
لا مشاحةَ أَن ...	It is incontestable that, indisputably ...
لا مشاحةَ في ذلك	That is incontestable
لا مَعْدَى عنه	Inevitable, unavoidable, inescapable
لا مفر منه	Unavoidable, inevitable
لا مناصَ منه	Inevitable, unavoidable
لا مندوحةَ له عن	It is imperative for him, absolutely necessary for him
لا مُنْصَرَفَ عنه	Indispensable, inevitable
لا مهرب منه	Inescapable, unavoidable
لا موجبَ لِـ	There is no reason for, one need not
لا ناقة لي في الأمر ولا جمل	I have no hand in this matter, I have nothing to do with it
لا نَدَحةَ عنه	It is indispensable, inevitable
لا نزاع فيه	Undisputed, unquestioned
لا نُكرانَ	It is incontestable
لا نهتز له كثيراً	This won't affect us greatly, this is not likely to disconcert us, this will hardly cause us any headache
لا وجه له من الصحة	It has no validity at all
لا وزن له (عديم الوزن)	Imponderable, insignificant, of no consequence, negligible
لا يأخذ الكَرَى بمعقد جفنه	No slumber closed his lids
لا يألو	To stop at nothing, be tireless in doing s.th.

He will go to any length, he spares no effort, goes out of his way for	لا يألو جهداً في
He never lets up giving him advice and guidance	لا يألوه نُصْحاً وإرشَاداً
He is constantly striving to make her happy	لا يألوها إسعاداً
Unconcerned, careless	لا يبالي
They don't want it otherwise, they ask for it	لا يبتغون عنه حِوَلاً
Unjustifiable	لا يُبَرَّرُ
It is not unlikely that …	لا يبعد أن …
This doesn't show him in a favourable light	لا يبيِّض من صحيفته
Unimaginable, inconceivable, unthinkable	لا يتصوره العقلُ
Not open to doubt, admitting no doubt	لا يتطرق إليه شك
The enemy's importance does not unduly impress him	لا يتعاظمه شأن العدو
It is not in agreement with their principles	لا يتفق ومبادئهم
Invaluable, priceless	لا يُثَمَّنُ
He can't find an opportunity to speak freely	لا يجد مفيضاً إلى الكلام
He must by all means	لا يجد مفيضاً من
It is of no use at all	لا يُجدي شَرْوَى نقير
It is of no use at all	لا يجدي فتيلاً
He can't think of a blessed thing to say	لا يُجديك فتيلاً
He won't let a word escape his lips	لا يجرّ لسانه بكلمة
(It is) no longer open to an appeal, incapable of revision, legally valid final (sentence)	لا يجوز نقضه

He doesn't want him to be happy, he grudges him everything	لا يحب الخيرَ له
He doesn't budge, he doesn't lift his finger, he remains immobile	لا يحرّك ساكناً
He is not capable of, he is not able to …	لا يُحسِن أن …
Innumerable	لا يُحصَى
It is limited to, it is nothing but	لا يخرج عن
It is well known that, as everybody knows, it is obvious that …	لا يخفى أن …
You know very well …	لا يخفى عليك
It is not without a certain beauty	لا يخلو من جمال
It is not quite useless	لا يخلو من فائدة
It is slightly exaggerated	لا يخلو من مبالغة
Immeasurable, innumerable	لا يدخل تحت الحصر
It is not within the bounds of reason	لا يدخل في حيّز المعقول
He feels no hesitation about, will not hesitate to, he doesn't see a problem with …	لا يرى حرجاً من
He wasn't worth a plug nickel	لا يساوي ملءَ أذنه نخالةً
It is not inconceivable, not improbable	لا يُستَبْعَدُ
Indispensable	لا يُستَغْنَى عنه
To be restless, undecided	لا يستقر له قرارٌ
Not to be sneezed at, not to be overlooked	لا يستهان به
I cannot say	لا يسعني أن أقول
He is unsurpassable, he is incomparable, there is no one like him he is unequalled, unrivalled, peerless	لا يُشَقُّ غبارُه

He is unsurpassable, he is unequalled, unrivalled, peerless	لا يُشَقُّ له غبار
It does not offend the eye, it is nice to look at	لا يَصُدُّ النَّظَرَ
Incredible, unbelievable, unreliable, untrustworthy	لا يُصَدَّقُ
Invincible, a great hero	لا يُصْطَلَى بناره
Unimportant, insignificant	لا يُعْبَأُ به
It does not (did not) take long until, before long, presently …	لا يعتّم أن …
Not to fail to do s.th., to do s.th. inevitably	لا يعدو أن يفعله
It is no more than	لا يعدو أن يكون
He doesn't know his knee from his elbow (proverbially of a stupid person)	لا يعرف الكُوعَ من البُوعَ
Irreplaceable, irreparable	لا يُعَوَّضُ
Unconscious	لا يعي
He doesn't know what he is saying	لا يعي ما يقول
Unforgiveable	لا يُغتَفَرُ
You will not have failed to notice that, you are no doubt aware (of the fact) that, you know very well that …	لا يغرب عنك أن …
Unpardonable, inexcusable	لا يُغفَرُ
It is of no use at all	لا يغني فتيلاً (من)
It won't help him a bit, it isn't worth a farthing	لا يغني عنه فتيلاً
Imperishable, inexhaustible	لا يفنى
To be negligible, be of no consequence	لا يُقَامُ له وزن
Irresistible	لا يُقَاوَم
Incontestable, indisputable	لا يقبل الجدال

لا يُقَدَّر	Inestimable, immeasurable, tremendous
لا يَقِرُّ له حالٌ	To be flighty, be of unstable temperament
لا يَقِرُّ له قرار	To be restless, restive, uneasy, wavering, undecided
لا يُقصيهِ البصرُ	Out of sight, not within view, invisible
لا يقطع عقلَه	It won't get into his head, he can't understand or believe it
لا يقف دونَه شيء	Nothing will stand in his way, nothing can stop him
لا يَقِلُّ عنه بالا	No less significant than this
لا يُقَوَّمُ بثمن	Inestimable, invaluable, priceless
لا يقيم له قيامة	He forestalls any resistance on his part
لا يكاد	(with negative, corresponding to English 'hardly, scarcely, barely, no sooner, as soon as')
لا يكاد يعي	(He is) almost unconscious
لا يَكِلّ	Indefatigable, untiring
لا يُلمس	Intangible, impalpable
لا يلوي على شيء	Not to care about anything, be utterly reckless
لا يلين	Unbending, inflexible
لا يُمحَى	Ineffaceable, indelible
لا يمكن	It is impossible
لا يمل	Indefatigable, untiring
لا يملك شَرْوَى نقيرٍ	He hasn't a penny to his name, he has absolutely nothing
لا يُنتهك	Sacrosanct, sacred, consecrated
لا ينضب	Inexhaustible, incessant
لا ينفع	Useless, of no use

Irrefutable, incontestable, irrevocable	لا يُنقَضُ
Irresistible, resistless, immeasurable	لا يُنكَف
Untiring, inexhaustible	لا يهن
Innocuous, harmless	لا يُؤذي
Indescribable, nondescript	لا يوصف
Not one inch, not one iota	لا ... قيد أنمُلة
Not only ... but	لا ... وحده بل
Not by a hair's breadth	لا ... قدرَ شعرةٍ
Indifferent attitude, indifference	لاأبالية
Scepticism: agnosticism	لاأدرية
The non-ego (philosophy)	اللاأنا
Selflessness, unselfishness	لاأنانية
It's too late to escape	لات حين مناص
Because of, on account of, for	لأجل
For your sake	لأجل خاطرك
For a short time	لأجل قريب
Stateless, being without nationality	لاجنسية
To observe or notice s.th. in s.o.	لاحظ عليه شيئاً
Exceedingly, in the highest degree	لآخر درجة
For the last time	لآخر مرة (للمرة الأخيرة)
Anti-religious, irreligious, without religion	لاديني
Irreligion, godlessness	لادينية
Anti-Semitic, anti-Semite	لاسامي
Wireless, radio	لاسِلكي
Because of the violence with which the disease struck	لاشتداد وطأة المرض
The unconscious, unconscious mind, unconsciousness	اللاشعور

لاشعوري	Unconscious, unaware
اللاشيء	The nothing
لاشيء	Nothing, nonentity, nil
لاشيئية	Non-existence, nothingness, nullity, nihility
لاطفه على كتفه	To pat s.o. on the shoulder
لاعب الجنباز	Gymnast, athlete
لاقط الألغام	Minesweeper
لاقى ترحيباً	To gain support
لاقى آذاناً صاغيةً	To find willing ears
لاك الكلام	To be inhibited in one's speech, stammer, express o.s. imperfectly
لاك سمعتَه	To bring into discredit (s.o.'s reputation)
لألأ بذنبه	To wag the tail
لامبالاة (لامبالية)	Indifference
لامّة	Evil eye
لأمر ما	Because of something or other, for some reason or other
لامركزية	Decentralisation
لامسؤولية	Irresponsibility
لأنَّ	On the grounds that, because, for
لأنْ	That, so that, in order that, in order to
لانت قناته	To show o.s. compliant, yield, relent, give in
لانظام	Lack of system, confusion
اللانهاية	The infinite
لانهائي	Infinite
اللاهوت	Godhead, deity: divinity
اللاهوتية	Theological
لأول مرة	For the first time

At first sight, right away, at once	لأول وهلةٍ
Timetable, schedule	لائحة السفر
Bill, draft	لائحة القانون
Bill, draft	لائحة قانونية
Physically fit (e.g. for military service)	لايق طبياً
To bring about a reconciliation, make peace between, reconcile	لائم بين (و)
Modesty, decency	لباس التقوى
Headgear	لباس الرأس
Uniform	لباس رسمي
Military uniform	لباس عسكري
To persist in an activity, keep doing s.th.	لبث (يفعل)
To abide, remain, stay	لبث بـ
He did it for a time	لبث يفعله
To take the veil, become a nun (Chr.)	لبست المسوح
To gallop about (animal)	لَبَطَ – الحصان
To throw s.o. to the ground	لَبَطَ – به الأرضَ
To fit, suit, (clothes) s.o.	لَبِقَ – القميص بـ
The mother caressed her child	لبلبت الأم بطفلها
Thick masses of cloud	لُبُود من الغمائم
To be called away by the Lord, pass away	لبّى نداءَ ربِّه
To bring up a problem time and again, harp on a question	لتّ وعَجَنَ في مسألة
In preparation of, for the purpose of	لتوطئة
(I have, she has) just ...	لتوها
(I have, she has) just ...	لتوي

لَجَّ – في	To persist, keep doing
لَجَّ على	To pester, trouble, bother, inconvenience s.o.
لجنة إدارية	Administrative board
لجنة الإمتحان	Board of examiners, examination board
لجنة الانضباط	Disciplinary board
لجنة التحقيق	Investigating committee
لجنة تنفيذية	Executive board
لجنة صلحية	Arbitration committee
لجنة فرعية	Subcommittee
لجنة قارة	Permanent committee, standing committee
لجنة قارة (مستديمة)	Standing committee, permanent committee
لحاجة في نفس يعقوب	For some unknown reason, from secret motives
لحالة أن ...	In case that, in the event that ...
لحد	Until, up to, to the extent of
لَحَدَ – إلى	To lean, incline, tend to
لحد الآن	Up to now, so far
لحساب فلان	To s.o.'s credit, to s.o.'s advantage
لحسن الحظ	Fortunately, luckily
لحسن طالعي	Luckily for me, fortunately
لحظات	For a few moments
اللحظة الراهنة	The present moment, the immediate present
لحظة خاطفة	A fleeting glance
لَحِقَ بخدمة	To enter a service
لحق بخدمته	To take up a position with s.o, enter the services of s.o.

To enter a school	لَحِقَ بمدرسة
On account of, because of	لِحكمةِ
For the benefit of	لِخير
For their own good	لِخير أنفسهم
Since, from the moment when …	لَدُنْ أن …
On demand, by request	لدى الطلب
In case of need, if necessary	لَدَى حاجة
He has	لديه
Rifle fire	لذع البنادق
Therefore, hence, that is why, for that reason	لذلك
Close to his side, close by	لِزقَه (بِلزقِه)
To keep silent, maintain silence	لَزِمَ الصمتَ
To be confined to bed	لزم الوساد
To stay home	لَزِمَ دارَه
To stay in bed	لَزِمَ فراشَه
The language which things themselves speak, silent language, mute expression (as distinguished from the spoken word)	لسان الحال
Bolt of the lock	لسان القُفل
Spokesman (of a crowd)	لسان القوم
Bit of the key (lit. key's teeth)	لسان المفتاح
Official organ	لسان رسمي
When seven nights of Shaban had passed	لسبع ليال خَلَون من شعبان
I can't do it	لست بفاعلٍ
I am unfamiliar with this field, I am not competent in this field	لست من فرسان ذلك الميدان
Let us not speak of, now, this is not the place to speak of …	لسنا في معرض الكلام عن …

لسوء الحظ	Unfortunately
لشدّما	How much...! Very often...! Very much, exceedingly
لشَدَّما كان سرورنا إذ ...	Tremendous was our joy when ...
لطائف النِّكات	Nice jokes
لطّف(ـه) من	To moderate, temper, lessen, reduce s.th.
لعاب الشمس	Air threads
لَعِبَ الأوراقَ	To play cards
لَعِبَ الشطرنج	To play chess
لعب العَصَا	Fencing (single-stick)
لَعبُ القُمار	Gambling
لَعِبَ الموسيقي	To make music
لَعِبَ دوراً	To play a part or role
لعب على الحبلين	To play a double game, work both sides of the street
لَعِبَ في عقله	To turn s.o.'s head
لَعِبَت به الهموم	To become the sport of sorrows
لعمر الله	By the everlasting of God! By the Eternal God!
لَعَمرُكَ	By your life!
لعمري	Upon my life!
لعنة الله عليه	God's curse be upon him!
لغاية	As far as, up to, until, till
لغة أجنبية	Foreign language
لغة الكتابة	Literary language
لغة المحادثة	Spoken language
لغة المهنة	Professional jargon, slang
لغة المولد	Mother tongue
لغة عامية	Colloquial language

Crossword puzzle	لغز الكلمات المتقاطعة
Lamentation over or for s.th.	لَغط عن
To do just like s.o., be of the same kind as s.o., belong to the same sort as s.o.	لفّ لفّه
Detours and evasions	اللَّف والدوران
Folding and unfolding, involution and evolution	لف ونشر
Parchment scrolls	لفات من الرَّق
Postal package	لفّة بريدية
To turn one's eyes or one's attention to	لفت (ألفت) نظرَه إلى
To attract, interest or captivate people	لفت الناسَ
To catch the eye, attract attention	لفت النظرَ
The Majestic Word (Allah, instead of saying the word 'Allah')	لفظ الجلالة
To breathe one's last, die, expire	لفظ النفس الأخير
To be in throes of death, breathe one's last	لفظ أنفاسه
Verbally, literally	لفظاً
In letter and spirit	لفظاً ومعنىً
To spit s.th. out like a date pit, brush s.th. aside, reject s.th., dismiss s.th.	لفظه لفظَ النواة
Grey hair covered his head	لَفَعَ (لفّع) الشيبُ رأسَه
To fabricate the most outrageous lies	لفق ما شاء له التلفيق
The Foreign Legion	اللفيف الأجنبي
Mob, rabble, riff-raff	لفيف الناس
A cluster, body, swarm, group of	لفيف من
On bail	لقاء كفالة

لقب البطولة	Title of champion (in sports)
لَقِس النفس	Annoyed, cross
لقّم القهوة	To stir ground coffee into hot water
لقمة سائغة	Titbit, choice morsel
لقي حتفَه	To find death, die
لَقِيَ سوءَ الحساب	He got a raw deal, he was in for it
لقي نجاحاً	To meet with success, to have success
لك عنه مندوحة	It is up to you, it is optional for you
لك هذا (لك ذلك)	You can have that! It's up to you, it's alright with me! All right! OK! Agreed!
لكانة في الكلام	Speech defect, faltering way of speaking
لكل ألف	Per (one) thousand
لكل سن حكمه	Every age has its own set of rules, must be judge by its own standards
لكونه (مجنوناً) ...	The fact that s.o. or s.th. is ...
لِكَي	So that, in order that, in order to
لكي (يفعلَ)	That, so that, in order that, in order to
لكي لا	In order not to, lest
لكيما	That, so that, in order that, in order to
للإيجار	For rent, to let
لِلتَّوِّ	At once, right away
للجنون فنون	Madness has many varieties, manifests itself in many ways
للضرورة أحكام	Necessity has its own rules, necessity knows no law
للغاية	Extremely, very much

For the first time	للمرة الأولى
For the sixth time	للمرة السادسة
For the study of, for further examination	للنظر في
To the greatest extent	للنهاية
Strange things can happen in this world! (lit. God has created all kinds of things)	لله في خلقه شؤون
At once, right away, immediately	للوقت (لوقته)
Why? Wherefore?	لمَ
Only, nothing but, just	لمَ – إلا
I could not stand it any longer	لم أعد أستطيع صبراً
I paid not the least attention to him	لم أعِرْهُ جانبَ اهتمام
He was no longer able to put up any resistance, he was as good as finished	لم تقم له قائمة بعد
He wouldn't be deceived by this ruse, this trick couldn't fool him	لم تنطلِ عليه هذه الحيلة
To put s.th. in order again, straighten s.th. out, put s.th. right	لَمَّ شعثَه
To round up the herd	لَمَّ شمل القطيع
We haven't yet attained a definitive position	لم نستقر بعد على حال
He hasn't come yet	لم يأت بعد
He is no longer a child	لم يبق طفلاً
My patience is at an end (lit. there is no arrow left for the bow of my patience)	لم يبق في قوس صبري مِنزَع
After that, he did not hesitate long before he, presently, he ...	لم يتأخر بعد ذلك من أن ...
He didn't budge from his position one bit	لم يتزحزح عن رأيه قيد أنملة

He couldn't do anything except, he had no other choice than …	لم يجد حيلةً إلا
Not to have enough time for	لم يجد متسعا من الوقت لـِ
To spare no effort	لم يدّخر جهداً
He saw nothing wrong in (doing it)	لم يرَ بأساً بـِ
To feel obliged, feel compelled to	لم يرَ مندوحةً من
(As) there has never been one before, (which is) unprecedented	لم يسبق له مثيل
I have never before …	لم يسبق لي أن …
Before he even realised it, there was all of a sudden, then all of a sudden, there was, it happened that …	لم يشعر إلا بـِ (و) …
It no longer existed	لم يصبح له وجود
He no longer did so	لم يصبح يفعل
The situation remained substantially unchanged	لم يطرأ على الحالة تبدل يُذكَرُ
He could not stand or bear it, he could not control himself	لم يطق صبراً
It does not (did not) take long until, before long, presently …	لم يعتّم أن …
There is no longer any possibility for it	لم يَعُد إليه سبيل
He no longer had any power over it	لم يَعُد له طاقةٌ به
He wouldn't let me give any excuses, he wouldn't take no for an answer, he kept insisting	لم يَعْذِرْني
He did not give me even a piaster, he did not give me as much as a piaster	لم يُعطِني حتى ولا قِرشاً
He did not fail to, he did not neglect to …	لم يَفُتْهُ أن …

He spared no pains or expense in or with, he left nothing undone to, he did not fail to	لم يقصّر في ...
No sooner – than ..., as soon as he – he ..., the moment he – he ...	لم يكد (ما كاد) - حتى
No sooner had he seen her, the moment he saw her	لم يكد يراها
He had no other alternative but to ...	لم يكن أمامه إلا أن ...
He was not what they expected	لم يكن عند رأيهم
Not to have enough time for	لم يكن في الوقت متسع لـ
He is (or was) not the right man for, he was not capable of, he was not in a position to (with foll. subjunctive)	لم يكن لـ(يفعلْ) (ما كان) لـ (يفعلْ)
They couldn't but, they had no other alternative but to ...	لم يكن لهم محيص من أن ...
It wouldn't have been difficult for him to ...	لم يكن لِيَصعُبَ عليه أن ...
He was unknown among his people	لم يكن معرفةً في قومه
He did not know what time of the night it was at that moment	لم يكن يعرف موقع وقته ذاك من الليل
He didn't pay any attention to what I said!	لم يلق لقولي بالاً
It did not take long until, before long	لم يمض غير قليل حتى
He could not refrain from, he couldn't help it, he had to ...	لم يملك أن ...
Not to hesitate	لم ينشب (ما نشب)
To remain without blossom and fruit, be without any effect and consequence	لم ينعقد له زهر ولا ثمر

لم ينفك	Keep doing, not to stop doing
لما	Why? Wherefore? For what reason?
لما	Why? For what reason?
لماذا؟	Why (on earth)?
لمجرّد أن ...	For the simple reason that ...
لمجرِّدِ أن ...	For the simple reason that ...
لمح البصر	Glance of an eye
لمحض صالحها	Solely in her own interest, only for her own good
لمس الحقائق	To take things as they are, face the facts
لمصلحة فلان	In s.o.'s favour, for the benefit of s.o., to s.o.'s advantage
لَمَعَ بسيفه	To brandish the sword
لَمَعَ بيده	To wave one's hand
لَمَعَ في رأسه خاطر	A though flashed through his mind
لَمْلَم (ه)	To gather, gather up s.th.
لندن بأكملها	All London
له إصبَعٌ في هذا الأمر	He has a hand in this matter
له الحق في	He is entitled to
له القدح المعلّى في	To be the principal agent in, have a major impact on, exert decisive influence on, be of crucial importance
له اليد الطولى في	To be in powerful in, have decisive influence on
له أن ...	He has a right to, he is entitled to, he may, he can, it is possible for him to ...
له بصرٌ بِـ	He is knowledgeable in, he is familiar with
له شأن في ذلك	He has s.th. to do with this, he has a hand in this

He has great influence on other people, he can accomplish a great deal with other people	له عند الناس يد
I am obliged to him for a favour	له عندي يد
He does not need it	له غناء عنه
It is connected with, it touches upon, it concerns	له مساس بِـ
To be versed, skilled, experienced in, to have the upper hand in	له يد بيضاء في
He has a hand in	له يد في
Death rattle, agony of death	لُهاث الموت
To extol s.o. fervently	لَهِجَ بالثناء عليه
To resort to humble pleas	لَهِجَ بالضراعة
To speak constantly of s.o., mention s.o.'s name continually with praise	لَهِجَ بذكره
To launch forth into profuse thanks or praises	لَهِجَ بشكره
Therefore, hence, that is why, for that reason	لهذا
Therefore, for this reason	لهذا
At this time	لهذا الوقت
Due to these circumstances, consequently, hence	لهذه المناسبة
O God! ('Dear Lord' invocations)	اللهم
If only	اللهم إذا
Unless, were it not that, or at best	اللهم إلا
In any case, I have fulfilled my task, done or said everything I could	اللهم إني بلَغتُ
They have a clean slate	لهم جباه ناصعة
By God, yes! Most certainly!	اللهم نعم
Here, over here, to this place, up to this point, so far,	لهنا

لو (فعلتَ)	If only …! would that …! I wish …!
لو أن	If (introducing nominal clauses)
لو كنت تفعل هذا لكان انفع	If you did this, it would be more useful (as a correlative of law)
لو كنت مكانَك	If I were in your place, if I were you
لو يعلم	I wish he knew! If he only knew!
لواعج (المحبة)	Ardent love, ardour (of love)
لُوثة في	Passion, weakness for
لوجه الله	For the sake of God, for nothing (in return)
لوح أَردُواز	Slab of slate
لوح الجليد	Block of ice
لوّح بيديه	To wave with the hands
لوحة الإسم	Name plate, doorplate
لوحة التوزيع	Switchboard
لوحة الشطرنج	Chessboard
لوحة الكتابة	Slate, blackboard, writing tablet
لوحة زيتية	Oil painting
لولا	If not
لولا تاب لَهَلَك	If he had not repented, he would have perished (as a correlative of law)
لولانا	If it weren't (hadn't been) for us
لوى فيه اللسانَ	To speak ill of s.o., backbite s.o.
لي عليه مال	He owes me money
لي قِبَله دين	He owes be a debt, he is indebted to me
لي كلمة معك	I've got to talk to you
لي معه شأن آخر	I still have a bone to pick with him

I have complete freedom to, I am at complete liberty to	لي ملء الحرية في
I wish I knew . . .! Would that I knew . . .!	ليت شِعري
In order to find out to what extent my words were meant seriously	لِيَتَبَيَّنَ مبلغَ قولي من الجد
Would God I had died for you!	ليتني مت لأجلك
I wish he were here! If only he were here!	ليته كان هنا
Long live the king!	لِيَحْيَى الملك
He is no better off than she is	ليس أحسن منها حظا
Only, no more, and nothing less	ليس إلا
To be unable to (+ participle)	ليس بِـ
It is not superfluous that . . .	ليس بالفضول أن ...
It is nothing, it is of no consequence	ليس بشيء
It is not my intention to . . .	ليس بي أن
There isn't	لَيْسَ ثَمَّةَ
That's improper, that isn't right	ليس ذلك بنوال
nothing but, only, merely	ليس سوى
There is not a grain of truth in it	ليس على شيء من الحقيقة
There is nothing to keep me from doing that, I am free to do that, it is no sin if I do that	ليس عليَّ في ذلك سبيل
He will be none the worse for	ليس عليه بأس من
He (it) is not reliable, one cannot rely on him (it)	ليس عليه معوَّل
And that's all, no more, only	ليس غيرُ
Not only – but also	ليس فقط بل
It is impossible, unthinkable, inconceivable	ليس في الإمكان
By no means, in no way	ليس في حال من الأحوال
He has no other possibility but, he cannot but	ليس في وُسعِهِ إلا

Not to have, not to possess	ليس لِـ
We know no more than what ...	ليس لدينا غير ما ...
We don't have anything	ليس لنا شيء
We cannot help doing it, we cannot but do it	ليس لنا منه مفيض
He has no right to, he mustn't ...	ليس له أن ...
It does not really exist, it is not real	ليس له حقيقة
He has no part in, he is not involved in	ليس له قدم في
Unequalled, one of a kind	ليس له مثيل
Unequalled, one of a kind	ليس له نظير
She has no brains at all	ليس لها حظ من عقل
I have no right to, it does not behove me to ...	ليس لي أن ...
I shall have nothing to do with that, that is none of my business, I shan't meddle in that	ليس لي شأن في ذلك
He doesn't side with the government	ليس مع الحكومة
It is illogical to ...	ليس من المنطق أن ...
It is not his affair or business to, it is inappropriate for him to, it does not tend to, is not conducive to ...	ليس من شأنه أن ...
No one will deny that ...	ليس من منازع في ...
He is not in the least involved in this affair, he has absolutely nothing to do with this affair	ليس من هذا الأمر في قبيل ولا دبير
All this is unfamiliar to him, he doesn't understand a thing about it	ليس من هذا كله على شيء
Not belong to, have nothing to do with ...	ليس من ...
To have absolutely nothing to do with s.th.	ليس منه لا بقليل ولا بكثير

There is nothing in it, it's worthless	ليس هذا على شيء
This has absolutely nothing to do with that	ليس هذا في شيء من ذلك
That's no coincidence	ليس هذا من باب الصُّدْفة
All is desolate and empty, there is nothing here	ليس هناك لا خَيْلَ ولا خيّالة
Down with ...!	لِيَسقُطْ ... (فليسقط ...)
Long live the king!	لِيَعِشْ الملك
(expressing an order, an invitation) He shall write, let him write (with preceding wa- or fa- contracted to wa-l- or fa-l- with elision of i)	لِيكتُبْ
Be it known to him, may he know, for his information	ليكن في علمه
Day and night	ليلَ نهارَ
At night	ليلاً
In order not to	لِئَلا
Tonight	الليلة
Premiere, opening night	ليلة الافتتاح
Wedding night	ليلة الدخلة
Twenty-seventh of Ramadan	ليلة القدر
Last night, yesterday evening	ليلة أمس
Charity night	ليلة خيرية
Evening party	ليلة زاهرة
Dark night	ليلة ليلاء
(In) that night, (on) that evening	ليلتئذٍ
Tractable, docile, pliant	لين الأعطاف
Gentle, compliant	ليّن الجانب
mild-mannered, gentle-hearted	ليّن العريكة
Soft, gentle	ليّن المكاسر
Sociability, tractability	ليونة الجانب

م

ما	What?
ما – طرفة عين	Not one moment
ما (لحظة) عين – طرفة	Not one moment
ما أبالي	I don't care! I don't mind!
ما أجمله	How handsome he is!
ما أحسنَه	How good he is! How handsome he is!
ما أحوجه إلى …	How much he stands in need of …! How urgently he needs …!
ما أحيلاه	Oh, how sweet is …, oh, how sweet he is!
ما أُحَيْلَى	Oh, how sweet is …, oh, how sweet he is!
ما أخفه من حمل	What a light burden it is!
ما أسرعَ أن رأيته	Before long I saw him, it did not take very long before I saw him
ما أسع ذلك	I can't do that
ما أشار بطرْفٍ	He didn't bat an eye
ما أغنى عنه شيئاً	To be of no use, be of no avail to s.o.
ما أفضل عمر	How excellent Omar is!
ما اكتحل غِمَاضاً (غُمضاً)	To find no sleep
ما الحِيلة	What's to be done?
ما العمل الآن	What's to be done now? What can you do?
ما إن	Not (negation)
ما إن … حتى	No sooner had he … than, he had hardly … when

ما أنت وذاك	What's that to you? What has that to do with you? What do you know about that?
ما أنزل الله به من سلطان	Futile, vain, preposterous (lit. God has given it no power)
ما أنس (لا أنسى، إن أنس، فلا أنسى)	I shall never forget
ما أهونه	How small, how worthless it is!
ما بالدار نافخ ضَرَمَةٍ	There is not a soul in the house
ما بالك؟	How about you? What do you think?
ما باله؟	Why is it that he …?
ما بَرِحَ غنياً	He is still rich
ما بَرِحَ في	He is still in
ما به الحاجة	The essentials
ما بِيَدي حيلةٌ	I can do nothing, I can get nowhere
ما بين النهرين	Mesopotamia
ما بين أيدينا من …	What … are before us or present themselves to us
ما بين جنبيه	What it contains, comprises, its contents
ما بين جوانبهم	Their hearts
ما بين يوم وليلة	Overnight, all of a sudden
ما ترك مجالاً للشك	To admit of no doubt
ما تعمد بإهانة	He was not out to insult her, he had no intention of offending her
ما تلوكه الألسن	What people say, what is generally rumoured
ما تمالك عن	He couldn't help (doing s.th.), he couldn't refrain from
ما جرت به الليلة	What the night brought, what happened in the night
ما جَنَتْ يَدَاه	The crime that he has committed

ما خطب ذلك؟	What's it all about?
ما خطبُك	What's happened to you? What's the trouble? What's the matter with you?
ما خطبه في	What concern of his is …? What has he to do with …?
ما خلا	Except, with the exception
ما دمت حياً	As long as I live
ما رأى مانعاً	To have no objections
ما رأيت من الكتب	The books that I have seen
ما رأيت من كتب	Whatever books I have seen
ما زاد الطينَ بِلَّةً	What made things even worse …
ما زال على عهده	To be unchanged, be as always
ما زال في الوقت فسحة	There is still time
ما زلت أنت كعهدي بك	You are still the same!
ما شأنك وهذا	What have you got to do with this? What business of yours is this?
ما شأنك؟	What's the matter with you? What do you want?
ما شأنَه والأمرَ	What has he got to do with the matter?
ما شأني في ذلك	What have I got to do with that? What business of mine is that?
ما شب (لم يشب) عن الطوق	To be still in its infancy
… ما شعر إلا بـ	Before he even realised it, there was all of a sudden, then all of a sudden, there was, it happened that …
ما شعر إلا و …	Before he even realised it, there was all of a sudden, then all of a sudden, there was, it happened that …
ما شقّ غبارَه	He never quite attained his (another's) eminence

ما صَغَرَني إلا بِسَنَةٍ	He was only one year younger than I
ما ضَنَّ بِمَشَقَّةٍ عَلَى	To shun no effort for the sake of
ما ظنك بِـ	What is one to think of
ما عبأ بِـ	Not to care about, not give a hoot for, pay no attention to, attach no importance to, not to insist on
ما عتَّم أن ...	It does not (did not) take long until, before long, presently ...
ما عَجَزَ عن أن ...	Not to fail to ...
ما عدا	Except, save, with the exception of, excepting
ما عسى ينفعُ هذا	Of what use could this possibly be?
ما عليك من	Don't worry about, don't mind, don't give ... a thought
ما علينا	What of it? What does it matter? Let's forget it!
ما عليه أن ...	He doesn't care if, it's of little importance to him ...
ما عندك	What do you think? What is your opinion?
ما عنه محيص	It is unavoidable
ما فاز بطائل	To fail, to be unsuccessful, to accomplish nothing
ما فتئ يفعل	Not to cease doing, do incessantly
ما قدّمتُ وما أخّرتُ	What I have ever committed
ما قدّمت يداك	What you have committed or perpetrated
ما كاد يقوم	No sooner had he got up
ما كان له أن ...	It is (or was) impossible for him to, he is (or was) unable to ...
ما كان من إمضاء المعاهدة	The fact that the agreement has been signed, the agreement having been signed

ما كان منه إلا أن ...	He had no other choice but to, there was nothing for him to do but to, he did no more than ...
ما كان منهم في	To what extent they were involved in, what part they played in
ما كذّب أن فَعَلَ	He did not hesitate to do so
ما كسبت يداه	What he has earned in the hereafter by his (good and evil) deeds
ما لبث (لم يلبث) أن ... (حتى)	It did not take long before he, presently he ...
ما لديك	The condition you are in, your state of mind
ما لك	What's the matter with you? What is it?
ما لك، ما لي	Why? Wherefore? What ... for? Why should I, (you, etc.)? (with foll. verb)
ما لله من شريك	God has no partner
ما لم	So long as, not, unless
ما له آخر	Endless, infinite
ما له ثاغية ولا راغية	He has absolutely nothing, he is deprived of all resources (lit. he has neither a bleating sheep nor a braying camel)
ما له عنه غنى	He cannot dispense with it, he cannot do without it
ما له وما عليه	His right and his duty, his credit and his debit, his assets and his liabilities
ما لي بذلك يدان	That is not in my power
ما معكم	What do you have with you! What's up your sleeve!
ما ملكت (تملك) يمينه	His fortune, his possessions, his property
ما من أحد يقدر	Nobody can ...

There is absolutely none who …	ما مِن شخصٍ
He didn't say a word	ما نَبَسَ بكلمةٍ
That's certainly not the way to do it! That's no way to handle it!	ما هكذا تُوَكَّل الكتف
To be delighted, take pleasure	ما هَنِئَ بِـ
Whenever I had a chance (lit. whenever opportunities came my way)	ما وأتتني الفرص
To take no offence at, have no objection to …	ما وجد غضاضةً في …
What is at the bottom of it, what's behind it	ما وراء الأكَمَة
Overseas	ما وراء البحر
The supernatural, the transcendental	ما وراء الطبيعة
The subconscious	ما وراء الوعي
What I had promised myself	ما وعدتُ به فيما بيني وبين نفسي
He can't think of a blessed thing to say	ما يبدئ وما يعيد
He can't think of a blessed thing to say	ما يُجديك عنك هذا
The way things are handled, what is customary practice	ما يجري عليه العملُ
What he is preoccupied with, what is on his mind	ما يجول في (بِـ) خاطره
S.th. very remarkable, s.th. outstanding (lit. that which is pointed out with the fingertips)	ما يُشَارُ إليه بالبَنَان
Irresistibly comical (lit. that which makes a woman who has lost her child laugh)	ما يُضحِكُ الثَّكْلَى
Appetising	ما يفتح الشهية
Approximately, about, circa (with foll. figure)	ما يقرب من …
The following, what follows	ما يلي

Underwear, underclothes	ما يلي البدنَ من الملابس
The outcome of the matter, what will come out of it	ما ينجلي عنه الأمر
More than fifty	ما ينوف على الخمسين
More than three years, over three years	ما يُنِيف على ثلاث سنوات
Prime of youth	ماء الشباب
Honour, dignity	ماء الوجه
Fresh water	ماء عذب
Holy water (Chr.)	ماء مُكرَّس
To starve to death	مات جوعاً
He died a natural death	مات حتفَ أنفه
He died leaving a large fortune	مات عن تركة كبيرة
He died at the age of eighty	مات عن ثمانين سنة
He died for his country	مات فدىً للوطن
Exploit, feat, glorious deed, memorable events, achievements (handed down from the past)	مآثر
Present before s.o.'s eyes	ماثل أمام عينيه
In front of s.o., in s.o.'s presence	ماثل في حضرته
Visible, conspicuous, evident, obvious	ماثل للعيان
He resembled him somewhat, to some extent	ماثله بعضَ المماثلة
The simplest, easiest approach	المأخذ الأقرب
In force, valid	مأخوذ به
To shake s.th. violently	ماد بـ
What (on earth)?	ماذا
What's got into him all of a sudden?	ماذا طرأ عليه؟
What could he possibly say?	ماذا عساه يقول
What should I do?	ماذا عسى أن افعل
What's up? what's the matter?	ماذا هنالك

To profess a religion	مارس شعائر الدين
Critical situation	مأزق حَرِج
Captivated by	مأسور بِـ
To drag or take s.o. or s.th. along to	مال به إلى
Non-fungible things, non-fungibles (Isl. Law)	مال قِيمِي
A hundred ships as compared with fifty the previous year	مائة سفية مقابل خمسين في العام السابق
Round-table conference	المائدة المستديرة
A final match (in sports)	مباراة نهائي
Directly and indirectly	مباشرةً وضِمنًا
Afflicted with, suffering from	مبتلى بِـ
Having no connection with, bearing no relation to	مبتوت الصلة بِـ
Principle of reciprocity	مبدأ المعاملة بالمثل
The crux (of a matter), the all-important factor (of s.th.)	المبدأ والمعاد
Stricken, afflicted, tormented	مبرّح به
The payment already effected	المبلغ السابق صرفُه
To have close ties with s.o., be related (by marriage) to s.o., to be connected with s.th., have to do with s.th.	مَتَّ بصِلة إلى
To be most intimately connected with s.o.	مَتَّ له بأقرب الصلة
Delight of the eyes	متاع العين
Corroded, eroded, worn	متآكل
Desert	متالف
A spokesman of the foreign ministry	متحدث بلسان وزارة الخارجية
Under control	متحكَّم فيه
The rich	المترَفون
Closely interlinked, closely connected	متصل الحلقات

متّع البصرَ	To gratify the eye
متع النهارُ	It was broad daylight, the sun was high
متعارف عليه	Common, usual, customary, commonplace, banal
المتعاهدان	The two contracting parties
متعدّد النواحي	Multifarious, variegated, varied, manifold, multifaceted, many-sided
متعلق بحبه	Affectionately attached to s.o.
متّعه الله	God grant him enjoyment throughout his life
المتقدمُ ذكرُهُ	The aforementioned
متقدم على إبّانِهِ	Premature, precipitate, untimely
متقدم في السن	Advanced in age, old
المتقدمون والمتأخرون	The earlier and the later = all
متقلب الأطوار (الأحوال)	Wavering, vacillating, variable, unsteady
متكاثر الرِّقاع	Patched in numerous places
متلبد بالغيوم	Overcast, heavily clouded (sky)
متلبساً بالجريمة	(He was caught, and the like) red-handed, in the act, *in flagrante delicto*
متلعثم اللسان	Stammering, stuttering
متمكن أمكن	Declinable with nunation, triptote (gram.)
متمكن غير أمكن	Declinable in two cases, diptote (gram.)
متمكن في جلسته	Firmly seated
متنازع فيه	Debatable, matter in controversy
متناسب الأجزاء	Even, regular, symmetrical
متناسب القياس	Fitting together, well-matched, equal in proportion, commensurate

Extremely thin	متناهٍ في الدقة
Extremely tiny, minute	متناهٍ في الصغر
Suspicious looking	مُتَّهَم المنظر
Fiery, impulsive, having a lively mind	متوقد الذهن
Whenever	متى ما
I wonder when …	متى يا تُرى
Well-off, in easy circumstances	متيسر الحال
Point of contention, object of controversy	مَثار الجدل
Point of contention, object of controversy	مَثار النزاع
Ideal(s)	مثال أعلى (مثل عالية)
Defects	مثالب
Idealist	مثالي النزعة
The weight of a dust speck, tiny amount, a little bit	مثقال ذرّة
A little of, a little bit of	مثقال من
Educated people, intellectuals, intelligentsia	المثقفون
Oppressed by	مُثقَّلٌ بـ
Ideal	مثل أسمى (أعلى)
To make a dreadful example of s.o., punish s.o. with utmost cruelty	مثّل به اشنع تمثيل
To have an audience with the king, be received in audience by the king	مثل بين يدي الملك
Just as, as well as	مثلَ ما
For example, for instance	مثلاً
He is comparable to …	مثله كمثل …
Two at a time, as a pair or duo	مَثنَى
Of his (its) kind, of her kind	مثيله (مثيلتها)

مُجَارَاةً لِـ	In conformity with, in accordance with, according to
مجازاً	Figuratively, metaphorically
مجال للتلاعب	Free play, latitude
مجلس النواب	House of Representatives
مجلس نيابي	Parliament
مَجَمُّ هذا الرأي ومستجمعُهُ	What this opinion amounts to
مُجمَع عليه	(That which is) agreed upon, unanimous
مجموعُ طولِه	Its total length
المحافظة على النفس	Self-preservation
محاولة على حياته	An attempt on s.o.'s life
محبة النفس	Selfishness, amour propre
محتاج إلى	In want of, in need of, requiring s.th.
محتويات النفوس	The innermost thoughts, the secrets of the heart
محجر العين	Eye socket
محجور عليه	One placed under guardianship, minor, ward
محدود المعنى	Unambiguous
مُحرزٌ على الشهادة العالمية	Holder of a scholarly degree
محسوس تقريباً	Barely perceptible
محصور في	Confined to
محضاً	Only, merely, solely
محطُّ الآمال	Object of hope
محطُّ الكلام	Sense, or meaning of one's words
محطّة إذاعة	Radio station
مَحْظِيٌّ بثقته	Enjoying s.o.'s confidence
محفوف بالمخاطر	Surrounded by dangers
محكوم عليه بالفشل	Doomed to fail

Scene of the accident	محل الإصابة
(Place of) residence, domicile, address	محل الإقامة
The substance, gist, crux, the interesting (part of an exposition)	محل الحاجة
Place of residence	محل السكنى
Object of controversy	محل النزاع
S.th. deserving attention, a remarkable thing	محل نظر
In his place, in his stead	محلَّه
Praised, laudable, commendable	محمّد
Burdened with, encumbered by	محمَّل بِـ
Having a good outcome	محمود العواقب
Subject (logic)	محمول عليه
For fear that, afraid that …	مخافةً أن …
Variegated, multicoloured, motley, varied, various	مختلف الألوان
Disputed, controversial	مختلف فيه (عليه)
Different from	مختلف من
Improper, unseemly, unbecoming	مُخِل الليَاقة
Immoral, indecent	مُخِلٌّ بالآداب
To prolong s.o.'s life (of God)	مد (الله) عمرَه
As far as the eye can see	مدّ البصر
Range of vision	مدُّ البصر
To turn one's eyes, direct one's glance to	مدّ البصرَ إلى
To lay a snare for s.o.	مد الحبالة له
To lay pipe	مد المواسير
Foresight, far-sightedness	مدُّ النظر
To extend one's hand to s.o.	مد إليه يده
To strike roots (tree)	مد جذراً في الأرض

مدّ رجله قدر كسائه	To cut one's coat according to one's cloth, make the best of it, adjust o.s. to the circumstances
مدّ رجليه بقدر لحافه	To cut one's coat according to one's cloth, make the best of it, adjust o.s. to the circumstances
مدّ سمعه	To prick up one's ears
مد في المشي	To take long strides
مدّ يد المساعدة (العون، المعونة)	To extend one's help, lend a helping hand
مدّ يدَ المعونة لـ	To extend one's help
مدافع جناح	Wing-back
مدبّر المكائد	Intrigant, schemer
مدة	Within, in the course of, during
مدة مديدة (زمن مديد)	Long time
مدة من الزمن	Period (of time), space of time, interval
مدةً من الزمن	For a while, for some time
مدخل خلفيّ	Back entrance
مدخل رئيسيّ	Main entrance
مدرّس الألعاب	Athletic coach, athletics instructor
المدّعي العام	Public prosecutor
مدفع مياه	Water gun, fire hose
مدفعيّة ثقيلة	Heavy artillery
مدى الأيام	Throughout the days, continually
مدى البصر	Visual range
مدى الحياة	Lifetime, for life
مدى الدوران	Continually, constantly, perpetually
مدى الصوت	Calling distance
مدى العمر	Lifetime
مديد البصر	Far-sighted
مذبحة جماعيّة	Mass massacre

A memorandum of understanding	مذكّرة تفاهم
An explanatory note	مذكّرة توضيحيّة
Mentioned above	المذكور أعلاه
Above-mentioned	مذكور أعلاه
Above-mentioned	مذكور بعاليه
Fatalism	مذهب القدر
To pass the examination	مر بالامتحان
The thought crossed his mind that ...	مرّ بخاطره أن ...
To turn out well, go off without mishap	مر بسلام
To overlook s.th. generously, pass over s.th. with dignity, treat s.th. with disdain	مر به (عليه) مر الكرام
It has been discussed, it has been previously mentioned	مر ذكر
To scan s.th., peruse s.th. hastily	مر عليه ببصره
To pass swiftly, flash past	مر مر البرق
To pass as if nothing had happened, brush past	مر مر الكرام
To continue to do s.th, keep, or go on, doing s.th.	مر يفعل
Frequently for English 'one' (e.g. one would think)	المرء (يظن المرء)
Repeatedly, several times, quite often	مراتٍ
Revision, correction of	مراجعة الحساب
A thorough revision	مراجعة دقيقة
Stages of her life	مراحل حياتها
Several times, at times, now and then	مراراً
Frequently, often	مراراً عديدة

Time and again	مراراً وتكراراً
Freelance	مراسل حرّ
Special correspondent	مراسل خاص
Sports reporter	مراسل رياضي
Personal correspondence	مراسلات شخصيّة
Coronation ceremonies	مراسم التتويج
Court etiquette	مراسم التشريفات
Social services	مرافق اجتماعيّة
Refining facilities	مرافق التكرير
Conveniences	مرافق الحياة
Medical institutions	مرافق صحّيّة
Public utilities	مرافق عامة
Once	مرةً
Once again, once more, anew	مرة أخرى (جديدة)
Time and again, again and again	مرة بعد مرة
Time after time	المرة تلو المرة
At once, at one time, eventually, finally, at last	مرة واحدة
Carefree	مرتاح البال
Of peaceful mind	مرتاح الضمير
Relieved	مرتاح النفس
Twice	مرتين
A decisive stage	مرحلة حاسمة
An early stage	مرحلة مبكّرة
Final stage	مرحلة نهائيّة
Recipient, addressee	مرسل إليه
Inlaid with gold	مرصّع بالذهب
Diabetes	مرض السكر
Body lotion	مرطّب الجسم

Sought after, desired, in demand	مرغوب فيه
Attached	مرفق بِـ
Head held high	مرفوع الرأس
To renege, renounce (esp. true faith)	مرق من الدين
Inferiority complex	مركب نقص
Shopping centre	مركز تجاريّ
Head office	مركز رئيسيّ
Epicentre	مركز زلزال
Expiration of the deadline	مرور الزمان
Public auction	مزاد علنيّ
To break up, dismember, dismantle	مزّق شمله
To tear s.th. to pieces or to shreds	مزّقه إرْباً إرْباً
More	مزيد من
Further explanation	مزيد من التوضيح
Attack of fever	مس الحمى
To be injurious, damaging to s.th., hurt, impair, prejudice s.th.	مس بسوء الشيء
To hit a mine	مس لغماً
Land surface	مساحة الأراضي
An unsettled, open question, unsolved problem	مسألة فيها نظر
The affair is subject to investigation, is being investigated	المسألة قيد البحث
Circumstances require, (it) is necessary, urgently needed	مست الحاجة إلى
Opinionated, obstinate, headstrong	مستبد برأيه
Bright future	مستقبل زاهر
Living standard	مستوى العيش
Birthplace	مسقط الرأس
To keep the books, keep the accounts	مسك الحسابات

مسك دفة الأمور	To be at the helm, be in charge
مسك لسانه	To keep one's tongue in check
مُسكة الأمل	That to which hope clings
مسلح بأحدث طراز	Equipped with the latest arms
مسه بأذى	To harm, wrong, hurt
مسه بسوء	To harm, wrong, hurt
مُشَادَّة كلامية	Battle of words, dispute, altercation
المشار إليه	The aforementioned, the aforesaid, the said
مشارق الأرض ومغاربها	The entire world
مشاكل حياتية	Problems of life
مشاهد الحياة	Aspects of life
مشتبه في صنعه	Of doubtful make
مشتبه فيه (مشتبه في أمره)	Suspicious, suspect, a suspect
مشتبه فيه بـ	Suspected of s.th.
مشتنك	Suspected of s.th.
مُشَرَّد البال	Confused, disconcerted
مُشَرَّد النفس	Confused, disconcerted
مشرف على الموت	Dying, in the throes of death, doomed to death, moribund
مُشْرِقُ الطلعة	Of radiant, splendid appearance
المشرقان والمغربان	The whole world
مشروع قانون	Bill, draft law
المشروع قيد الدرس	The project is being studied, is under consideration
مشغوف بـ	Fascinated by, passionately fond of, madly in love, infatuated with
مشغول البال	Anxious, apprehensive
مشكو (منه)	Accused, charged, defendant, complained of
مشكوك في أمره	Suspect(ed)

Doubtful, dubious, uncertain	مشكوك فيه
Appetisers, hors d'oeuvres	مُشَهِّيَات
His academic career is full of achievements	مشواره الأكاديمي زاخر بالانجازات
Troubled with worries	مَشُوبٌ بِالهُموم
Bewildered, confused, baffled	مُشَوَّش الفكر
Disabled veteran	مُشَوَّه الحرب
To scatter slanderous rumours	مشى بالنميمة
Stricken, afflicted by	مصاب بـ
Incandescent light, light bulb	مصباح الإضاءة
Searchlight	مصباح كشاف
The undersigned	المصحح أسفله
Copy of the Quran	المصحف الشريف
Legalised, officially certified	مُصَدَّقٌ عليه رسميا
Dismissed, discharged	مصروف من الخدمة
Generally accepted, conventional, customary, technical term, terminus technicus	مصطلح عليه
With an empty hand	مُصْفِر اليد
Without any possession at all, completely destitute	مصفر اليد من كل شيء
Public welfare, commonwealth	المصلحة العامة
Handmade	مصنوع باليد (مشغول باليد)
The way of all flesh	مصير كل حي
He went to his destination, he left in order to do what he had in mind, he went his way	مضى (ذهب) لطِيَّته
He went his own way, he went off on his own	مضى إلى حال سبيله
To stride ahead, continue forwards	مضى أمامه
To pass away, die	مضى سبيله (لسبيله)
To conclude a bargain	مضى على البيع
Months have passed since then	مضى على ذلك شهور

مضى فقال	And he went on to say, and he added
مضى في كلامه	To go on talking
مضى في مهنة	To purse, practise, exercise (in a profession)
مضى ما مضى	Let bygones be bygones! No more of that!
المضي في الحرب	The continuation of war
مُطْبِقٌ بِالذهب	Coated with gold, gold-plated
مطبوع بطابعه	Bearing the stamp, being characterised by
مطبوع على	Being by its very nature, having the innate property of
مطرد النسق	Uniform (adj.)
مطرد النغم	Monotonous (song)
مطعم الشعب (شعبي)	Soup kitchen
مطلع على	Acquainted with, familiar with, cognisant of, privy to
مطلق التصرف	Having unrestricted right of disposal, invested with full power
مطلق السراح	Free, at large, at liberty
مطلقاً	Absolutely, unrestrictedly, without exception, in any respect, under any circumstances
مطوي الضلوع على	Harbouring s.th. in one's bosom
مطوي على	Bearing within itself, harbouring, containing
مظاهر الحياة	Manifestations of life
مع التحفظ	With full reservation
مع التوسع	In a wider sense, by extension
مع الحائط	Along the wall
مع المعرفة	Knowingly, deliberately (jur.)

مع الوقت	In (due) time, in the course of time, gradually
مع أن	Although
مع بُعْدِ الفارق	In spite of the great difference
مع تقادمِ الزمن	In the course of time
مع ذلك	In spite of it, nevertheless, still
مع عدم الإخلال بِـ	Without prejudice to, without detriment to
مع كل هذا	In spite of all that
مع كونه غنياً	Although he is rich, rich as he is
مع كونه مجنوناً	Although he is mad
مع مرور الزمن	In time, as time goes by
مع هذا	In spite of it, nevertheless, still
مع هذا	Herewith, in spite of it, nevertheless
معاً	Together, at the same time, simultaneously, with one another
المعادن الكريمة	The precious metals
معاذ الله	God forbid
معاش التقاعد	Pension
معاليم النقل	Transfer fees
معاهد الذكريات	Places fraught with memories
معاهدة (اتفاق) عدم الاعتداء	Pact of non-aggression
معاول الإفساد والتقويض	Destructive and subversive elements
مَعَاوِل هدّامة	Destructive elements
المعتقد أن ...	It is believed that, it is held that ...
معجب بنفسه	Conceited, vain
معدود في الطبقة الثالثة	Regarded as third-rate
معرض الصحف	Press review
مُعَرَّضٌ للخطر	Endangered, jeopardised
معرفة الجميل	Gratitude
مُعَرَّق في القِدَم	Very old, ancient

المعروف أن ...	It is (well) known that, as is well known, it is commonly held that, it is generally understood that ...
معصوم من الزلل	Infallible
مَعْقِد آماله	The object on which s.o. pins his hopes
معقود اللسان	Tongue-tied, incapable of speech
المعمورة (المعمور)	The inhabited world
المعهود	The said ..., the ... in question
معيار الذهب	Gold standard
معيار العيش	Living standard
معيشة الريف	Rural life, life in the country
مغدى ومراح	An ever-frequented place, an aspired goal
مغرب الشمس	Time of sunset, sunset
مغزى دقيق	Subtle meaning
مغضوب	Object of anger
مغضوب عليه	Object of anger
المغفور له	The deceased, the late ...
مغلول اليد	Inactive, idle
مفترق الطرق	Crossroads, intersection
مفتول الساعد	Muscular, brawny
المفتي الأكبر	Grand Mufti
مفروغ منه	Finished, settled (question, problem and the like)
مفصّلاً	In detail, elaborately
المفهوم أن ...	It is said, it is reported that ...
مفهوم ضِمْناً	Tacitly comprised, implicit
مقابل تقديم الكوبون	Upon presentation of the coupon

Accordingly, in accordance with that, in return for that, in exchange for that	مقابل ذلك (في مقابل ذلك)
Reprisal, retaliation	مقابلة المثل بالمثل
Requital, retaliation, reprisal	المقابلة بالمِثل
In return for that, in exchange for that, in compensation for that	مقابلة ذلك (في مقابلة ذلك)
Revenue	مقابيض
The reins of government or power	مقاليد الحكم
Topic of the conversation	مقام الحديث
Air defence	مقاومة جوية
Passive resistance	مقاومة سلبية
Early at night	مقتبل الليل
A minimum	مقدار أدنى
A maximum	مقدار أقصى
Military potential	المقدرة الحربية
Applicant	مُقَدِّمُ الطَّلَب
Place of employment	مقر العمل
Headquarters	مقر القيادة
Official seat, seat of office	مقر الوظيفة
Decisions	مقررات
Demure, chaste (of a woman)	مقصورة الطرف
Decision, judgement	مقطع الرأي
Incomparable	مقطوع (منقطع) النظير
Matchless, peerless, unrivalled	مقطوع النظير
Decided, settled (matter or affair)	مقطوع به
Eyeball	مقلة العين
Powerless, helpless, weak	مُقَلَّم الظُّفْر
Elements, constituents, components, formative agents, basic factors	مُقَوِّمَات

مقومات الجمال	Cosmetics
مقومات الحياة	Means of subsistence, earthly possessions
مقومات العمران	Cultural factors
مقياس الحرارة	Thermometer
مقياس الزلازل	Seismometer
المقيم الأسبق	The ex-resident
مقيم بواجباته	Dutiful, conscientious, loyal
مكارم الأخلاق	Noble manners
مكارم الأخلاق	Noble characteristics, noble traits of character
مكالمة تليفونية	Telephone conversation
مكانَ	In the place of, in lieu of, instead of
مكان الحادث	Site of action, scene of the crime, locus delicti
مكان الشيء من نفسه	The importance of s.th. for s.o., the place that s.th. has in s.o.'s mind
مكانة الصدر	First place, precedence, priority
مكانة الصدر	First place, precedence, priority
مكانة مرموقة	A prominent place
مكانَك	Stop!
مكانَه	On the spot, at once
مكبّر الصوت	Loudspeaker
مكتب الأخبار (الأنباء)	News agency, press agency, wire service
مكتب الاستعلامات	Information desk, information office, press agency
مكتب البريد	Post office
مكتب التحرير	Editorial office
مكتظّ بـ	Crammed, full, jam-packed
مُكَسَّرات	Almonds and nuts
مكشوف الرأس	Bare-headed, hatless

Guaranteed	مكفول به
Obligated to observe the precepts of religion (Isl. Law)	مكلّف
Commissioned with, liable to, responsible for	مكلّف بِـ
Place where s.th. is hidden, ambuscade, ambush, hiding place	مكمن
Surnamed	مكنّى
Composed of, made up of, formed by	مُكوَّن من
Air conditioner	مُكيِّفة الهواء
A handful	ملء اليد
He is all pride and arrogance	ملء إهابه الكبرياء
As much as one can eat	ملء بطنه
A cupful	ملء قدح
The angels, heavenly host	الملأ الأعلى
His (its) fame spread far and wide	ملأ الدهرَ
To wind up a watch or clock	ملأ الساعةَ
To satisfy completely, please	ملأ العينَ
To fill the air with complaints, voice loud laments	ملأ الفضاءَ بالشكوى
To puff one's cheeks	ملأ شدقيه بالهواء
To satisfy s.o., to please s.o.	ملأ عينه
Underwear and outer clothes	ملابس داخلية وخارجية
Lights and shades (in painting)	ملاح وظلال
Matches, contests, events (in sports)	ملاعب
Adapted, suited, appropriate (to)	ملائم لِـ
Overcast, heavily clouded (sky)	مُلبَّد بالغيوم
Protective clothes	مَلبس الوقاية
A black-bearded man	مُلتَح بلحية سوداء
Day nursery, children's home	ملجأ الأطفال

ملجأ الأيتام (دار الأيتام)	Orphanage
ملجأ الشيوخ	Elderly home
ملجأ العَجَزة	Infirmary
ملجأ العُميان	Institution for the blind
ملحوظ الجانب	Noticeable, conspicuous
ملزوم بالأداء	Liable for taxes, taxable
مِلَف الكتاب	Book cover
مُلفِت النظر	Attracting attention, striking, conspicuous
ملفوف على	Twisted, wound
ملقّب بـ	Nicknamed, surnamed, called
ملقيات الالغام البحرية	Mine layers
ملك العينين من البكاء	To hold back the tears
مِلك شائع	Joint property
ملك على نفسه أمرَها	To have o.s. under control
ملك عليه جميع مشاعره	To dominate s.o.'s every thought and deed
ملك عليه حسَّه	To take possession of s.o.'s feelings
ملك عليه لبه	To preoccupy s.o.'s heart
ملك عليه نفسَه	To lay hold of s.o.'s soul, affect s.o. deeply
ملك مقيد	Constitutional monarchy
ملك ناصيتَه	To be or become the master of s.th., have or get s.th. under control
ملك نفسَه	To control o.s., restrain o.s.
ملكه الغيظ	Anger overwhelmed him, got the better of him
مُلِم بـ	Completely familiar, conversant with
ملم بالقراءة والكتابة	Literate
ملموسات	Tangible things
ملوك الأرض عند الله تراب	The kings of this world are mere dust in comparison with God

Laxatives	ملَيِّنات
It will be noticed that, obviously, evidently ...	مما يُلاحَظُ أن ...
Fat, stout, corpulent	ممتلئ الجسم
Senseless, meaningless, inane	ممسوح من المعنى
Attainable	ممكن المنال
Amply provided with	مملوء الوطاب بـ
No smoking	ممنوع التدخين
No entry! Keep out! Off limits!	ممنوع الدخول
From – to	من – إلى
From nearby, at a short distance	من (عن) كثب
For that reason, on this account	من أجل هذا
He belongs to his clique, he is of the same breed	من أحزابه
From behind, from the rear	من آخره
From one end to the other, throughout, everything without exception	من أدناه إلى أقصاه
Previously convicted	من أصحاب (ذوي) السوابق
From the depth of his soul	من أعماق النفس
From the bottom of his heart, from the depth of his soul	من أعماق قلبه
It must be admitted that, admittedly ...	من الاعتراف أن ...
From now on, henceforth	من الآن فصاعداً
Obvious, it is immediately apparent, goes without saying that ...	من البديهي أن ...
It would be very unwise to ...	من الخُرْقِ في الرأي أن ...
It is (would be) wrong to ...	من الخطأ أن ...
From behind	من الخلف
From head to toe	من الرأس إلى أخمص القدم

من الشجاعة بمكان	He is extremely brave
من الطراز الأول	First-class, first-rate
من الطراز القديم	Old-fashioned, outmoded
من الظاهر	From outside
من العبث أن ...	It is foolish and useless to ...
من ألفه إلى يائه	From beginning to end, from A to Z
من الفور	Immediately
من القعر صاعداً	From the ground up
من الليل	At night
من المحتمل أن ...	Probably ...
من المحقَّق أن ...	It is certain that, it is a fact that ...
من الممكن أن ...	Possibly, perhaps, maybe ...
من المهد إلى اللحد	From cradle to grave
من الواضح أن ...	It is obvious that ...
من آن إلى آخر	From time to time
من أول أمره	From the outset, right from the beginning
من أوله إلى آخره	From beginning to end, from A to Z
من باب الضرورة أن ...	It is necessary that ...
من باب الفضل	As a favour
من باب أولى	With all the more reason, the more so
من بعد	From a distance, from afar
من بعض الوجوه	In some ways
من بعض خدامه	To be one of his servants
من بعيد	From afar, from a distance
من بين أظهرنا	From our midst, from among us
من تحت	From under, beneath
من تحت الدلف لتحت المزراب	From one calamity to another
من تدخل فيما لا يعنيه سمع ما لا يرضيه	Keep your nose out of other people's business

Designed by so-and-so	من تصميم فلان
Made to measure by, tailored by …	من تفصيل …
Of one's own accord, spontaneously, automatically	من تلقاء ذاته
Of one's own accord, spontaneously, automatically	من تلقاء نفسه
Hence, therefore, for that reason	مِن ثَمَّ
Then, thereupon	مِن ثَمَّ
On the one hand – on the other hand	من جانب ومن جانب آخر
On his part	من جانبه
I alone	من جبيني
Anew, again	من جديد
Because of, due to	من جرّاء
Because of you, on your account, for your sake	من جرَّاك
Because of you, on your account, for your sake	مِنْ جرائك
Because of	من جَرَّى
Because of, on account of	من جريرة
In every aspect	من جميع النواحي
On the one hand … on the other hand	من جهة … ومن جهة أخرى
For my part, as for me, I for one	من جهتي
With his own cash, with funds at his disposal	من حُرِّ ماله
Fortunately, luckily	من حسن الحظ
Luckily for me	من حسن حظي
Around him, about him	من حوله
From their vicinity, from their surroundings (dual)	من حوليهما
From where, whence	من حيثُ

من حيثُ الثقافة	With regard to education, as far as education is concerned
من حيث المبدأ	In principle, basically
من حيث أن	Inasmuch as
من حيث لا	Without being, doing, etc.
من حيث هو	As such, in itself
من حيث يدري ولا يدري	Whether he knows it or not, knowingly or without his knowledge
من حين إلى حين	From time to time, now and then, once in a while
من حين لآخر	From time to time, now and then, once in a while
من خاطره	Of one's one accord, voluntarily
من خلال	Across, right through the middle of, from within
من خلايا	From within, out of, from inside
من خلف	Behind
من خَلْفُ	At the back, in the rear
من دون (بدون شرط)	Unconditional
من ذلك الحين	From that time, from then on
من ذلك أن ...	Among other things ...
مِن ذِي قبل (عن ذي قبل)	(after a comparative) ... than before
من ساعته	At that moment, right away
من سنة إلى أخرى	From year to year
من سنة مضت	A year ago
من شأنه أن ...	It is in his (its) nature that, he (it) tends to, it is his business to ...
من شهر	For a month
من صلبه	His own son, his offspring
من صميم القلب	From the bottom of the heart, wholeheartedly, most sincerely

Dreamed up by him, a product of his fantasy (of a story)	مِن صيد خياله
Included in, implied in, belonging to, falling under	مِن ضِمْنِ
Among them	مِن ضِمْنِهِمْ
On the part of	مِن طرف
From one end to the other	مِن طرف إلى طرف
Secretly, furtively, discreetly	مِن طَرْفٍ خفي
By means of, through	مِن طريق
From an old, respectable family	مِن عائلة عريقة
The remarkable thing about the matter is that …	مِن عجائب الأمر أن …
To belong to the common people	مِن عُرض الناس
From above	مِن على..
From, from the home of, away from	مِن عند
In his turn, for his part	مِن عنده
For a short time (past), of late, recent	مِن عهد قريب
Without	مِن غير
Frictionless	مِن غير احتكاك
Without account	مِن غير حساب
Without any reservation, without qualification	مِن غير قيد أو رابط
Without much ado, without ceremony	مِن غير لف
Without compensation, for nothing, gratis	مِن غير مقابل (بدون مقابل)
Please! If you please	مِن فضلك
It would be needless talk to, it would be a waste of words if …	مِن فضول الكلام أن …
Immediately	مِن فوره (ها)
Above it	مِن فوقه

مِن قُبُل	In front, from the front
مِن قِبَل	On the part of, on the side of, from, by
مِن قبل (قَبلاً)	Previously, formerly, earlier
مِن قِبَلِ نفسه	By himself, of his own accord
مِن قَبِيل الإيضاح	By way of illustration, as an explanation
مِن قديم	From times of old
مِن قريب	From near
مِن قِمَّة الرأس إلى أخمَصِ القدم	From head to toe
مِن كل الوجوه	In every aspect, every way, completely
مِن كل أوب	From all sides or directions
مِن كل بد	In any case, at any rate
مِن كل جهة	From all sides
مِن كل حدب وصوب	From all sides, from all directions, from all quarters, from everywhere
مِن كل خاطر	With all one's heart, most gladly
مِن كل فج عميق	From all sides, from all directions, from everywhere
مِن كل فج وصوب	From all sides, from all directions, from all quarters, from everywhere
مِن كل قَبيل ودبير	Of every origin (whatsoever)
مِن كل قلبه	With all his heart
مِن كل وجه	In every aspect
مِن لَدُن	From, on the part of
مِن له سوابق	(One) previously convicted, recidivous convict
مِن له نظر	A noteworthy man
مِن متعلقاته	Depending on s.o. or s.th., pertaining to s.o.'s authority
مِن مدة	For some time (in the past)

From a reliable source	من مصدر موثوق به
With regard to, in respect to, as for	من ناحية
On the other hand	من ناحية أخرى
De jure	من ناحية قانونية
De facto	من ناحية واقعية
It goes without saying that …	من نافلة القول أن …
As far as I am concerned, as for me, for my part, I for one	من نحوي
Of this kind, like this, such	من هذا القَبيل
As seen from this angle, from this viewpoint	من هذه الجهة
In this respect, from this point of view	من هذه الوجهة
From here, hereof, hence, for this reason, therefore	من هنا
From there, from that place	من هناك
According to the date contained in these registers	من واقع هذه السِجلات
In many aspects	من وجوه كثيرة
Behind, beyond, over and above (with foll. genitive)	من وراء
Behind the scenes, backstage (fig.)	من وراء الستار
From time to time	من وقت لآخر
On the very same day	من يومه
From … on, from … upwards	من … فصاعداً
Research methods	مناحج البحث
All walks of life	مناحي الحياة
Contested, disputed	منازع عليه
The highest heavens, as far as the Pleiades or Gemini	مناط الثريا (مناط الجوزاء)
Sanitary facilities	منافع صحية

Public services	منافع عامة
Self-contradictory	مناقض ذاتَه
The untouchables (in India), the pariahs	المنبوذون
Of ill repute, of dubious reputation	منثلم الصيت
From time immemorial	منذ أزمنة غابرة
From now on, henceforth	منذ الآن
From the very beginning	منذ البدء
From times of old, by long tradition, of long standing	منذ القِدَم
From times of old	منذ القديم
As of today, from this day on	منذ اليوم
For a long time	منذ أمد بعيد
For the past few days, a few days ago	منذ أيام
For many years	منذ سنين بعيدة
For a month (past), a month ago	منذ شهر
For the past ten years	منذ عشرِ سنواتٍ خلت
A long time ago	منذ عهد بعيد
Of late, lately, recently	منذ عهد قريب
For the last hundred years and more	منذ قرن وبعض قرن
Since I was a child	منذ كنت طفلاً صغيرًا
From (the days of) his earliest youth	منذ نعومة أظفاره
From his earliest youth, since his tender age	منذ نعومة أظفاره
Weakened, debilitated, exhausted	منسرق القوة
Position of power	مِنَصَّة الحكم
At their departure, when they left	مُنصَرَفَهُم
Stipulated, determined, laid down in writing	منصوص عليه
Sphere of influence	منطقة النفوذ

Demilitarised zone	منطقة مجردة من التجهيزات الحربية
Self-absorbed, low-spirited, depressed	منطو على نفسه
Exact terms of the contract	منطوق العقد
Legal text	منطوق القانون
Literal meaning of a word	منطوق الكلمة
General view, panorama, landscape, scenery	منظر عام
A heart-rending sight	منظر يُشَقُّ له نياط القلوب
One under supervision, underling, subordinate, protégé	منظور إليه
Dejected, low spirited, crestfallen, disheartened, depressed	منقبض الصدر
Matchless, peerless, unrivalled, singular	منقطع القرين
Place of execution	منقع الدم
With bowed head	مُنَكَّس الرأس
Unfortunate, unlucky	منكود الحظ
Curriculum	منهاج التعليم
Some of them	منهم من
Some of them – others ..., there are those who – and others who ...	منهم من – ومنهم من
You must do it this way	مِنوالك أن تفعل كذا
To indulge in the hope of, have every hope that ...	منّى نفسَه بِ
Important matters	مهام الأمور
Official duties, official functions	مهام المنصب
The cradle of Islam	مهبط الوحي
Slowly, leisurely, in no hurry	مهلاً
Easy does it! Take it easy!	مَهْلَكَ
Whatever it may cost him, at any cost	مهما كلّف الأمر

مهما يكن من الأمر	Be it as it may, whatever the case may be, whatever may happen
مهمل التوقيع	Unsigned
مواقع الإطلال	(Sites of) ruins
مواقيت الأقلام	Business hours
موت أبيض	Natural death
الموت الأحمر	Violent death
موت الغفلة	Sudden death
مؤتمر (منعقد) على أعلى مستوى	Top-level conference
المؤتمر المزمع انعقاده	The conference to be held
مؤثرات صوتية	Sound effects
موثوق به	Reliable, dependable
مؤخراً	Recently, lately, the other day
المُودَع لديه	Keeper, consignee, depository
موزع الخواطر (موزع الفكر)	Absent-minded, distraught, scatter-brained
الموصى إليه	Executor
الموصى به	Bequest, legacy, decreed, recommended
الموصى عليه	Legatee, heir
موضع الاعجاب	Object of admiration
موضع الحنان	Object of sympathy
موضوع مطروق	A much-discussed, frequently treated subject
موطن الضعف	Soft or sore spot
موطن العبرة	The salient point, the crucial point
الموطن الوضيع	The lowest point, the lowest mark, the bottom
موظف كتابي	Clerk, clerical worker (of a government office)

Having many wishes	موفور المطالب
Temporarily, provisionally, for the time being	موقتاً
Advanced position	موقع متقدم
Hostile attitude	موقف عدائي
His attitude towards	موقفه من
The one referred to, the above-mentioned	المومأ إليه
Sewage, sullage, waste water	المياه العادمة
Fresh water	مياه عذبة
A hundred times as much, the hundredfold of it	مِئَةُ ضِعْفِهِ
Death in battle, death of a hero	ميتة الأبطال
Initiative	مِيزَةُ السبق
Favourable, auspicious	ميمون الطائر
Desperate (cause)	ميؤوس منه

ن

ناء بالحِملِ	To bear a burden with difficulty, to be weighed down by a burden
ناء بكلكله	Oppress s.o. gravely, weigh heavily upon s.o.
ناب منابه	To represent s.o., substitute for s.o., act in s.o.'s behalf
نابذه بالحرب	To declare war on s.o.
نابض بالحياة	Vibrant with life
ناجى بنفسه	To soliloquise, talk to o.s., say to o.s.
نادر المثال	Unparalleled, singular
نادراً	Rarely
نادى (دعا) بالويل والثُبور	To wail, burst into loud laments
ناشده أن يفعل	To adjure, implore s.o. to do s.th.
ناصبه الحربَ	To declare war on s.o.
ناصبه الشر	To show o.s. openly hostile to s.o., open hostilities against s.o.
ناصبه العداءَ	To declare o.s. the enemy of s.o.
ناعم الظُفُر	Youthful, of tender age
ناعم الملمس	Soft to the touch
نافذ المفعول	Valid, effective, in force
نافق ضميرَه	To act contrary to the dictates of one's conscience
ناكر الجميل	Ungrateful
ناكر المعروف	Ungrateful
نال بسوء	To harm s.o. or s.th.
نال بضر	To harm s.o. or s.th.
نال حظوةً عند (لدى)	To find favour with s.o.

To cause damage, do harm, impair	نال من
To depreciate, discredit, defame, malign	نال من عرضه
It made the deepest impression on him	نال من نفسه أبلغ منالٍ
To do s.o. untold damage, harm s.o. grievously	نال منه أوفر منال
To attain (the age of) maturity	ناهز البلوغَ
He was close to fifty, he was pushing fifty	ناهز الخمسين
It is enough to mention …	ناهيك بِـ
Let it suffice you to know that, aside from the fact that …	ناهيك بأن …
How excellent is …!, to say nothing of, not to mention, let alone …	ناهيك من (عن، بِـ) …
To be hostile to s.o., treat s.o. with hostility	ناوأه العداءَ
Assistant magistrate (Isl. Law)	نائب
Vice chairman, vice president	نائب الرئيس
Viceroy	نائب الملك
He felt unable to remain in the place	نبا به المكانُ
Insubordination	نبذ الطاعة
To pay no attention to s.th., not to care about s.th., disregard s.th.	نبذه (طرحه) ظهريّاً
To reject or dismiss s.th. or s.o. with disdain, spurn or scorn s.th. or s.o.	نبذه نبذَ النواة
To excel, be outstanding in	نبغ في
To save one's life, save one's skin	نجا بحياته
To save o.s. from	نجا بنفسه (بروحه) من
To pass the exam	نجح في الامتحان
To comb, card, tease (cotton)	نجّد القطنَ

نَجَمَ قرنُه	To begin to show
نجوماً	In instalments
نحا به نحو الباب	To show s.o. to the door
نحا نحو الباب	To walk towards the door
نحا نحوه	To follow s.o., to follow s.o.'s example, to be of the same nature, on the same line as
نحن أقارب في أقارب	Our social relations are those of kinsfolk
نحن خليقون أن ...	It is only fair that we ...
نحن في واد وأنتم في واد	We belong to different camps, we stand worlds apart
نحواً من	Approximately, circa (with foll. figure)
نَدِى الكف	Open-handed, liberal
نذر على نفسه	To vow to o.s., make the solemn pledge to ...
نذرت لله أن ...	I vow to God that, I swear by God that ...
نرجع إلى ما نحن بصدده	We return to what is our present concern or to what we are just discussing
نزّله عن العرش	To dethrone, depose
نزا به قلبه إلى	To long, yearn for
نزح به	To emigrate, be away from home, live abroad
نزر الحديث	Taciturn, of few words
نزر قليل	Tiny amount
نزع السلاح	Disarmament
نزع منه نازع إلى	He felt a desire for, he discovered his inclination to
نزغ الشيطان	Insinuations of the devil
نُزِفَ دَمُه	To lose much blood, bleed (to death)

To disembark, go ashore, land	نزل إلى البَرِّ
To sink low (fig.)	نزل إلى الحضيض
To take the field	نزل إلى الميدان
To demote s.o., reduce s.o. in rank	نزّل درجَته
To avail o.s. of s.o.'s hospitality, stay as a guest with s.o.	نزل ضيفاً على
To defer, give in, yield, submit to s.o.	نزل على حكمه
To comply with, or fulfil, s.o.'s wish or demand	نزل عند (طلبه، رغبته)
To defer to s.o.'s will, do s.o.'s bidding	نزل عند إرادته
I lost all respect for him	نزل من عيني
To occupy a place or position, get to a place or position	نزل منزلاً
To hold the position of, serve as	نزل منزلة فلان
To occupy one's due place	نزل منزله اللائق
In accordance with	نزولا على
In compliance with his wish	نزولا عند رغبته
In compliance with his demand	نزولا عند طلبه
Death rate	نسبة الموت
In respect to, with regard to	نسبةً إلى (لـ) (بالنسبة إلى)
Percentage	نسبة مئوية
To imitate s.o., walk in s.o.'s footsteps, act like s.o.	نسج على منواله
In regular order, in rows	نَسَقاً
To start by itself, arise spontaneously	نشأ نشوءاً ذاتياً
To propagate a religion	نشر ديناً
To be freed from one's shackles, be unfettered	نشط من عقاله
To toil hard, to pester s.o.	نشّف ريقَه

In letter and spirit	نصاً وروحاً
Before my eyes	نُصْبَ عيني
To declare war on s.o.	نصب له الحربَ
To lay a trap for s.o., trap s.o.	نصب له شركاً
To set a trap for s.o.	نصب له شَرَكاً (فخاً)
To set a trap for s.o., to prepare an ambush for s.o.	نصب له كميناً
To hatch a plot, devise a clever plan	نصب مكيدةً
They made every effort in order to, they struggled hard to	نَصَبُوا أنفسَهم لـِ
Hemisphere	نِصف الكُرة
Fortnightly, biweekly	نصف شهري
To get undressed	نضا عن نفسه
Orion's Belt	نطاق الجوزاء
Pronouncement of sentence	نطق بالحكم
To say a word	نطق بكلمة
Magnifying glass	نظّارة مكبّرة
Public order	النظام العام
Traffic laws	نظام المرور
To tray a case (jur.)	نظر (في) القضية
To regard s.o. with contempt, look down on s.o.	نظر إليه بعين الاحتقار
To give s.th. sympathetic consideration	نظر إليه بعين الالتفات
To give s.o. a sidelong glance, look askance at s.o.	نظر إليه شَزراً
He looked askance at him, he gave him a slanting glance (contemptuously)	نظر إليه عن عُرضٍ
To look with satisfaction	نظر برضى
To foresee, foreknow, divine s.th.	نظر بعين الغيب إلى

To look askance, glare distrustfully, angrily or malignantly at s.o.	نظر شَزْراً إلى
To process s.o.'s application	نظر في طلب فلان
To peep through the keyhole	نظر من فرجة المفتاح (فوهة المفتاح)
In view of, with respect to	نظراً إلى
Telling glances, glances full of meaning	نظرات كلها معانٍ
No more than a quick glance is apt to convince us that …	نظرةٌ يسيرةٌ خليقةٌ أن تُقنِعَنا بأن …
Quantum theory (physics)	نظرية الكم
Euphoria, death song, swan song	نعشة الموت
What an excellent man Zayd is!	نِعمَ الرجلُ زيدٌ
What a wonderful youth they have!	نِعمَ الشبابُ شبابُهم
To feel serene and confident about	نَعِمَ بالاً بِـ
Well done!	نِعمَ ما فَعَلتَ
To harbour resentment against, hold a grudge against	نَغِلَ قلبُه على
Perspicacity, acute discernment	نفاذ البصيرة
Erotic poetry	نَفث
Literary productions	نَفَثات الأقلام
To blow out a candle	نفخ الشمعة
To be puffed, become inflated	نفخ شِدقَيه
To blow the trumpet	نفخ في البوق
To rouse s.o.'s temper	نفخ في زَمَّارةِ روحه
To bring s.th. into being	نفخ في صورته
To be at the end of one's patience	نَفَذ لديه معين الصبر
The essence of the matter, the nature of the affair	نفس الأمر
The thing itself, the very thing	نفس الشيء
To recover from	نَفَضَ من
Reversal of a sentence	نفض الحكم

نفض عنه الكسلَ	To shake off one's laziness
نفض عنه الهم	To shake off one's sorrows, shed one's anxiety
نفض غبارَ كسله	To flick one's laziness
نفض غبارَه	To shake off its dust, i.e. to have reached the end of, be finished with
نفض في لعب الأوراق	To gamble away at cards
نفض يدَه من الأمر	To chuck s.th., shake off s.th., rid o.s. of, refuse to have anything to do with
نفض يدَه من يد فلان	To break with s.o., dissociate o.s. from
نفوذ مطلق	Unlimited authority
نفير عام	General call to arms, levy en masse, general alarm
نقد ذاتيّ	Self-criticism
نقص المواليد	Falling birth rate
نقص عن	To fall short of
نقصه الشيء	He lacked, needed the thing, was in want of the thing
نقض السلام	Breach of the peace
نقض الولاءَ	To renounce allegiance, to revolt
نقطة أساسية	Key position
نقطة الاتصال	Junction (of traffic lanes)
نقطة الارتكاز	Fortified position, pocket of resistance
نقطة التحول	Turning point
نقطة العنبر	Beauty spot, mole
نقطة القتال	Combat zone
نقطة المطافئ	Fire station
نقل الدم (نقل الدماء)	Blood transfusion
نقّل خطاه	To stride along, move along

Based on, according to	نقلاً عن
Head of the Alids, head of the descendants of the Prophet	نقيب الأشراف
In defiance of him, to spite him	نكايةً فيه
Misfortune	نَكَد الطالع
Ingratitude	نكران الجميل
Self-denial	نكران الذات
To bow, tilt one's head	نكس برأسه
To retreat, climb down, give up one's intention	نَكَصَ على عقيبه
Refusal to testify in court (Isl. Law)	نُكُول
First-class, first-rate	نمرة واحد
A wonderful day	نهار أنهر
By day and night	نهاراً وليلاً
News of the day	نهاريات
Opportunist	نَهَّاز الفرص
The ultimate goal	نهاية الأرَب
Minimum	النهاية الصغرى
The best grade, the highest rating	النهاية العليا
Maximum	النهاية الكبرى
At last, finally	نهائياً
To cover the distance	نهب الأرضَ (إلى)
To cover the distance quickly	نهب الطريقَ (إلى)
To pursue a plan, to assume an attitude	نهج خطةً
To follow s.o.'s example	نهج على منواله
Tigris	نهر السلام
The Jordan River	نهر الشريعة
To take all burdens upon o.s., carry all burdens	نهض (قام) بالأعباء كلها

نهض بالأمر	To assume power, take command
نهض بالخسائر والضحايا	To take losses and sacrifices readily upon o.s.
نهض بشيء	To boost, further, promote s.th. (lit. to rise with s.th.)
نهض قائماً	He got on his feet, he got up
نهضت الحجةُ بـ	Proof has been established for
نَهَكَ عرضَه	To injure s.o.'s honour
النهي والأمر	Unlimited, absolute power, dictatorial command
نواتي السفينة	Ship's crew
نوالك أن تفعل كذا	You must do this
نوبات المطر	Rainy spells
نوبات غضبه	His fits of anger
نوبة قلبية	Heart attack
نودي به رئيساً	To be proclaimed president
نور برّاق	Flashing light
نور كشاف	Searchlight
نوع الإنسان (النوع الإنساني)	The human race
نوعاً ما	Somehow or other, somewhat
نوعاً وكمّيَّةً	Qualitatively and quantitatively, in nature and quantity
نيابة عمومية	Prosecution, the district attorney's office
نيابةً عن	Instead of, in place of, in lieu of
نَيِّف وعشرون	Twenty-odd

Ha! Look! There!	ها
You there!	ها أنتم
Look, there he is!	ها هو
This one, that one, that	ها هو ذا
Give me (us) ...! Bring me (us), let me (us) have ...!	هات (هاتوا)
Inner voice	هاتف القلب
This theory is rather weak	هاته النظرية من الضعف بمكان
Composed(ly), with one's mind at ease	هادئ البال
Calm, composed, confident	هادئ السرب
Calm(ly), confident(ly)	هادئ القلب
Here, take it! There you have ...!	هاك
There he is ...	هاكه
To let one's eyes wonder	هام بأنظاره
To wander aimlessly about	هام على وجهه
He was no longer himself, he was floating in higher regions, he was beside himself, he was out of his senses	هام في وديان
He was no longer himself, he was out of his senses	هام في وديان
To attach no importance to the fact that ...	هان عليه أن ...
You there!	هأنتذا
I (emphatic form)	هأنذا
To burst into laughter	هأهأ
To blow (wind), to rage (storm), to break out (fire)	هبّ (الريح)
To take up arms, to enter the war	هب للحرب

هب للمقاومة	To rise in arms, to take up arms in opposition
هب واقفًا	To stand, to plant o.s., station o.s.
هبّ واقفاً	To get on one's feet
هب ...	Suppose that, assuming that ...
هباء منثورا	Atoms scattered in all directions
هبت ريحه	He is in luck's way, he has a lucky hand in everything
هبني فعلتُ	Suppose I had done it
هتاف الحرب	Battle cry, war cry
هتف بحياته	To cheer s.o.
هتف به	To call to s.o.
هتف به هاتف	A voice called out to him, an invisible force told him, made him (do s.th.)
هتف ثلاثًا لـ	To give (s.o.)
هتف ضد	To jeer, boo
هتك الاستار	Disclosure, uncovering of s.th. hidden
هتك عرض	To disgrace s.o.
هدَأ أعصابه	To soothe the nerves
هَدَأ من روعه	To become composed, calm down
هدف تتقطع دونه الأعناق	A goal which remains unattainable (lit. a goal on the way to which throats are slit)
هَدِّئ روعَك	To calm down! Take it easy! Don't worry! Don't be afraid!
هذا الضعيف	My own insignificant self, I (as an expression of modesty)
هذا إلى أن ...	Besides, moreover, furthermore, what's more
هذا بـ (خمسين دينار)	That costs, amounts to (e.g. fifty dinars)

Now we are even, we are quits	هذا بذاك
You owe this to me	هذا حقي عليكم
That's tough look!	هذا خازوق
That's what you need, what you deserve	هذا خَرْجُك
That is sheer fantasy!	هذا خيال في خيال
Here is a man to fill any man's shoes	هذا رجل ناهيك من رجل
That's his affair	هذا شأنه
He is always that way	هذا شأنه دائماً
This and that are two entirely different things (or matters)	هذا شيء وذاك شيء آخر
This equals that	هذا عديد ذاك
That's pretty strong! That's laying it on thick	هذا كثير
That won't help you, that will be no use (to you)	هذا لا يُجديك
This does not concern me, this is none of my business	هذا لا يَخُصُّني
This is not to my taste	هذا لا يوافق مزاجي
That is very kind of you, that is proof of your goodness	هذا من بعض ما عندكم
Besides, moreover	هذا و
Besides, there is	هذا ويوجد
To flee from s.o.	هرب من وجه فلان
Confusion, jumble, tumult, turmoil, confusion, chaos	هرج ومرج
To wag its tail	هز ذيله
To nod, shake one's head	هز رأسه
To shrug (one's shoulders)	هز كتفيه
He shook his shoulder	هز من منكبه
He suffered a complete defeat	هُزِم

He brought utter defeat upon them	هزمهم شر هزيمة
It occurred to him all of a sudden, it flashed across his mind	هف على باله
He yearned for	هفّت نفسه إلى
Would you like …? Do you want …? Do you feel like …?	هل لك في (ألك في)
Do you feel like …? Would you like to …?	هل لك في …
Anything new?	هل من جديد؟
Come on!	هلم بنا
Now then, quickly to him!	هلمي إليه
They are masters of disputation	هم أساتذة في الجدل
They are of one stamp, they are all alike	هم على منوال واحد
They are of the same stamp, they are all alike	هم على نَمَط واحد
They stick together, they assist each other	هم على ولاية واحدة
They are united against him, they are sworn to oppose him	هم عليه إلْبٌ واحد
They, in themselves, they alone	هم في حد ذاتهم
They are alike in this	هم في هذا شرع واحد
They are as good as unanimous about it, they are practically agreed on it	هم كالمجمعين على ذلك
They are like him, they are of his kind	هم مثلُه
They and the likes of them	هم وأشكالهم
They are in league against me	هم يد واحدة عليّ
They are like day and night, they are diametrically opposed	هما كالتنوين والإضافة
Innuendoes, defamatory insinuations, taunts, gibes, sneers	همز ولمز
To whisper in s.o.'s ears	همس في أذنه

That's where the secret lies	هنا مكمن السر
Here and there	هنا وهناك
There, over there, in that place, there is (are)	هناك
There is a proverb	هناك قول مأثور
There, over there, in that place, there is (are)	هنالك
May it do you much good!	هنيئاً لك
May it do you much good! I hope you will enjoy it!	هنيئاً مريئاً
He is the originator of this development	هو أبو عذر هذا التطور
He is better than you	هو خير منك
He does not need it	هو في غناء عنه
He and the likes of him	هو وأضرابه
The plague	الهواء الأصفر
Open air, fresh air	هواء طلق
Compressed air	هواء مضغوط
Take it easy! Don't get excited! Never mind!	هوّن عليك
Slowly, gently, leisurely, imperceptibly	هوناً
Sexual intercourse	الهوى الأحمر
To degrade s.o.	هوى بمقامه
He fell in her arms, he embraced her	هوى على رقبتها
It is more natural for her than for him, she is more entitled to it than he is	هي أولى به منه
To pave the way for	هيأ الأسباب لِـ
To prepare o.s. (at heart) for	هيأ ذاته لِـ
To offer a good opportunity for	هيأ فرصة ملائمة لِـ
Simple and nice	هين لين

هيهات أن يفعل كذا	How far he is from doing so!
هيهات أن ...	It is absolutely out of the question that ...
هيهات بين هذا وذاك	What a difference between them! How different they are!

و

Oh what a pity! It's too bad! Alas!	وا أسفاه
To make a firm resolution on, intend firmly (to do s.th.)	واثق نفسَه على
It is your duty	واجب عليك
Front line	واجهة القتال
One by one, single, one after another	واحد بعد الآخر
Each of them	الواحد منهم
One by one, single, one after another	واحداً فواحداً
What a pity! Too bad!	واحسرتاه
I mention, among them, especially	وأخُصُّ منهم
To bury s.o.	واراه التراب
Imports and exports	واردات وصادرات
Widespread	واسع الانتشار
Abounding in mercy (in justice)	واسع الرحمة (العدل)
Patient, forbearing, generous, magnanimous	واسع الصدر
Comprehensive, extensive, far-reaching, large-scale	واسع النطاق
Very well-off!	واسع النعمة
To work by day and night	واصل الليلَ بالنهار
To make untiring efforts for	واصل جهدَه (سعيَهُ) في
Self-evident, self-explanatory	واضح بذاته
Occupier	واضع اليد
His fate overtook him	وافاه أجله
Reality, the real, material world	الواقع
Factual findings, facts	واقع الحال
Let alone that, not to mention that, to say nothing of …	وأقل من هذا وذلك أن …

Under these circumstances, such being the case, things being as they are	والحالة هذه
One may say, it must be admitted, it's only fair to say, say what you will...	والحق يقال
In short, briefly	والخلاصة
And vice versa	والعكس بالعكس
And the rule is, as a rule...	والغالب أن ...
By God!	والله
Obviously, evidently	والملاحظ أن ...
In the following, the reader will find what...	وإلى القارئ ما
The matter is, as follows	وإليكها بالإيجاز
And why shouldn't he?	وأنّى له إلا
(with على to express regret) Too bad for...!	وَاةَ (على) ...
With him	وإيّاه
And everything else that belongs to it	وتوابعه
Official documents	وثائق رسميّة
To make smooth (s.th. esp. the bed)	وَثَّرَ (ه) – (السرير)
To have self-confidence	وَثِقَ من النفس
It is his duty to, he is duty bound to, he has to, he must	وجب عليه أن ...
He became distracted from it in	وجد شاغلاً عنه في
Toothache	وجع السن
That much, at least, can be said that...	وجُلُّ ما يقال أنه ...
In short, to sum up, briefly stated...	وجملة الأمر أن ...
In short, to sum up, briefly stated...	وجملة القول أن ...

To address (a question, letter, etc.) to	وجَّه (ه) إلى
The state of affairs	الوجه الحال
Point of resemblance	وجهُ الشبه
To turn one's eyes to	وجَّه النظرَ إلى
To raise an accusation against him, bring a charge against s.o.	وجَّه عليه تهمةً
Apparently	وجهًا
Face to face, personally, directly	وجهاً لوجهٍ (بوجه)
In no way whatsoever (with preceding negation)	وجهاً من الوجوه
Point of view	وجهة النظر
He is on his way to Paris	وجهته باريس
Prominent people	وجوه الناس
Masked faces, hypocrites	وجوه مستعارة
To consolidate, or fund, debts	وحَّد الديون
To declare God to be one, be a monotheist	وحَّد اللهَ
He alone, he by himself	وحده (على وحده)
But enough of all these negative aspects!	وحسبك بهذا كلِّه شرّاً
How well that I did that I …!	وحسناً فعلتُ إذ
By the truth of	وحقّ
Predatory animals	الوحوش الضاربة
Her parents' only daughter	وحيدة أبويها
And the like	وخلافه
Of evil consequences	وخيم العاقبة
To wish o.s. far away from	ودَّ نفسَه بعيدًا عن
Goodbye	الوداع (وداعاً)
I wish he were rich	وددت لو كان غنياً
To give s.o. a free hand, wide scope of action	ودع المجالَ أمامَه فسيحاً

To leave s.th. aside, omit	ودعه جانباً
Something's fishy! There is more to it than meets the eye	وراء الأكَمَةِ ما وراءها
Behind the scenes, backstage (also fig.)	وراء الكواليس
Always the same old story	الورد الذي طالما التسبيح به
Always the same old story	الورد الذي يتلى في الغُدُو والآصال
Writing paper	ورق الكتابة
Banknotes, paper money	ورق النقد
To annoy, vex, infuriate s.o.	وَرَمَ أنفَه
To be puffed up, conceited	وَرَمَ بأَنفِهِ
To flow (water)	وزب الماءُ
The foreign minister in his capacity as senior minister	وزير الخارجية باعتباره أقدم الوزراء
Minister of public works	وزير النافعة
Means of communication and transportation	وسائط المواصلات والنقل
Precautionary measures	وسائل الاحتياط
Means of transportation	وسائل النقل
To hug s.o.	وسّد صدره
To lay s.o. or s.th. to rest in the ground	وسّده التراب
To make room for	وسّع المكانَ لِـ
To take long strides, quicken one's pace	وَسَّعَ خُطاه
What he can do, what is in his power	وُسعُه
To be written in s.o.'s face	وُسِمَ جبينُه بِـ
To brand s.o. as infamous, stigmatise s.o.	وَسَمَهُ بالعار
And the likes of them, and their sort (of people)	وشبههم
Doomed to early ruin	وشيك الزوال

الوصايا العشر	The Ten Commandments
وصل أسبابه بأسبابه	To join forces with s.o.
وصل إلى الصفحة الحاسمة	To enter the decisive phase
وصلني خطاب	I have received a letter
وصله الخبر	He received the news
وصلوا بالألوف	They arrived by the thousands
وضع أساساً	To lay a foundation, lay a cornerstone
وضع اقتراحات	To draw up proposals, make suggestions
الوضع الحالي	The present situation
وضع الحق في نصابه	To restore justice
وَضَعَ السِّلاحَ تَحْتَ الضَّرْبِ	To level a weapon, hold a weapon ready to fire
وضع الفكرة موضع الفعل	To translate the idea into action
وضع تقريراً	To write or make a report
وضع ثقته في	To place one's confidence in
وضع حداً لـ	To put an end to s.th.
وضع حياته على كفه	To risk one's life
وضع ختماً على	To place a seal on
وضع شيئًا تحت تصرفه	To put s.th. at s.o.'s disposition
وضع في حيز التنفيذ	To put s.th. into force
وضع لفظًا لـ	To coin a word
وضع للفظ معنى خاصاً به	To give a special meaning to an expression, place a particular construction on an expression
وضع مشروعاً	To make or form a plan
وضع من قدره	To depreciate s.th., lower the value of s.th.
وضع نظارته على عينيه	To put on one's glasses
وضع نُظُماً	To lay down rules
وضع نفسَه	To abase o.s., humble o.s.

To put o.s. in s.o.'s position	وضع نفسَه موضع فلان
To take possession of, lay hold of	وضع يده على
To take a thousand prisoners	وضع يده على ألف أسير
To lay one's hand over one's heart	وضع يده على ضميره
To lay one's finger on a sore spot	وضع يده على موطن العلة
In words and deeds	وضعاً وقولاً
The war has come to an end	وضعت الحرب أوزارها
To have a millstone about one's neck, be seriously handicapped	وُضِعَت السلسلة في عنقه
To put s.th. in s.o.'s power	وضعه تحت يده
To put s.th. aside	وضعه جانباً
To set s.th. apart, single out s.th.	وضعه على حدةٍ
To put s.th. in one's pocket	وضعه في جيبه
To misplace	وضعه في غير موضعه
To devote particular attention to s.th., make s.th. one's foremost concern, give priority to s.th.	وضعه في مُقَدَّمَةِ اهتمامه
To lay s.th. aside	وضعه من يده
To doubt s.th., question s.th.	وضعه موضع الشك
To put s.th. into action	وضعه موضع العمل
To put s.th. in the place of s.th. else	وضعه موضعَه
To point out, demonstrate s.th. to s.o.	وضعه نصب عينه
The low and high	الوضيع والرفيع
To lower the voice	وطّأ صوتَه
To gain a footing in	وطّد اقدامه في
To resolve firmly to …	وطّد العزمَ أن …
To rely firmly on, put one's faith in	وطّد ثقته في
To strengthen the bonds of friendship	وطّد عُرَى المحبة
To get used to, adjust o.s. to, put up with, to make up one's mind to (do s.th.)	وطّن نفسَه على

Having strong hopes of, confident of	وطيد الأمل بـ
To pledge o.s. on one's honour, give one's word of honour	وعد بشرفه
To promise o.s. to ...	وعد نفسَه بأن ...
And so forth, and so on	وعلى هذا النحو
To dawn on s.o., become clear to s.o.	وَعَى على نفسه
National consciousness	وعي قومي
To boil with anger against s.o., harbour malice against s.o.	وغر صدرَه على
And the like, and so forth, etc.	وغير ذلك
And the like, and so forth, etc.	وغيره
In fulfilment of, as a compensation for	وفاءً لـ
In accordance with	وفاقاً لـ
To save s.o. a lot of expenses	وفّر عليه مصاريفَ كثيرة
To succeed completely in, have every success in or with	وُفِّقَ كلَّ التوفيقِ إلى
In accordance with, in conformity with	وفقاً لـ
Baghdad time is two hours ahead of Central European time	وقت بغداد متقدم ساعتين عن وقت اوربا الوسطى
At once, at one time, one day	وقتاً
For some time, for a short time	وقتياً
Then, at that time, by then	وقتئذٍ
To him it was an established fact that ...	وَقَرَ في نفسه أن ...
The picture stood vividly before his mental eye	وقرت الصورة في نفسه
And so forth	وقِس عليه
The matter pleased him very much	وقع الأمر منه موقعاً حسناً

وقع الحافر على الحافر	To coincide, happen to correspond exactly
وقع الحق	The law has been determined
وقع الحق عليه	He was found guilty
وقع القول عليه	He was called upon to speak, he was given the floor
وقع الكلام في نفسه	The words impressed him, touched him
وقع الكلام منه موقعا	The words moved him
وقع بأيديهم	He fell into their hands
وقع تحت حواسه	To enter s.o.'s range of perception, become palpable, tangible for s.o.
وقع تحت طائلة القانون	To be subject to punishment by law
وقّع حجزاً على	To seize, confiscate, impound s.th.
وقع ضحيّتَه	To fall victim to, become a victim of s.th. or s.o.
وقع على عاتق فلان	To be at s.o.'s expense, fall to s.o.
وقّع على وَتَر الحساس	To touch the sensitive spot
وقع عنده موقع الرضى	It met his approval
وقع فريسةً لِـ	To fall victim to s.o., become a prey of s.o.
وقع في إساره	To be subjected to s.th., fall into the clutches of s.th.
وقع في الفخ	To walk into the trap, get caught in the snare
وقع في النفوس موقعاً جليلاً	To leave a strong impression
وقع في حَيْصَ بَيْصَ	To get into a bad fix, meet with difficulties
وقع في غير موقعه	To be misplaced, stand in the wrong place, be used in the wrong context
وقع في قبضته	To fall into s.o.'s hands
وقع في نفسه أن ...	It came to his mind, it occurred to him ...

He fell in love with her	وقع في هواها
To take s.th. to heart, to make s.th. one's business	وقع من قلبه في مكان
To cause raised eyebrows, cause astonishment	وقع موقع الاستغراب
To stand in place of	وقع موقعه
To give o.s. up	وقّع نفسه
Fighting broke out	وقعت العين على العين
War broke out	وقعت حرب
She fell in love with him	وقعت في حبه
She has made an impression on him, she has bewitched him	وقعت في نفسه
To initialise s.th.	وقّعه بالأحرف الأولى
They fell to quarrelling, they fell out with one another	وقعوا في بعضهم
Ceasefire	وقف إطلاق النار
To be on s.o.'s side	وقف إلى جانبه
To stand at his left	وقف إلى يساره
To oppose, resist, stop, check s.th.	وقف أمامَه
To be in a quandary, at a loss as what to do	وقف حائراً
To stand in the way of s.th., rise as an obstacle in the way of s.th.	وقف سدّاً دون
To be a stumbling block for s.o., obstruct s.o.'s way	وقف عثرةً في سبيله
To stand in the way of s.th., obstruct s.th.	وقف عقبةً دون
To remain neutral, observe strict neutrality	وقف على الحياد
To apply o.s. with diligence to, take pains in, make every effort to, throw o.s. into s.th., go to great lengths	وقف على ساق الجد لِ
To be on the brink of ruin, be about to perish, on the verge of destruction	وقف على شفير الهلاك

وقف عند حد ...	To stop at or short of ...
وقف في وجه فلان	To offer s.o. resistance, stand up against s.o.
وقف موقفاً ملؤه الحزم	He assumed a posture that was all determination
وقف موقفاً من	To assume an attitude, take a stand with regard to
وقف وقفاً	To assume a posture
وقف وقفةً	To stand still, assume a posture
وقفه عن العمل	To suspend s.o. from duty
وقّفه عند حده	To put s.o. in his proper place
وقل مثل هذه في	The same must be said about, the same can be said of, the same applies to
وكأس شربتُ	Many a cup have I emptied, how many cups I have drunk
وكفى	And that's all! Enough of that! That's enough!
وكفى حزناً أن ...	It is sad enough that ...
وكيل النيابة	Prosecuting attorney
ولا	Nor, ... either, not even (with preceding negative)
ولا جَرَمَ	Certainly, surely
ولا مشاحة	Incontestably, indisputably
ولا واحد	Not one, not a single one
ولا يقال إن ...	One cannot say that, let no one say that ...
ولاة الأمور	The leaders
ولّاه دبرَه (ظهرَه)	To turn one's back on s.o. or s.th.
ولّاه كشحَه	To turn one's back on s.o.
ولاية العهد	Succession to the throne
ولَجَ البابَ	To go in by the door, to enter the door
ولَدَتْ بطناً واحداً	She gave birth only once

To have child by s.o. (woman)	وَلَدَت منه
While he seemed to say, with an expression as if he wanted to say ...	ولسان حاله يقول
To taste blood, become bloodthirsty	ولغ في الدم
But he couldn't give him an answer	ولكن عبثاً استطاع أن يجيبه
Let us suppose that ...	ولنَهب أنَّ ...
Although, though, even if	ولو
They turned their backs on him, they turned away from him	ولّوا عنه الأدبارَ
To direct one's glances towards s.o.	ولّى أنظارَه شطرَه
To take flight, run away	ولّى هارباً
To turn, face (towards)	ولّى وجهه
To turn one's face towards s.th.	ولّى وجهه شطرَه
The man in charge	ولي الأمر
To take over the government, come into power	وَلِيَ الحكمَ
Avenger of blood	ولي الدم
Heir-apparent, crown prince, heir to the throne	ولي العهد
Benefactor	ولي النعمة
His benefactor	ولي نعمتِهِ
Conceived on the spur of the moment (idea, plan, etc.)	وليد ساعته
And the like	وما أشبه ذلك
And the like, etc.	وما إليه
And the like, etc.	وما شابه ذلك
And the like, etc.	وما في معناه
Before long he, presently, It was not long until ...	وما هو إلا أن ...
Before long she, presently, It was not long until ...	وما هي إلا أن ...

No sooner had he … than …, he had hardly … when …	وما هو إلا أن … حتى
Although – nevertheless …, it is true – but …	ومع أن – إلا أن …
And other people like that	ومَنْ إليه (إليهم)
She gave herself unreservedly to him	وهبته من ذات نفسها
And so on, and so forth, etc.	وهُلَمَّ جَرّاً
And how impossible is this to you!	وهيهات لك ذلك
Unfortunately	ويا للأسف
Woe to …	ويحاً لـ
Woe unto you!	ويحك
Woe to this fool!	ويحه من مخبول
Woe to …	ويل لـ
Woe unto you!	ويل لك
Slowly, gradually	وئيداً

ي

يا أبتِ، أبتاه، يا أبتاه	O my father!
يا الله مِن …	What a calamity is …! How unfortunate is …!
يا تُرى	What's your opinion? Would you say …? I wonder …? (in interrogative sentences)
يا حبذا الحالُ	That's just wonderful
يا حسرتي	What a pity! Too bad! Oh my misfortune!
يا خسارة	What a pity!
يا سلام	Good lord! Good heavens! Oh dear!
يا ضيعَانَهُ!	What a loss!
يا طالما	How often, how many times …
يا طولها من ليلة	What a long night it is!
يا لطيف	O my God! Good heavens!
يا للتعس ويا للشقاء	What a calamity!
يا للحسرة	Alas! Unfortunately!
يا لَلْخَجَل	O disgrace! The shame of it!
يا لِلْخِزْيَ	What a shame!
يا للعجب	Oh, how wonderful!
يا للهول	Oh, how terrible!
يا له من رجل	What a man!
يا لَهفَ	Oh, what a pity! What a pity! Too bad!
يا لهفا	Oh, what a pity! What a pity! Too bad!
يا لَهفِي عليك	Oh, how sorry I feel for you!
يا ليت كان يذهب	I wish he had gone!

يا معشر الشباب	O ye young men!
يبدئ ويعيد	He says or does everything conceivable
يَبِسَ الثَّرَى بينَهم	They became enemies
يبقى على حاله	It remains unchanged, just as it is
يجدر بالذكر	It is worth mentioning
يجدر ذكرُه	It is worth mentioning
يجري على هذه السنن	He acts in accordance with this rule, follows this principle
يجمع الكتابُ بين صفحاته	The book contains, lists
يُجْمَعُ بيت على بيوت	The plural of *bayt* is *buyūt*
يُحْتَمَلُ	It is conceivable, probable, likely
يحدوهم الأملُ في	The hope of ... spurs them on
يحسُن بك أن ...	It is to your advantage that you, you ought to ...
يُحِقُّ في	To be right in s.th.
يَحِقُّ له	He is entitle to it, he has a right to it
يحق له أن ...	He has every reason to ...
يَخْبِطُ خَبْطَ عَشْوَاءَ	He acts blindly, thoughtlessly, at random, haphazardly
يختلفون جدَّ الاختلاف	They differ widely
اليد الشمال	The left hand
اليد العاملة	Labour force
يد النكاح	Conjugal authority (Isl. Law)
يد بيضاء	Favour
يد مبطلة	Unrightful possession (Isl. Law)
يد مُحِقَّة	Rightful possession (Isl. Law)
يداً بيدٍ	Personal(ly), from hand to hand
يدخل في خُوَيصَةِ أمري	He meddles in my private affairs
يدع محلا	To leave room

He is incapable, his powers are limited	يده قصيرة
He calls on her time and again or constantly	يراوحها ويغاديها
Deplorable, regrettable	يرثى له
The reason is to be found in	يرجع السبب إلى
The merit thereby is his due, he deserves all credit for it	يرجع الفضل في ذلك إليه
He considers it his duty	يرى من واجبه
To (at, on) the left	يساراً (على اليسار)
He is responsible, answerable for	يُسْأَلُ عَنْ
Worth mentioning, noteworthy	يستحق الذكرَ
To pave the way for s.o. to, enable s.o. to do s.th.	يسّر السبيلَ أمامَه لِـ
He is a famous man (lit. he is pointed at with fingers)	يُشَار إليه ببنان
He drags her by the hair	يشد بشعرها
Worthy of thanks, deserving, meritorious, praiseworthy	يُشْكَرُ عليه
He attends to it morning and evening, he is constantly, incessantly occupied with it	يُصَاحِبُهُ وَيُمَاسِيهِ
One proceeds to, one will eventually, one will wind up with	يصار إلى
It may serve as a basis	يصح الاعتماد عليه
It is rightly said of him	يصح أن يقال فيه
This gets to the point where	يصل هذا إلى حد كذا
It has (absolute) validity for, it applies to	يُطلَق على
This will take me too long	يطول بي هذا
He knows it from A to Z	يعرف ألفَه وياءَه
He understands it most thoroughly, he grasps its very essence	يعرفه كُنةَ المعرفة

يعلم من أين تؤكل الكَتِف	He knows how to take the matter properly
يُعمَلُ به	It is valid, is effective, is in force
يعني	That is, i.e.
يَعْيَا بأمره	He is at his wit's end, is in utter despair, despairs of himself
يعيد القولَ ويبدأ	He keeps talking of it, he continues to bring up the subject
يغلب عليه الكرم	His predominant or foremost quality is generosity
يُفَتِّتُ القلبَ (الأكباد)	Heart-breaking, heart-rending
يفعله إذا أصبح ويفعله إذا أمسى	He does it morning and evening, he does it all the time, incessantly
يُفهَمُ أن ...	It is reported, it is said that, we understand that ...
يفوق الحصرَ	Immeasurable, innumerable
يَفُوقُهُ أشواطاً	He surpasses him by far
يقدّم رِجلاً ويؤخّر أخرى	To hesitate, waver, be undecided
يُقَطِّعُ القلبَ	Heart-rending
يقينيات	Established truths, axioms
يكاد أن (يفعل)	It wouldn't have taken much more, he (it) all but, he (would have) almost (with imperfect)
يكاد أن ...	To be on the point of doing s.th.
يكاد يكون في حكم العدم	It is almost as good as non-existent
يكون جواز السفر قابلاً للتجديد أربع مرات	The passport can be renewed four times
يُلَخَّص في أن ...	It can be summed up to the effect that ...
يلوح لي أن ...	It seems to me that ...
يمكن أن ...	It is possible that, it maybe that ...
يمكنه (أن) ...	He can (do s.th.)

To resort, wend one's way	يَمَّمَ (صوب، نحو، شطر)
To venture into the lion's den	يَمَّمَ في فم البركان
To turn or face towards	يَمَّمَ وجهه شطر
Oath of allegiance	يمين الأمانة
Perjury	يمين الصبر
Oath of allegiance	يمين الولاء والإخلاص
Official oath	يمين قانونية
False oath	يمين كاذبة
To assent, to place confidence in s.o.	ينام إلى
To forget about s.th., overlook	ينام عن
He is sound asleep, he sleeps the sleep of the just	ينام ملء جَفنِه (جفنيه)
It behoves him, it is incumbent upon him, he must, he ought to	ينبغي عليه (له)
I must …	ينبغي لي أن …
Trustworthy	يُوثَقُ به
He almost, he all but …	يوشك أن …
The Day of Resurrection, the Day of Judgement	يوم القيامة
Some day, some day or other	يوم من الأيام
Day after, from day to day	يوماً عن يوم
Day after day, day by day	يوماً فيوماً
Some day, sometime in the future	يوماً ما
He likes the thing	يؤنقه الشيءُ

www.ingramcontent.com/pod-product-compliance
Lightning Source LLC
LaVergne TN
LVHW022332070225
803225LV00050B/1705